E-Learning Companion:

A Student's Guide to Online Success

Ryan Watkins and Michael Corry

The George Washington University

Houghton Mifflin Company
Boston   New York

Senior Sponsoring Editor: Mary Finch

Development Editor: Shani B. Fisher

Editorial Assistant: Andrew Sylvester

Senior Project Editor: Tamela Ambush

Senior Production/Design Coordinator: Sarah Ambrose

Manufacturing Manager: Florence Cadran

Marketing Manager: Elinor Gregory

Marketing Assistant: Donna Laverdiere

Cover photograph: © Daniel Arsenault/The Image Bank

Printed in the U.S.A.

Library of Congress Catalog Card Number: 2003110122

ISBN: 0-618-379703

1 2 3 4 5 6 7 8 9-QWE-08 07 06 05 04

Contents

1 E-learning Vocabulary   1

2 Technology Tips for Online Students   24

6 Developing Positive Online Relationships 111

7 Study Tips for Online Students 131

8 Getting Motivating, Staying Motivated   171

HOW TO TUTORIALS   T1

Everyone talks about the weather, but no one does anything about it; just as everyone thinks Mark Twain wrote or said this, but he didn't. Likewise, everyone talks about the potential of computers and the Internet to enhance education, but not until now has anyone produced a useful guide that students can use to do something about it.

The hypothesis that if enough monkeys pounded away at enough computer keyboards for a sufficient length of time they would surely write *Hamlet* is laughable. But that's the way a lot of people have gone about trying to advance their knowledge electronically. Lots of trials, lots of errors, but no *Hamlet*.

The tuition at the *School of Trial and Error* is too high. To avoid paying it, anyone seriously interested in online success would be well advised to use this companion as a trusted guide. In it you will learn not just how to use the technology but how to master it; not just how to select courses, but how to get the most out of them. Here you'll find tips and tutorials, exercises and checklists; but you'll find more than that—you'll find ways to harness your time and talent to ensure success.

This companion is more than a how-to guide; it is a reference, a toolkit, a mentor. You'll find it a lot easier to succeed in school with it than without it.

Stephen Joel Trachtenberg
President, The George Washington University

Catalog of Contents: Common Obstacles to Success in Online Coursework

Success in the traditional classroom doesn't always translate into success when college courses require the use of online technology. There are barriers that often prevent normally high achieving students in the classroom from achieving the same levels of success when online technologies replace the traditional lecture hall. Being aware of these barriers is the first step in overcoming them and being successful.

Below are several common obstacles that many students must overcome on their path to success in online coursework. Despite all of these barriers thousands of students each semester successfully supplement their college courses with online coursework. The challenge for most students will be adapting previously mastered learning skills and developing new study habits to ensure that they can also overcome these obstacles and be successful in their online college coursework.

Technical Terminology

The rapid growth of technology in the daily lives of people around the world has brought with it a host of new vocabulary that each of us must know in order to communicate effectively with our classmates, instructors, technical support, and, in many cases, even our family. Overcoming the obstacle of technical terminology is more challenging for some students than others since our experiences commonly define our vocabulary. For example, if your roommate is a dance major, then you will likely become familiar with many terms that are used frequently within that community of learners, likewise if you are an engineering major, you will learn a certain vocabulary for communicating with other engineers.

As students, however, you will want to build a broad vocabulary of general technical terms that will allow you to communicate effectively with your fellow students and professors. Understanding the basic functionality of computer components (without being overwhelmed with the details of how the components function or why) and discerning what online resources to use when given an assignment for class will increase the likelihood of your success in today's college classroom.

In Chapter 1, E-learning Vocabulary, we will present common technological terms as well as their typical application in the context of online coursework. In addition, the glossary provides definitions of many terms and phrases, which are underlined throughout the companion, that you may not be familiar with as they relate to online technologies.

Utilizing the Technology

As you have likely discovered from your own experiences with computers, cell phones, the Internet, and all other technologies, they will inevitably stop working at the most inopportune times. It may seem like the Internet is never slow when your roommate is downloading music, but when the time comes for you to do your research for an upcoming term paper the pace of information coming into the computer is outpaced by a snail. Knowing the many features and options of your computer's software applications can help you fully utilize the technology to achieve success in college.

Chapter 2, Technology Tips for Online Students, will focus on the how to avoid and overcome many of the common obstacles that technology can place between you and college success.

Unfortunate Choices

Too often in life we put ourselves in situations where the odds of being successful are not in our favor. In selecting college courses students regularly make unfortunate choices about which courses to take and when; often taking the most challenging courses that require the use of online technologies in the semesters when they have the least time available to concentrate on their studies.

Chapter 3, Selecting the Right Opportunities for Success, provides a guide for making decisions that will balance your many academic, work, and personal commitments in order to improve the likelihood of your success in online coursework.

Lack of Planning for Success

The odds for success in online coursework are dramatically improved when you have a plan that outlines your goals as well as your strategies for being successful. The challenges associated with starting each new semester in college, from creating a class schedule that doesn't overlap with other commitments to figuring out how to log into the college's Internet portal, are typically overlooked when planning for success.

Chapter 4, Creating a Plan and Following It, will not only focus on how to quickly develop a useful plan for your success in college, but also offers many suggestions for how to follow through with your plans and achieve your goals.

Time Mismanagement

Procrastination and other mishandlings of time are common obstacles to success for online students and on-campus students alike. The temptations for time mismanagement associated with the flexibility of college courses are only magnified when you are assigned online coursework, but don't be fooled; online coursework typically requires as much, or more, time of students.

Chapter 5, Time Management Strategies, will discuss many strategies for how you can use long-standing time management techniques, as well as today's technologies, to help you avoid time mismanagement and achieve success in your online coursework.

Online Isolation

Being outside of the traditional classroom can be an isolating experience for many students. For most of us, we have had years of experience working with other students and our instructors in the conventional classroom, and we have developed many useful strategies for being successful in that environment. Yet, transferring those talents and developing positive relationships with other students in an online learning environment is not a skill that most of us have developed.

In Chapter 6, Developing Positive Online Relationships, the suggestions, tips, tools, and techniques will focus on providing you with the skills for developing a positive online relationship with your professors and classmates.

Lack of Training for Online Success

Few high schools (and only a small number of colleges or universities) adequately prepare students for being successful in their studies and even fewer provide students with necessary learning skills and study habits for success in online coursework. Even though online technologies have become more universal in their use in education, their application rarely affords students with the opportunities to build effective strategies for success in college courses that require greater critical thinking and independent learning. Yet, surmounting this obstacle and achieving success in online coursework only requires that you adapt many of your study habits, as well as adopt a few new learning skills, for the online classroom.

From tips on how to avoid miscommunications to suggestions for getting the most out of online readings, Chapter 7, Study Tips for Online Students, will provide you with a comprehensive guide to success in a quick and easy-to-access format that you can use throughout your college experience.

Decreasing Motivation

Maintaining motivation throughout the semester is an obstacle for countless students taking on-campus or online courses. Although most students are typically excited about their college courses each semester, by Thanksgiving or spring break many of us are exhausted from the long hours of studying and find it difficult to remain focused on the exams and term papers that still have to be completed. The added potential for online isolation can sometimes only further undermine motivation. Through planning and practical motivational strategies, however, each of us can build skills for maintaining our motivation throughout the semester.

In Chapter 8, Getting Motivated, Staying Motivated, we will discuss several strategies that will help you prevent a decrease in motivation throughout the semester.

Technical Know-How

The final obstacle to success in online coursework is acquiring the necessary technical skills to take advantage of the many features offered by today's computer software applications and the Internet. While most online coursework will only require minimal computer skills (such as locating a Webpage, writing a paper in a word processing application, and sending an email), success in college comes much easier for students who know how to utilize the numerous features of software applications that can improve the quality of their college assignments and activities. Features that can help you stay organized, promptly find files, quickly identify useful online resources, share information between software applications, and many others, are all common in most of today's software applications.

In the How To Tutorials section you will find detailed guides for completing many of the tasks you will require in order to be successful in your online coursework. These guides provide step-by-step instructions for effectively using many of the features you will want to use in software applications like Microsoft Word and Internet Explorer, as well as the Web portals like WebCT and Blackboard. Take a few minutes to review the tutorials and then keep this book next to your computer so you can quickly find the guides you want, when you require them. As a quick reference guide, a list of the How To Tutorials, along with a summary list of useful tips, is available on the inside cover of this book.

Introduction for Instructors

Whether it is in the traditional classroom or the online classroom, the fundamentals of success are rooted in the effective learning skills and study habits of students. From knowing the acronyms used to memorize the spectrum of color (such as, r.o.y.g.b.i.v. or h.o.m.e.s)[1] to utilizing computer-based systems for learning complex foreign languages, these skills are used in the traditional college environment by students around the world. Whether students are enrolled in an English course that meets on-campus and requires some additional online assignments, or they are taking a completely online biology course, using the skills that led to their success in the traditional classroom by no means guarantees their success in this new and challenging online learning environment.

The online classroom is a new learning environment for almost all students. And while many students have been very successful in the traditional classroom, the online learning environment presents to them an array of obstacles and opportunities that must be addressed in order to be successful. This book is intended to provide students with the appropriate strategies and tactics for achieving success with any online coursework, whether it is for an entirely online course or for a course that simply uses online tools to supplement on-campus experiences. Throughout this companion we will address specific steps that can be taken by any student to realize their goals and gain the most from the online course experiences.

Based on our years of experience in both taking and teaching online courses, we have identified two fundamental skills that are essential to the success of online students. Each chapter in this book will guide and assist students in developing these skills as they apply to the e-learning success.

The first skill of successful students doing online coursework is to *adapt old skills and habits from the traditional classroom for use in the online classroom.*

Students enter the online classroom with a range of learning skills and study habits that they have developed through their years of experience in the traditional classroom. While some of these skills and habits are not useful in achieving goals (for example, day dreaming while giving the appearance of paying attention to the instructor), many of these skills and habits will provide students with an excellent foundation for adapting to the new characteristics of the online learning environment. In this book we will build upon these skills and habits whenever possible.

The second skill of successful online students is to *develop and apply new skills and habits for the online classroom.*

The learning skills and study habits necessary for success in the online classroom are not always the same as those utilized in the conventional classroom. The new technologies that offer students the opportunity to expand their education at a distance, also produce barriers to success that are dealt with by successful students through the development of new skills and habits specific to the online environment. Throughout this book we will provide guidance and directions for developing these new learning skills and study habits that can help your students to be successful in any college course that utilizes online technologies.

Success in online coursework requires the effective integration of online strategies and student success skills (see the figure below). By combining the learning skills and study habits that are required for success in any college course with the distinctive skills required in online learning environments, your students can build the expertise to be successful in any online coursework that may be required throughout their college education.

Each day professors, instructors, multimedia developers, Web-masters, and many other professionals around the world are working to develop online learning environments that can offer students the necessary tools and resources for being successful. But their work can only provide students with the opportunities for success; the real work is still on the shoulders of the learner. In order to be successful in these new learning environments, students must also work on developing the necessary learning skills and study habits that can translate into success in the online classroom. This book is intended to provide the foundation for that success though the implementation of study habits and learning skills unique to the online environment.

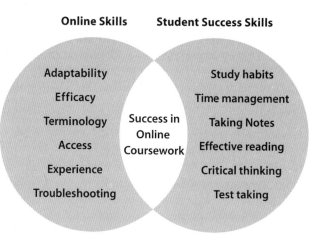

The integration of online skills and student success skills.[2]

Introduction for Students

Getting the Most from This Book

Being successful in today's college courses requires that you not only develop effective learning skills and study habits for use in the on-campus classroom, but that you also develop the skills necessary for success when your courses use online technologies (such as, real-time chats, online discussion boards, email, etc.) to supplement your education. The *E-learning Companion* is intended to provide you with a course resource and quick-reference guide for developing the necessary technology skills and study habits for achieving success in any college course that uses online technology. As a result, you will want to get the most out of this book by using it as college textbook, workbook, and user manual for all of your college courses.

Who Should Use This Book?

The integration of online technologies with conventional teaching strategies is significantly changing the learning skills and study habits required of today's college and university students. From those attending large state universities to those enrolled at local liberal arts colleges or community colleges, first year students and seniors alike are finding that developing the knowledge and skills for effectively using Internet technologies in their studies is a crucial element of their education. College professors are increasingly using online technologies to supplement (or even replace) many of the course requirements that had traditionally been confined to the classroom. The resources, tools, ideas, activities, suggestions, tips, examples, and recommendations included in this book can nonetheless be useful to students at any time in their education: high school, college, graduate school, or even on-the-job training.

As with any book, however, in order for the examples and illustrations to be useful in developing the knowledge and skills for success, they cannot be as broad and general as to apply to all students at any level of their educational experience. Therefore, in an effort to provide useful skills, resources, and suggestions, we have attempted to focus on the widespread abilities required of college and university students.

How do you know if this book is for you?

✔ Are you currently or do you plan to enroll in a course at a **community college, career school, or junior college?** If so, then yes this book is for you.

(continued)

✔ Are you currently or do you plan to enroll in a course at a **liberal arts college** or **university?** If so, then yes this book is for you.

✔ Are you currently or do you plan to enroll in a **college level distance education** course? If so, then yes this book is for you.

✔ Are you currently a **high school student** preparing for the rigors of college? If so, then this book is a wonderful resource that will help you prepare for success in online college coursework. Although some of the examples and suggestions may not directly apply to your present setting, the tips and suggestions provided throughout this companion will supply you with useful skills for any online activity.

✔ Are you currently an employee who is or will be taking an **online training course?** If so, then the *E-learning Companion* is a wonderful resource to help you prepare to be successful in online training or work related activities. While some of the illustrations may not directly apply to your present setting, the recommendations and tips for success with online technologies are as equally useful in the workplace as they are in the classroom.

What is Online Coursework?

As the Internet has become a beneficial and widely used tool by students, the introduction of online technologies for course assignments and activities has become widespread at most colleges and universities. From required online discussions with your instructor to Internet-based quizzes, the use of online technologies to move education outside the boundaries of the classroom will require that you sharpen many of your skills.

The term *coursework* can be used to describe any of the assignments, activities, research requirements, exams, or other tasks that are required of students in successfully demonstrating their mastery of course topic. When coursework can be completed using the computer and the Internet then it can be considered *online coursework*. Examples of online coursework could include:

▶ Using email to contact your professor with a question on an upcoming assignment,

▶ Using your college's Web portal to review a course syllabus,

▶ Using your computer's word processing software to edit a collaborative research paper,

▶ Using instant messaging to organize a group project,

▶ Using the World Wide Web to access online library resources from your home computer.

When Should I Use This Book?

For many students this book will likely be a practical and valuable resource starting in their first year of college. Just as the transition from high school to college requires many changes in the study habits of students, the use of online technologies in courses will require that you not only adapt some of your earlier study habits for this new environment, but that you also develop some new skills for being successful in online coursework.

The *first year experience* or *college survival* course that may be offered at your college or university will likely provide you with a wealth of skills and resources for being successful in the college classroom. As a companion to the many resources you have available as a college student, the numerous tools and techniques for translating those skills into successful habits for the online learning environment can be found in this book.

If your college or university doesn't offer a course focused on building the skills for being successful in college, then this book will be a priceless resource in developing the variety of skills that have helped thousands of students to be successful.

Accordingly, even if you are buying this book part way through your college experience, it is a wonderful time to gain additional skills for ensuring your current success as more faculty adopt online technologies for use in their courses as well as to build habits that you can apply in training programs in the future. It is never too late to start fostering new and useful study habits that can ensure your success in the emerging online classroom and provide you with the skills necessary for a successful transition to using technology in the workplace.

Where Should I Use This Book?

Our hope is that this is not just another book in which you read only those chapters that an instructor assigns as required readings for a course. This book is intended to be valuable resource that you can keep next to your computer as a reference guide when you have questions or concerns in completing online activities and assignments. Take notes throughout each chapter, fold down the corners of pages that you may want to come back to, complete the activities to gage your progress, and even tear out pages that you think would be good reminders and post them on a bulletin board. Please take this book with you to the library and the computer lab; leaving this book to collect dust on your bookshelf (or selling it back to the bookstore at the end of the semester) will do little to guarantee that you are successful when your courses later in college require online participation.

Why Should I Use This Book?

There are many reasons why we believe you should be using this book as you prepare to be successful in college. Here are just a few:

▶ Merely applying the same learning skills and study habits that made you successful in the past does not guarantee your success in the future.

▶ Today's college classroom is no longer confined to a traditional lecture hall.

▶ Simply making it through college is no longer enough to ensure that you are prepared for success in the future.

▶ You can't assume that your instructor will provide you with the knowledge and skills for being successful in online course activities and assignments.

▶ Other books on student success may not adequately address how learning online differs from that in the conventional classroom.

Key Features of this Book

Hot Tips

While there are hundreds of essential tips and suggestions for how to be successful in online coursework throughout this book, we have identified many that we consider to be critical for success. When you see one or more "hot tips" icons, take some extra time to think about how you can use that specific recommendation in your college courses. The more "hot tips" icons, the greater significance of the tip.

Activities

Throughout this book we have included a variety of activities that you can do in order to practice many of the strategies and skills of successful students. Completing these activities as you read through each chapter can help build your comprehension and increase the likelihood that the skills discussed in this book will become successful study habits that you use throughout your college experience.

Exercises

In addition to the activities included within each chapter of this book, there are also longer exercises found at the end of chapters. These exercises often require that you have access to a computer that is linked to the World Wide Web, while the chapter activities can be done without any additional resources.

How To Tutorials

Included in this book are thirty-two How To Tutorials, providing you with step-by-step instructions for completing many of the online skills that are discussed in each chapter. When you see the How To Tutorials icon with a number, this indicates that there is an associated tutorial for the skills being discussed on that page. For quick-reference there is also an index of the How To Tutorials on the inside front cover of this book. Each How To Tutorial is also available on the *E-learning Companion* Website with additional illustrations: **<http://collegesurvival.college.hmco.com/students>**.

Student-to-Student-Tips

Included in this book are more than 50 tips that we have received from successful students from around the world. Each of these recommendations is based on these students' experiences in completing online course assignments and activities.

Glossary

We have selected words or phrases that you may not be familiar with to include in the glossary of this book. Terms that are defined in the glossary can be identified throughout this book since they will be underlined. If you come across an underlined term that you are unfamiliar with, take a minute to review how the term is defined in relation to online coursework before continuing. In addition, there are online flashcards available for terms provided in the glossary at the *E-learning Companion* Website: **<http://collegesurvival.college.hmco.com/students>**.

How Should I Use This Book?

Don't be afraid to write in this book.

Fill in each of the activities, checklists, and exercises with your responses. Take notes in the margins and update any information that you may find to be slightly different at your college or university. The *E-learning Companion* is intended to be a resource that you will use throughout your college experience.

Use the How To Tutorials

The How To Tutorials in the back of the book provide step-by-step instructions for completing many of the tasks required for being successful in your online coursework. From attaching files to an email to participating in an online chat, the How To Tutorials are an essential resource that you should keep near your computer. When you see the How To Tutorials icon in the margin, refer to the related tutorials section at the end of the book for easy steps to help you develop that skill. Online versions of the How To Tutorials, with additional illustrations, are also available at **<http://collegesurvival. college.hmco.com/students>**.

Apply the skills whenever you can.

None of us were born with all of the skills and knowledge for being success-ful in college. Actually, for most of us, developing these learning skills and turning them into successful study habits requires a good deal of practice. Be sure to take the time to apply the techniques, tips, and methods de-scribed in this book whenever you can, even when using the Internet for ac-tivities that have nothing to do with your courses. Only by practicing useful skills will they develop into study habits that become an inherent part of your college education.

After reading the book, keep it nearby as a resource.

Some books you can read and then put on the shelf for the rest of your col-lege career, while others will be valuable resources that you will want to refer back to often. In helping you to be successful in college, we hope that this book is the latter. Keep the *E-learning Companion* near your computer or in the book bag that you take to the computer lab; you never know when you will want to refer back to a chapter, illustration, tutorial, or resource that may be useful in your studies.

One size does not fit all.

Applying each and every study strategy that we describe in this book may not be beneficial for everyone. As a result, if there are tips and techniques that just don't seem to work for you, skip over them and move on to the next. After all, your individual success is the goal.

Each student should develop their own unique set of learning skills and study habits that work best for them. And while you should highlight, cir-cle, or otherwise mark the strategies that will be useful to you immediately, don't forget to come back to this book as the online demands of your courses change each semester and throughout your college experience. The strategies and tips that may not sound useful this semester may be very helpful a year or two from now.

NOTES

1. r.o.y.g.b.i.v. is an acronym for the colors in the visible spectrum: red, or-ange, yellow, green, blue, indigo, and violet; and h.o.m.e.s. is an acronym for the five Great Lakes: Huron, Ontario, Michigan, Erie, and Superior.
2. Based in part on Anderson and Kanuka, 2003

E-learning Readiness Self-Assessment

Self-assessments are tools that we can use in developing learning skills and study habits for college success. Take a few minutes now to complete the E-learning Readiness Self-Assessment starting on the next page.[1] The E-learning Readiness Self-Assessment will provide you with individual feedback on your readiness to be successful in online course assignments and activities, helping to guide your path as you develop necessary skills and habits. This individualized feedback can also be useful in determining how to use this book and where you should focus additional time and energy in developing necessary skills for success.

After completing the E-learning Readiness Self-Assessment follow the guidelines provided at the end of the assessment for scoring and interpreting the results;[2] make special note of those chapters which may require that you spend some additional time and energy studying the strategies and suggestions provided in this book. By using the Self-Assessment as a guide to your development of online study skills, you will better be able to build on your prior experiences in order to improve your online proficiencies.

An online version of the E-learning Readiness Self-Assessment is also available on the *E-learning Companion* Website at **<http://collegesurvival.college.hmco.com/students>.**

For each item below indicate your agreement with the statement by circling the corresponding value. For each category of statements, calculate your average response by dividing the total value of your responses by the number of items. When you have calculated your average response for each category, complete the interpretation table provided at the end of the Self-Assessment.

1 = Completely disagree
2 = Strongly disagree
3 = Not sure
4 = Strongly agree
5 = Completely agree

Technology Access

I have access to a computer with an Internet connection.	1 2 3 4 5
I have access to a fairly new computer (e.g., enough RAM, speakers, CD-ROM).	1 2 3 4 5
I have access to a computer with adequate software (e.g., Microsoft Word, Adobe Acrobat).	1 2 3 4 5
Average response (total ÷ 3)	

Technology Access

I have the basic skills to operate a computer (e.g., saving files, creating folders).	1 2 3 4 5
I have the basic skills for finding my way around the Internet (e.g., using search engines, entering passwords).	1 2 3 4 5
I can send an email with a file attached.	1 2 3 4 5
I think that I would be comfortable using a computer several times a week to participate in a course.	1 2 3 4 5
Average response (total ÷ 4)	

Online Relationships

I think that I would be able to communicate effectively with others using online technologies (e.g., email, chat).	1	2	3	4	5
I think that I would be able to express myself clearly through my writing (e.g., mood, emotions, humor).	1	2	3	4	5
I think that I would be able to use online tools (e.g., email, chat) to work on assignments with students who are in different time zones.	1	2	3	4	5
I think that I would be able to schedule time to provide timely responses to other students and/or the instructor.	1	2	3	4	5
I think that I would be able to write clearly in order to ask questions and make comments.	1	2	3	4	5
Average response (total ÷ 5)					

Motivation

I think that I would be able to remain motivated even though the instructor is not online at all times.	1	2	3	4	5
I think that I would be able to complete my work even when there are online distractions (e.g., friends sending emails, Websites to surf).	1	2	3	4	5
I think that I would be able to complete my work even when there are distractions in my home (e.g., television, children, roommates).	1	2	3	4	5
Average response (total ÷ 3)					

Online Video/Audio

I think that I would be able to relate the content of short video clips (1-3 minutes typically) to the information I have read online or in books.	1	2	3	4	5
I think that I would be able to take notes while watching a video on the computer.	1	2	3	4	5
I think that I would be able to understand course-related information when it's presented in video formats.	1	2	3	4	5
Average response (total ÷ 3)					

(continued)

Internet Discussions

I think that I would be able to carry on a conversation with others using the Internet (e.g., Internet chat, instant messenger).	1 2 3 4 5
I think that I would be comfortable having several discussions taking place in the same online chat even though I may not be participating in all of them.	1 2 3 4 5
I think that I would be able to follow along with an online conversation (e.g., Internet chat, instant messenger) while typing.	1 2 3 4 5
I sometimes prefer to have more time to prepare responses to a question.	1 2 3 4 5
Average response (total ÷ 4)	

Importance to Your Success

Regular contact with the instructor is important to my success in online coursework.	1 2 3 4 5
Quick technical and administrative support is important to my success in online coursework.	1 2 3 4 5
Frequent participation throughout the learning process is important to my success in online coursework.	1 2 3 4 5
I feel that prior experiences with online technologies (e.g., email, Internet chat, online readings) are important to my success with online course.	1 2 3 4 5
The ability to immediately apply course materials is important to my success with online courses.	1 2 3 4 5
Average response (total ÷ 5)	

Scoring and Interpretation

After completing the E-learning Readiness Self-Assessment you should calculate your average response for each section of the assessment. This is calculated by dividing the total (i.e., sum) of each section by the number of items included in that section. Based on your average score in each section of the Self-Assessment there may be particular chapters of this book where you should focus more of your time and attention (see the table below).

We recommend that for any section of the Self-Assessment in which your average response score was a 3 or below, you would benefit from spending additional time studying the strategies and suggestions provided in the related chapters of this book.

Relating self-assessment results to chapters in the *E-learning Companion*.

Your Average Response	Section of Self-Assessment	Focus Chapter (s)
_____	Technology Access	Chapter 1
_____	Technology Skills	Chapter 2
_____	Online Relationships	Chapters 6 and 7
_____	Motivation	Chapter 8
_____	Online Video/Audio	Chapters 2 and 7
_____	Internet Discussions	Chapters 2 and 7
_____	Importance to Your Success	Chapters 3, 4, and 5

When you have completed your initial reading of the learning skills and study habits discussed throughout this book, we suggest that you again complete the E-learning Readiness Self-Assessment to evaluate your progress and to help you further develop strategies for strengthening the skills necessary for success in online college coursework.

NOTES

1. Based in part on Watkins, 2003.
2. Funding for research regarding the reliability and validity of E-learning Readiness Self-Assessment was provided through a grant from the International Society of Performance Improvement.

E-learning Vocabulary

Either as a supplement to traditional on-campus courses or as part of entirely online courses, online coursework is today an essential ingredient in an education for students at all stages of their academic and professional careers. No longer are students limited by the boundaries of geography and time that once characterized the traditional college classroom. Educational technologies (such as the computer, World Wide Web, and audio/video conferencing) have transformed colleges, universities, libraries, and other training centers from 9:00 to 5:00 organizations (with some limited evening and weekend opportunities) into institutions that have the opportunity to serve your ever-growing educational requirements 24 hours-a-day, 7 days-a-week, 365 days-a-year.

The first step to success in online college coursework is, therefore, being prepared to take advantage of the learning opportunities supported by the technology. From being able to retrieve your <u>email</u> to viewing video lectures on your computer, to being prepared to meet the technology requirements, you have to know the basic terminology of online coursework. In this chapter we will discuss many of the frequently used words and phrases that you are likely to find when you enter the online classroom. Beginning with words like "email" and "instant messaging," building your e-learning vocabulary will help you understand the online requirements of your college courses and be the first step on your journey to success.

E-learning Experiences

It was a fall evening in 1995 when I was introduced to the Internet as a practical tool for education. Sitting in our rental house in a student-ghetto near campus, my college roommate and I decided to push the modem on his first "real" computer to its limits. As English and Education majors, respectively, he and I had both used computers to write term papers and play simple learning games. But for me, I figured that the primary use for the computer was as a replacement for a typewriter or secretary.

Until that evening we had only used the modem to access a few online discussion boards, and with the discussions dominated by computer scientists, this quickly lost its appeal. But with that evening's introduction to the World Wide Web our perceptions of the computer were about to change, or so we hoped. Over the next few hours we largely worked to overcome a host of network errors. After two hours of searching for a site with more than just text, the image that would be our first glimpse of the future finally started to appear, one line at a time.

With each line taking nearly 20 minutes to download it was sometime around 3:00 A.M. when my roommate woke me up to see the last line of the picture come through. The small black-and-white picture of a Russian skyline that finally appeared was not much to behold, the image quality was poor, and the total image size was no bigger than one inch by two inches, and yet the memory of seeing that picture remains with me. For the first time I realized that the computer and especially the Internet had the potential to give me access to more information than I ever could have imagined.

Understanding the Basic Lingo

The basic lingo (or terminology) of online coursework is woven into the fabric of our daily conversations. From Website addresses being included in lemonade commercials to discussions of the wireless networks in many college dorms, today most students are more familiar with the technology lingo than those students entering college just a few years before them. Yet there are many terms that are frequently used in relation to online coursework with which you may be less familiar.

To be successful in online coursework you will want to be familiar with terminology that your instructor may use in defining assignments or discussing online supplements to course materials. This chapter provides an abridged dictionary of common technology terms and is supplemented by additional e-learning vocabulary contained in the glossary.

What follows is a short list of terms commonly used in describing the technologies of online coursework:[1]

Web Portal

Definition: A <u>Website</u> considered as an entry point to other <u>Websites</u>. <u>Web portals</u> commonly provide links to a variety of online tools, resources, and links. Many colleges and other educational institutions will use <u>Web portals</u> (also called <u>educational portals</u> or course management systems) that include online tools like grade books, real-time <u>chat</u>, <u>discussion boards</u>, online whiteboards, and other course resources and links.

#18

Typical Uses in Online Coursework:
College courses will utilize <u>Web portals</u> (called <u>educational portals</u> when used as online course management tools) to provide students with easy access to multiple resources through a single <u>Website</u>. WebCT, BlackBoard, Ecollege, and other <u>Web portals</u> are commonly used <u>educational portals</u> at many institutions.[2] These services also provide the structure in which instructors can create course materials, interact with students, grade tests, and even maintain an up-to-date grade book. These <u>Websites</u> commonly require that students use a password for access and they typically include links to tools including real-time <u>chats</u>, <u>discussion boards</u>, <u>email</u>, as well as access to lectures and assignments. For students, these online software applications can provide you one-stop access to most all of the resources that you will require in completing online coursework.

#25

Real-Time Chat (Internet Rely Chat or IRC)

Definition: A network of <u>Internet</u> servers through which individual users can hold real-time online conversations. <u>Instant messaging</u> is a type of real-time <u>chat</u>.

#21

Typical Uses in Online Coursework:
<u>Chats</u> are commonly used when an instructor wants to encourage synchronous (at the same time) discussions. These discussions can be between individual students and the instructor, groups of students, or even the entire class. Real-time <u>chats</u> do, however, require that all of the participants be linked to the <u>Internet</u> at the same time. Areas within <u>educational portals</u> that are designated for real-time <u>chats</u>

#28

are typically called <u>chat</u> rooms, and most educational <u>Web portal</u>s will offer features including whiteboards for sharing graphics, multiple <u>chat</u> rooms for side discussions among student groups, and even whisper functions that allow students to <u>chat</u> with just one other individual within a larger group <u>chat</u>.

Discussion Board (Bulletin Board System or BBS)

#22

Definition: An electronic communication system that allows users to leave messages and to review messages, as well as upload or <u>download</u> software.

Typical Uses in Online Coursework:

#29

<u>Discussion board</u>s are likely to be one of the most frequently used tools for online interactions that you will have with other students and instructors. Like the name implies, students and the instructor can leave messages for others to view on a virtual bulletin board. These messages can be viewed at different times by different members of the learning community and are thus considered a form of <u>asynchronous</u> course communication. Like with real-time <u>chat</u>s, most <u>educational portal</u>s will include <u>discussion board</u>s within the online classroom. Common features in many portals include <u>threaded</u> discussions (where you can visually see which messages are replies to other messages), file <u>attachment</u>s, restricted access to messages defined by the instructor, and the ability to link to <u>Webpage</u>s outside of the portal.

Email

#19

Definition: A feature that lets a computer user send a text message to someone at another computer using the <u>Internet</u>. <u>Email</u>, or electronic mail, can duplicate most of the features of paper mail, such as storing messages in "in boxes" and "out boxes," message forwarding, providing delivery receipts, and sending multiple copies.

Typical Uses in Online Coursework:

#26

As with <u>Internet</u> <u>chat</u>s and bulletin boards, <u>email</u> is commonly used by instructors to communicate with students (as well as by students to interact with other students and the instructor). Instructors will frequently use <u>email</u> to make announcements regarding course assignments, discuss individual grades with students, and to manage other course related activities.

Email Attachments

Definition: A file of any <u>file format</u> (such as, a <u>word processing</u> document or picture) that is attached to an <u>email</u>. The contents of an attachment usually do not appear within the body of the <u>email</u> message, but can be accessed by <u>email</u> recipients by clicking on an appropriate <u>icon</u>.

#19

Typical Uses in Online Coursework:

From term papers to doctoral dissertations, <u>email</u> <u>attachments</u> are regularly used to send larger files (for example, text files that are more than a few pages long or that include graphics). In completing assignments, instructors will often request that related files be <u>email</u>ed to them as <u>attachments</u>. These files can be in most any <u>file format</u> (for example, Microsoft Word, <u>Adobe Acrobat PDF</u>, Microsoft Excel, etc.) and as a courtesy you should include the <u>file name</u> and <u>file format</u> in the text of the <u>email</u> accompanying the <u>attachment</u>. Depending on the software you use to access your <u>email</u> the process for attaching a file to the <u>email</u> may differ.

#26

Instant Messaging

Definition: A type of real-time communications that enables you to conduct a private <u>chat</u> with one or more other users. Typically, the instant messaging software will allow you to create a list of individuals that you want to have private <u>chat</u>s with and alert you whenever somebody on your list is online. You can then initiate a <u>chat</u> session with that particular individual or multiple individuals.

Typical Uses in Online Coursework:

<u>Instant messaging</u> offers students in online courses synchronous (i.e., real-time or simultaneous) communications with other students and/or the professor. From asking quick questions of the instructor to working in collaborative teams on a pro-

> **STUDENT-TO-STUDENT TIP**
>
> When working on group projects instant messaging saved me time and frustration since I could always know when other group members were online and working.

ject, <u>instant messaging</u> services (like Microsoft Messenger, ICQ, Yahoo Messenger, AOL Messenger, and many others) can provide you with a communications resource that can facilitate many of the discussions you will want to have while taking an online course. Most <u>instant messaging</u> programs will also allow you to include <u>attachments</u> with your messages. Traditionally each user had to use the same <u>instant messaging</u> software in order to communicate, but in recent releases of software several companies now offer <u>instant messaging</u> software that can communicate through multiple <u>instant messaging</u> programs (for example, you could instant message with classmates that use AOL Messenger as well as classmates that use Microsoft Messenger).

Videoconference

Definition: Conducting a meeting or conversation between two or more participants at different sites by using computer networks to transmit video and audio files.

Typical Uses in Online Coursework:

Sometimes used as the primary means for communication in some distance education courses, videoconferences are most typically limited to only those instructional activities that require synchronous (at the same time) two-way interactions among participants, due to the expenses involved. Often instructors will use videoconferences for guest speakers or to provide unique opportunities for students in multiple locations to interact with regards to a specific topic. Videoconferences use satellites or high-speed computer networks to link to two (or more) sites so that participants can communicate both verbally and visually with each other in a synchronous format. Typically videoconference equipment utilizes television technology that is supplemented with computer technology.

Desk-top videoconferencing is also available for participants to exchange both audio and video information through their personal computers. The quality of audio and video using desk-top videoconferencing equipment is dependent on the speed of <u>Internet</u> access available at each computer engaged in the conference and the computer itself.

Streaming Audio and Video

Definition: A technique for transferring data from one computer to another such that it can be processed as a steady and continuous stream. Streaming technologies are becoming increasingly important with the growth of the <u>Internet</u> because most users do not have fast enough access to <u>download</u> large multimedia files quickly. With streaming audio and video your <u>Web browser</u> can start displaying the audio or video data before the entire file has been received.

Typical Uses in Online Coursework:

Audio or video segments are often used by professors to supplement classroom instruction or to provide complete lectures to students at a distance. Like other forms of video or audio (for example, DVDs, video tapes, compact discs, etc.), students have access to watch or listen to the instructor any time they wish. Given file size and cost limitations, streaming audio and video are most commonly used when the instructor wishes to convey a large amount of course content, in the same format, to all students in the course (rather than individualized instruction for particular students).

Listserv

Definition: A mailing list manager used for the distribution of <u>email</u> among the list's members.

Typical Uses in Online Coursework:

Today's college instructors typically use <u>listservs</u> when they want to communicate the same message to all students in a course or when they want to facilitate discussions that can include multiple students outside of the classroom. Most <u>listservs</u> require that you subscribe or register before you can send or receive messages with other members of the <u>listserv</u>. Often, however, instructors will subscribe all of the students in a class to a course <u>listserv</u> to facilitate communications. Although <u>listservs</u> do not allow instructors or students to limit the recipient list for broadcast <u>emails</u>, they can be effectively used to facilitate online coursework (especially when students have limited access to the <u>Internet</u> and their <u>email</u>).

ACTIVITY 1-1   **Have you missed something?**

As a review, answer the following questions by circling True or False for each statement.

1. **True–False**   A <u>listserv</u> uses <u>email</u> to communicate the same message to many members of a group.

2. **True–False**   Instant messaging allows you to communicate online using similar techniques to those that you would use on a <u>discussion board</u>.

3. **True–False**   You must use a separate software application to send <u>attachments</u> with an <u>email</u>.

4. **True–False**   <u>Educational portals</u> provide a single <u>Website</u> that students can use to link to many online resources.

5. **True–False**   A <u>discussion board</u> offers a form of synchronous conversation for students.

Checking Technology Requirements

Many of the courses you will take as part of your college education will require the use of some form of computer technology. From finding books in the college library to continuing discussions of class topics well after the on-campus lectures, technology today is interwoven into the curriculum of most courses. Some coursework may require that you have access to video conferencing equipment, while others may require specific software applications. In all cases, though, when classes begin each semester you should explore the course requirements to make sure that you have adequate access to all of the necessary resources to be successful.

It is also often useful, when possible, for students to contact their course instructor prior to starting classes to review the technology requirements. During this introductory conversation (either using <u>email</u> or the telephone) you will not only want to determine what technology resources are required for the course (such as <u>Internet</u> access, <u>email</u>, <u>word processing</u>), but also the extent of previous online experiences the instructor recommends for students. Depending on your access to technology you may also want to ask the instructor about the technologies available through the institution rather than purchasing them yourself for personal use.

Important technology questions to ask your instructor:

✔ What online technologies will be used in the course (for example, the <u>Internet</u>, <u>email</u>, online <u>discussion boards</u>, online library databases, etc.)?

✔ What minimum computer specifications are recommended for students in the course (such as, current versions of software applications)?

✔ How much experience should students have with online technologies in order to be successful in the course?

✔ Do the college's computer labs have the necessary software?

For most college students financial considerations are part of course enrollment decisions each semester. Additional hardware or software requirements should also be considered as part of the cost associated with a course. However, there are alternatives to purchasing the hardware or software for your personal use. Many students unfortunately do not take full advantage of the computer technologies (including <u>Internet</u> access) commonly available in college or public libraries. Many local recreation centers and public schools also offer free (or low cost) access to <u>Internet</u> or other technologies that you may require. These, and other alternative resources, can be used to reduce the costs of technology requirements.

STUDENT-TO-STUDENT TIP

Even though you may think you have prepared for a course by having accessed the software application previously and familiarized yourself with the tools and technology, always expect the unexpected.

Not all minimal hardware requirements will apply to all courses offered under an umbrella organization (a community college, university, or corporation). For example, while broadband access (for example, DSL or cable modem connection) may be required for courses that use synchronous video and audio <u>chat</u> software (for example, Microsoft Netmeeting), the course you are interested in may only require dial-up <u>modem</u> access since the instructor only uses <u>asynchronous</u> discussions (such as, <u>discussion boards</u>) for course communications. Therefore it is important to examine the hardware requirements of both the individual course you are considering as well as the requirements of the institution offering the course.

Additional hardware that may be required for online coursework could include desktop video systems, digital cameras, scanners, access to video-conferencing equipment, and other technologies. Whatever the technologies that you will be required to use, you should become familiar with the requirements as early in the semester as possible. This will give you time to identify alternative resources if you do not own or wish to purchase the required technologies, and it will give you time to try them out once or twice before your course assignments are due.

Familiarizing Yourself with Required Hardware

The hardware requirements necessary for online coursework should be examined in detail as soon as they are available. Typically they will be specified in a syllabus or other information provided by the instructor during the first week of classes. Also, you shouldn't be afraid to contact the instructor prior to the first day of class to identify what hardware may be required for success in the course. You will want to spend whatever free time you have before the course begins to verify that you meet the specifications and to get familiar with the required hardware in order to make sure that it works correctly when the time comes to participate online.

A few terms related to computer hardware that you should be familiar with in determining if the technology you have available meets the minimal requirements include:

CPU (Central Processing Unit)

Definition: The part of a computer that interprets and executes instructions (i.e., the brains of the computer). Sometimes referred to as the processor or chip, the CPU is where most calculations take place. In terms of computing power, the CPU is not the only critical element of a computer system, though it is likely the most important element.

What Is Important and Why:
As the central control unit for the calculations that are the foundation of computer technologies, the faster the CPU works, the more quickly the computer will be able to start software applications, project Webpages on the monitor, save large files to the hard disk, and so forth. In recent years the accelerated capabilities of this component have allowed computer technologies to perform more and more complex tasks in shorter time spans than ever before.

Typically software will require a minimum CPU speed rating that is calculated in Megahertz (Mhz). Typically the greater the Megahertz rating, the faster the CPU, though this is not always true with newly designed CPUs that offer greater speeds at fewer Megahertz (for example, a 400Mhz Intel Pentium IV CPU may be faster than a 500 Mhz Intel Pentium III CPU). Getting more <u>CPU</u> speed with fewer Megahertz is desirable since that will reduce the amount of heat produced by the <u>CPU</u> and provide for greater efficiency. All of which is important to long-term performance of the component.

As a student you will want to make sure that you have a <u>CPU</u> installed in your computer that meets the minimum requirements for the software applications that you will be using for your coursework. For example, the application Microsoft Office XP (released in 2002, described in "Familiarizing Yourself with Required Software" on page 14) requires a minimal <u>CPU</u> for computers running Microsoft Windows software of the equivalent to a Pentium III CPU (third generation of the Pentium brand CPU manufactured by Intel). For those with Macintosh computers, the equivalent software package is Microsoft Office v. X (released in 2002), which requires the Macintosh G3 CPU, at a minimum, to function properly. If your coursework requires the use of these software applications then these would be minimum hardware requirements for computers that you could use to complete your assignments.

Hard Disk Drive

Definition: A rigid metal disk fixed within a disk drive and used for storing computer data even when the computer is turned off. Hard disks provide considerably more storage space and quicker access than most other data storage devices.

What Is Important and Why:
The hard disk drive provides for the long-term storage of data in the computer. <u>Operating system</u>s and other software applications are each stored in the memory that is part of the hard disk drive. Though the user can erase data that is stored on the hard disk drive, it is not lost when the computer's power supply is turned off.

#2

#4

Using the tools of the <u>operating system</u> you will want to create <u>folder</u>s on the hard disk drive to store data that you may want to find again. If you don't store data on the disk drive in some orderly fashion, it can easily be misplaced and hard to find again when you are ready to retrieve it. The larger the hard disk drive, the more data you can store in your computer. Recent advances in technology have allowed the storage capacity of hard disk drives to increase to such a size that it is unlikely that you will run out of storage space on most modern computers. Hard drives that can store multiple Gigs of data (a Gig is equivalent to approximately eight billion single characters representing data as either a one or a zero) will typically provide you with more than enough storage space for your college coursework. Expanded memory may be required, however, if you store large sound and/or video files on your computer's hard disk drive.

RAM (Random Access Memory)

Definition: All data does not require storage on the hard disk drive for later use. Storing data that is only required for a short time, while the computer is making calculations, is done using Random Access Memory (RAM). RAM allows the CPU to access the data it requires without having to go through other data first, making RAM faster than memory that offers sequential access (such as a hard disk drive or CD-ROM). When a computer is turned on, the information from the start up is immediately loaded in RAM. New or changed data will be stored in RAM until it can be written to a hard disk or other storage device. Data stored in RAM is, however, lost every time the computer is turned off or loses power.

What Is Important and Why:
RAM provides the short-term memory for your computer. When the supply of power to the computer is turned off, however, any data that is stored in the RAM memory will be lost forever. Increasing the amount of RAM memory you have available in your computer will increase the performance of your computer since data that could be stored temporarily on the hard disk drive can instead be stored in the RAM memory. Since data in RAM memory can be stored and re-trieved at a much faster rate than that stored on the hard disk drive (which requires the spinning of multiple metal disks in order to lo-cate and retrieve data), the computer's CPU can use the information in RAM memory to make more calculations in a shorter period of time.

The amount of RAM memory you have available is calculated in megabytes (with each megabyte, MB, being equivalent to approxi-mately eight million single characters representing data as either a one or a zero). Typically software applications will require a mini-mum amount of RAM memory that should be available in your computer in order to operate effectively. For example, Microsoft Of-fice XP, 2002 release, requires more than 128 MB of RAM to function properly when using their Microsoft Windows XP operating system (also described in the following section).

Though the proficiency of your computer in retrieving data from the Internet is primarily determined by the type of access you have to the Internet or World Wide Web (such as, dial-up modem, DSL modem, or network interface card), additional RAM memory can also improve download speeds since more data can be stored in short-term memory. Websites that have multiple graphics and other complex features will require more RAM memory in order to appear quickly on your computer monitor. Access to information contained within your school's Web portal (for example, WebCT or BlackBoard) will typically require at least 64 megabytes of RAM memory.

Modem or Network Interface Card (for access to the Internet and World Wide Web)

Definition: A dial-up **modem** is a device or program that enables a computer to transmit data over telephone lines. A dial-up modem converts data from digital signals to analog signal and vice versa, so that computers can communicate over telephone lines, which transmit analog waves. Newer modems can also provide similar service through cable television lines, or high-speed Internet access through fiber-optic phone lines.

Network Interface Card, often abbreviated as NIC, is a device that allows your computer to be connected directly (i.e., without using phone lines) to a network of multiple computers that are linked together, and then the entire network can be linked to the Internet and World Wide Web. Most NICs are designed for a particular type of network, protocol, and media, although some can serve multiple networks.

The **Internet** is a massive network that connects millions of computers together globally, forming a network in which any computer can communicate with any other computer as long as they are both connected to the Internet. Information that travels over the Internet does so via a variety of languages known as protocols.

The **World Wide Web,** or simply Web, is a way of accessing information over the medium of the Internet. It is an information-sharing model that is built on top of the Internet. The Web uses the hypertext transfer protocol (or HTTP), only one of the languages spoken over the Internet, to transmit data. Web documents using HTTP can contain graphics, sounds, text, and video.[3]

What Is Important and Why:
The type of hardware you use to connect to the Internet and the World Wide Web will directly impact the speed at which you can access materials available online. If you associate your Internet access with that of a hose attached to the spigot at your house, the bigger the diameter of the hose, the more water that can come through the hose at any given time (this is known as bandwidth). Likewise, the diameter of the nozzle that you hold in your hand will also control the amount of water that can come out of the hose (as does the nozzle attached to the spigot). The modem in your computer works much like the nozzle in your hand, the faster the modem, the faster information can flow from the Internet into your computer.

The nozzle attached to the spigot also controls the flow, and with a computer linked to the Internet, the server (or host computer) that you link to through your Internet Service Provider (ISP) will regulate the flow of information. If you link to the Internet with an ISP that offers high-speed Internet access (for example, DSL or cable) then you will be able to have a much greater flow of information into your computer than those students that connect using conventional phone lines and a dial-up modem.

But the control over the flow of information doesn't end there; several other factors will also dictate how fast you can receive information. The speed of the computer <u>host</u>ing the <u>Website</u> you are accessing (these computers are called servers since they serve data to many users), the speed of your computer (see previous definitions), as well as the number of users attempting to access information at the same time are all factors that affect the rate of flow of information. Each of these variables plays a role in how fast you will be able to access course related <u>Website</u>s.

Making a decision about how you will access online coursework doesn't have to be complicated. If you have access to the <u>Internet</u> through a network on campus (for example, through your dorm) then you will likely have a fast enough connection to be successful in coursework. If you are, however, accessing the <u>Internet</u> and World Wide Web from another location that isn't connected to a campus network, then you will want to choose the method by which you can best access coursework based on your demands. If you are taking a completely online course that does not meet on campus, then you will likely have greater demands for a faster connection to the <u>Internet</u> and would want to choose a high speed connection by DSL or cable <u>modem</u>. These connections cost more per month, but when you are accessing a variety of interactive media files (for example, video, audio, etc.) the faster flow of information can make a difference in your course performance.

If you are taking classes that meet on-campus and use the World Wide Web to facilitate learning activities, you may want to remain with the less expensive dial-up <u>modem</u> connection to the <u>Internet</u>. When the class demands for online activities and assignments is greater, you can always utilize alternative resources, like the computers in the lab at college or those in a public library, to access online materials.

ACTIVITY 1-2   Have you missed something?

As a review, mark the phrase that correctly completes each of the following statements.

1. Data stored in Random Access Memory (RAM)...

   a. is erased when the computer is turned on.

   b. is erased when the computer is turned off.

   c. can only be erased by the user.

(continued)

ACTIVITY 1-2   **Have you missed something?**

  2. The hard disk stores information on...

    a. a plastic disk called a plate.

    b. a metal disk called a platter.

    c. a length of plastic tape.

  3. A <u>modem</u> converts...

    a. analog data into digital data.

    b. digital data into analog data.

    c. analog data into digital data and digital data into analog data.

Familiarizing Yourself with Required Software

Determining if you have the software required for online coursework can be as confusing as the hardware. You should take the time prior to enrolling in an online course to resolve what software, if any, you require. While many courses use only <u>Internet</u>-based software that is purchased, administered, and maintained by the institution offering the course (see <u>Internet</u> portals defined previously), there may be other required software that must be installed on your computer in order to complete course requirements. For example, many instructors will only accept research papers and other documents in Microsoft Word or <u>Adobe Acrobat PDF</u> formats.

No matter what software is required, you will want to be familiar with the functionality of the software prior to starting the course. There are

many similarities in how you can access analogous features in different software programs; as a result, learning to utilize the functions of your software is not as challenging as it may seem at first. With a healthy amount of curiosity and some patience you should be able to quickly learn to use most of the software features that you will use most often throughout college.

Operating Systems (Macintosh and Windows)

Description: Operating system: The foundational software installed on a computer that negotiates the basic functions between the hardware (such as, hard disk drive, modem, CD-ROM, etc.) and the software (such as, Microsoft Word, Adobe Acrobat PDF Reader, Netscape Navigator, etc.). Modern operating systems also offer a variety of features that can be used to organize files, search for files, edit basic text, repair damaged files, and so forth.

The two leading operating systems for personal computers are described below:

Macintosh Operating System (OS). Installed on a popular model of computer made by Apple Computer, the Macintosh OS was the first to feature a graphical user interface (GUI) that utilizes windows, icons, and a mouse to make it relatively easy for novices to use without learning a complex set of text commands.

As a result of the GUI operating system, all applications that run on a Macintosh computer have a similar user interface. Once a user has become familiar with one application, he or she can learn new applications relatively easily. The success of the Macintosh OS led to the widespread use of graphics-based applications and operating systems. The Windows operating system interface copies many features from the Macintosh OS.

Windows operating systems. Like the Macintosh OS, Microsoft Windows provides a graphical user interface (GUI) that allows users to easily learn to use a variety of software applications. Although released after the Macintosh OS, to gain market share Microsoft permitted other companies to develop software applications that would run within the Windows operating system while Macintosh maintained proprietary control over the Macintosh OS allowing few software applications to be created by other companies. The greater number of software applications available for the Windows operating system has made it the most used operating system in the world. By some estimates, nearly 90% of all personal computers in the world utilize a Windows operating system.

What Is Important and Why:

For the typical user, the functionality differences of today's operating systems are not as distinctive as in earlier versions. For the majority of students a computer utilizing either the Windows or Macintosh operating system will provide them with the necessary operations for success in their online coursework. Typically Internet-based software (for example, Web portals like WebCT and Blackboard) will function equally as well on computers utilizing either operating system (or even the Linux operating system which is a low cost alternative operating system for more computer savvy users).

Microsoft Office Suite

Description: A suite of Microsoft's primary software applications for computers running either Microsoft Windows or the Macintosh Operating System. Depending on the package, it includes some combination of Word, Excel, PowerPoint, Access, and Schedule along with a host of Internet and other related utilities. The applications share common functions, such as spell checking and graphing, and objects can be dragged and dropped between applications.[4]

Typical Uses in Online Coursework:
The Microsoft Office suite provides a variety of software applications in one package.[5] While competing companies offer software with similar functionality, to ensure compatibility, many colleges and universities (as well as individual instructors) require that course-related materials be submitted in the file formats associated with the products included in the Microsoft Office Suite. This isn't to say that you can't use alternative software to create the files, but the copy of the file submitted to the instructor will most often have to be saved in Microsoft Office format.[6]

Within the Microsoft Office Suite, the software program that you will most likely use is Microsoft Word. Using this word processing software you can create documents that include text, images, graphics, tables, and other features. The Microsoft Office Suite also includes Microsoft PowerPoint, which facilitates the creation of graphical images that can be used as slides in a presentation or as handouts for class discussions. Like with Microsoft Word, PowerPoint files can be saved in a HTML file format for publishing to the World Wide Web. Other software included in the Microsoft Office Suite can be used for creating databases (Microsoft Access), organizing data (Microsoft Excel), and completing the requirements of many of your course assignments. Even if you have experience with one or more of the programs available in the Microsoft Office Suite, you will want to review the technology tips provided in chapter 2 and complete How To Tutorials 5 and 6, as well as examine the online tutorials available through links provided on the *E-learning Companion* Website at **<http://collegesurvival.college.hmco.com/students>**.

> **STUDENT-TO-STUDENT TIP**
>
> Get to know the various functions of the software you will be using and test drive it every chance that you get until the features are second nature.

Web Browser (Netscape and Internet Explorer)

Description: A software application used to locate and display Web pages. The two most popular browsers are Netscape Navigator and Microsoft Internet Explorer. Both of these are graphical browsers, which means that they can display graphics as well as text. In addition, most modern browsers can present multimedia information, including sound and video, though they require plug-ins for some formats.[7]

Typical Uses in Online Coursework:

Throughout your college education you will most likely use <u>Web browser</u>s for at least one assignment in each course. From finding resources required for a term paper to participating in a group project hosted in the college's <u>Web portal</u>, you will want to be familiar with the functionality of the <u>Web browser</u> that you decide to use. The <u>Web browser</u> software will provide you with a variety of resources for expanding your educational experience including the ability to save <u>bookmark</u>s so you quickly come back to your favorite <u>Website</u>s again and viewing <u>Web page</u>s even when you are not connected to the <u>Internet</u>.

Choosing either Microsoft's Internet Explorer or Netscape's Navigator is not a critical decision. Newer versions of both software programs have few differences in functionality for the average user. Our primary recommendation to students is, however, to select one browser and stay with it. By using one <u>Web browser</u> for your online coursework you can customize the software so it is easy to find the <u>Website</u>s that you use most (using the "favorites" function in Internet Explorer or <u>bookmark</u>s in Netscape Navigator). Organizing these favorite <u>Website</u>s in <u>folder</u>s that allow you to easily find information when you require it can save you time. Finding these <u>folder</u>s can be a challenge if you have some <u>Website</u>s noted in one program and additional sites identified in the other. In addition, by staying with the same <u>Web browser</u>, you will not discover the night before a term paper is due that your <u>Web browser</u> requires additional software (i.e., a plug-in) for accessing the files you want to use.

Plug-In (or Add-In)

Description: An accessory program designed to be used in conjunction with an existing application (especially common with <u>Web browser</u>s) to extend its capabilities or provide additional functions.

Typical Uses in Online Coursework:

Most colleges use a variety of software applications to host the many resources that are used in completing online coursework. From real-time <u>chat</u>s to streaming video, often the software used to create and distribute information to students will require additional software that is not included with a <u>Web browser</u> or other software applications. When necessary, you should be able to <u>download</u> and install required plug-ins (typically for free) to ensure that you have access to all of the software functions necessary for your success in online coursework. Examples of plug-ins that are commonly required to access online resources include Macromedia Flash Player, Apple QuickTime, and <u>Adobe Acrobat PDF </u>Reader. (See chapter 2, table 2-5, for a

#14

#10

#15

list of plug-ins and other software applications that are available for free.)

Antivirus Software

Description: A utility that checks <u>emails</u>, memory, and disks for computer viruses and removes those that it finds. Since new viruses corrupt, you should periodically update the <u>antivirus</u> program's virus definitions on your computer; though some programs will now do this automatically over the <u>Internet</u>.

Typical Uses in Online Coursework:
Throughout your college experience you will be receiving numerous <u>emails</u>, as well as <u>downloading</u> many files from course <u>Websites</u> and other sources, which may contain virus applications that can destroy data stored in or disrupt the performance of your computer. Installing an <u>antivirus</u> software application (such as, McAfee Antivirus, Norton Antivirus, etc.), and keeping the virus definitions file up-to-date can protect you from these potential threats by scanning each file that enters your computer for known computer viruses. Many colleges provide <u>antivirus</u> software to students at no charge, and many others require that students purchase <u>antivirus</u> software.

Adobe Acrobat PDF (Reader and Writer)

#7

Description: Document exchange software from Adobe that allows documents created on one platform to be displayed and printed exactly the same on another no matter which fonts are installed in the computer. The fonts are embedded within the Acrobat document, which is known as a PDF (Portable Document Format) file, thus eliminating the requirement that the target machine contain the same fonts.[8]

Typical Uses in Online Coursework:
As discussed earlier, instructors are commonly concerned with the compatibility of files from differing software programs. When twenty-five students submit essay answers to online exam questions, those submitted in file formats that the instructor cannot access can lose points (if for no reason other than the negative feelings on the part of the instructor who has to install software to convert a file from one format to another). The Adobe Acrobat program attempts to facilitate the sharing of files by moving documents into a standardized <u>file format</u> (PDF) that can be viewed and printed using software made available for free by the company to users.

Many institutions and individual instructors therefore require that files submitted to them be in the PDF format. The <u>Adobe Acrobat PDF</u> Reader[9] can then be used to view and print the documents submitted by students without any worries concerning file formats. However, in order to create a document in the PDF format students

#18

must have access to (or purchase) the Adobe Writer that facilitates the creation of PDF documents.[10] When the Adobe Acrobat Writer software (also called Adobe Acrobat Distiller) is installed, you can then create PDF files from many other software programs through the print function (for example, using Microsoft Word, Microsoft PowerPoint, Corel WordPerfect, etc.).

File Transfer Protocol (FTP)

Description: A protocol (File Transfer Protocol) used to transfer files over a network (Internet, UNIX, etc.). For example, after developing the HTML pages for a Website on a local machine, they are typically uploaded to the Web server using FTP.[11]

Typical Uses in Online Coursework:

A variety of software programs facilitate the transfer of files from one computer to another using FTP.[12] In addition to software programs that you can install for transferring files, most of the Webportals that you will use in online coursework (for example, WebCT, Blackboard, etc.) will have FTP software built into the Web-based applications. This will facilitate your moving files (such as term papers, pictures, and other course related documents) from your computer to the course Website for the instructor or other students to view (this is called "uploading"), or moving files from the course Website to your computer (this is called "downloading").

Typically you will not be aware that an FTP program is being used when you want to up-load (or post) files to the course Website. These Web-based FTP options will be a common tool that you will use when submitting assignments to your professors or sharing files with fellow students through the college's Web portal.

FTP software that is not Web-based will be used primarily when you have created Webpages of your own. To make these Webpages accessible to others using the World Wide Web, you will want to move Webpages or other documents from your computer to a host computer (or server). As you gain more experience in completing online coursework you will likely want to install and become familiar with the operations of an FTP software program that is not Web-based since it provides additional flexibility for storing files on servers and accessing Internet resources.

Web Authoring Software (HTML Editors)

Description: A software program that allows you to create Webpages using similar tools and resources as you would use when developing a new document in a word processing program. It generates the required hypertext mark-up language (or HTML) code for the pages and is able to switch back and forth (in varying degrees) between the page layout and the HTML.

Typical Uses in Online Coursework:

Some, but not all, courses may require that you submit your coursework through a <u>Website</u>, outside of the <u>Web portal</u>, that you design, maintain, and control. If this is the case, or if you just want to create a <u>Website</u> for some other reason, then you will likely want to become familiar with Web Authoring Software. Software programs like Macromedia's Dreamweaver and Microsoft's Frontpage can be used to create a single <u>Webpage</u> or a complete <u>Website</u> (the Netscape Web browser also includes free software for creating basic <u>Webpages</u> called Netscape Composer). These software programs (as well as many other programs offered by other software companies, some of which can be <u>download</u>ed for free) provide for the development of <u>Webpages</u> using an interface that allows you to see the page as it will look on the World Wide Web at the same time that you are creating it (also called "what you see what you get" or WYSWYG technology). These programs make it much easier to create a <u>Webpage</u> that has the look that you intended since they function much like a <u>word processing</u> program.

<u>Webpages</u> created with Web authoring software will have to be uploaded to a server using an FTP program (described previously) in order to be viewable to the public. Server availability is typically provided to students by colleges, so you should check with your college's technical support services before purchasing server space from another provider.

ACTIVITY 1-3   Have you missed something?

As a review, match the word, phrase, or acronym with the correct definition.

_____ 1. GUI

a. A software application that allows you to view files available on the World Wide Web.

_____ 2. <u>HTML</u>

b. Software designed to control the hardware of a specific computer system in order to allow users and application programs to employ it easily.

_____ 3. <u>Web browser</u>

c. The <u>file format</u> for files available on the World Wide Web.

_____ 4. PDF

d. An interface that uses icons to illustrate objects such as files, folders, and other computer resources.

(continued)

ACTIVITY 1-3   Have you missed something?

_____ **5.** Operating system   e. The file format that allows files to be shared between users of computers with different operating systems.

CHAPTER SUMMARY

Success in online coursework requires at least a basic understanding of the terminology used in relation to computer hardware, software, and the Internet. In this chapter we examined many of the fundamental words and phrases that you are likely to hear when being assigned or completing online course assignments and activities. Reviewing these terms, as well as those defined in the glossary, periodically throughout you college experience can help prepare you for success in online coursework.

CHAPTER ONE   EXERCISE

To begin the following exercise you will want to access your Web-based course materials (i.e., educational portal) using a Web browser (such as, Netscape Navigator or Microsoft Internet Explorer, etc.). In addition, you will want to open a new document in a word processing program (for example, Microsoft Word).

STEP ONE: Using the Web browser access your course Website using the login and password provided to you by the instructor or institution. When you have entered the Web-based course site you will want to enter the area that includes the course syllabus. Within the course syllabus identify the assignments that will be used to grade your performance in the course.

STEP TWO: Highlight (by dragging your mouse over the text describing the assignments) and copy (by selecting copy from the "edit" menu at the top of the screen) the text.

STEP THREE: When you have copied the assignments you will want to enter the area that includes the discussion boards for the course. Typically within discussion boards you will have links to a variety of topics for discussion that have been created by the instructor. For this activity you can select any one of these areas by clicking on it.

STEP FOUR: Though each Web-based course program is slightly different, you should see a button that says "post" or "reply." Click on that button and a <u>window</u> should appear where you can post a message. Typically your name and the date will automatically appear with the message, but you can create a title of your own. Title this message "course assignments." You should then put the cursor in the message <u>window</u> by clicking in the space provided.

STEP FIVE: Paste the course assignments you have copied into the message <u>window</u> (by selecting paste from the "edit" <u>menu</u>). When you have done this continue to step six.

STEP SIX: Select the "submit" ("upload," "ok," or similarly named) button from the message <u>window</u>. The message should then be included within the <u>discussion board</u> topic you have selected.

CHAPTER ONE   SKILLS CHECKLIST

After completing this chapter you should be able to do the following. If there are skills below that you may not be able to do, take a few minutes to review the chapter, focusing on those areas that you may have missed the first time through.

❏ I can define (and give an example) of an <u>Internet</u> portal that may be used for online coursework.

❏ I can describe the different uses for real-time <u>chats</u>, bulletin boards, and <u>instant messaging</u> for online communication.

❏ I have checked to ensure that I have access to a computer with a <u>CPU</u> that meets the minimal requirements for the required online coursework software.

❏ I have checked to ensure that I have access to a computer with enough RAM memory to access online course materials.

❏ I have checked to ensure that I have access to a computer with adequate <u>Internet</u> bandwidth to access online course materials.

❏ I am familiar with my computer <u>operating system</u> and the basic skills required for organizing my coursework files.

❏ I have checked to ensure that I have access to the software required for completing online coursework.

❏ I have completed each of the chapter 1 activities.

ADDITIONAL RESOURCES

Additional resources on topics covered in this chapter are available on the Website: <u>Website</u>: **<http://collegesurvival.college.hmco.com/students>.**

NOTES

1. Definitions based on Kleinedler, 2001.
2. For additional information and links to these services you may visit http://www.e-learningcentre.co.uk/eclipse/vendors/campusportals.htm
3. http://www.webopedia.com/
4. From http://www.techweb.com/encyclopedia/
5. Software suites from companies like Corel or Lotus also offer similar functionality, though they have a smaller number of users than Microsoft.
6. If you use an alternative software program to the one included in the Microsoft Office Suite you will likely want to ensure that you can save files into the Microsoft format before assignments are due in the course. See the help menu for this information in most software programs.
7. From http://www.webopedia.com
8. From http://www.techweb.com/encyclopedia/
9. Available for free at http://www.adobe.com/
10. Other software programs for creating PDF files are available, though compatibility can vary.
11. From http://www.techweb.com/encyclopedia/
12. A variety of companies offer FTP software. Several are available for free through sites like http://ww.shareware.com or http://www.tucows.com

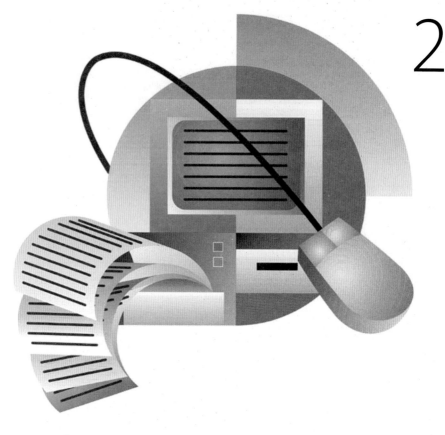

2

Technology Tips for Online Students

Computer technologies are just one of the keys to the recent increase in the use of online coursework in many colleges and universities. Much of the growth in the utilization of technology in education is also a direct result of the adaptability of students. Gaining the most from the use of computers in college courses, does however, require that you become a skilled user of the many tools and resources available in computer software.

While much of the responsibility for developing and supporting these technologies is left to the institution offering the course, successful students must also have an adequate knowledge of technologies in order to take advantage of the learning opportunities (and to overcome some of the learning barriers) that are part of any online coursework experience. As you become familiar with many of the time and energy saving tips for making the best use of software applications, you can improve both the efficiency and quality of your study habits.

Before Online Coursework Begins

Most of us do not actually rely on user manuals when learning new software applications; rather we attempt to complete a series of task using the software; learning through our successes and failures. While this is not always considered the most efficient process for learning new software, for most of us the familiarity with other software programs (such as Microsoft Word or Internet Explorer) has provided us with many foundational skills that we can apply to most other applications. Having tasks to perform is, however, essential to learning software operations; just "playing" with the software with no goals in mind usually results in an ineffective and dull experience.

Learning how to use your college's educational portal (i.e., Web portal) for completing your coursework is analogous to learning any other new software application. It is equally challenging to discover the functionality of online course resources, such as chat rooms or tools for sharing files with other students, without activities that utilize multiple functions of these resources.

- ❑ Before classes begin you can often access your college's Web portal for courses to **complete tutorials** and **view sample courses**. Take the time to explore the resources that will be available before the semester even begins.

- ❑ **Contact both the library and technical support services** to identify any training they may offer regarding the online tools used at your college.

- ❑ If possible, **select a single computer** that you will use for completing your online assignments and activities. If you use a computer lab this may not be possible, but you do want to make sure that you have adequate access to computers with similar software configurations throughout the semester.

- ❑ **Review your course syllabus** carefully to determine when and how online resources will be utilized throughout the semester.

- ❑ If adequate information is not available in your course syllabus, **contact the instructor** (either by email or phone) during the first week of classes to determine how online technologies will be used in your courses. Be sure to ask when and how students will be able to access the online resources.

❏ As soon as online resources are made available in your courses, visit the <u>Websites</u> to **verify your access**. If you have technical problems (for example, your login and password do not work properly) you will now have time to get the problems resolved before online assignments or activities are required.

❏ When you access your courses' online tools and resources, **follow each link** and verify that you can access each component of your online learning environment. For example, does the <u>chat</u> room appear to function properly on your computer and does the link to online lecture materials seem to function as it should.

❏ If you have not previously used one or more of the online tools that are available, you should **familiarize yourself with the functionality of each online tool** during the first week of the course. Take a few minutes to review tutorials provided on the <u>Website</u>, post messages to a synchronous <u>chat</u> room, or post your introduction of yourself to other students in the online <u>discussion board</u>.

❏ **Contact technical support services** if you have any problems or questions regarding the use of the online resources at your college.

Time-Saving Technology Tips

In completing your online assignments and activities you will want to take advantage of the many timesaving features that are common in today's software applications. While utilizing these functions will take some practice, you can use your time more efficiently by using just a few of the following timesaving features.

Make use of keyboard shortcuts. Keyboard shortcuts (or hot keys) are combinations of the keys that you can use to accomplish specialized functions. By using the keyboard shortcuts rather than taking the time to complete each step with the computer's mouse you can efficiently do everything from copying-and-pasting to switching between your <u>email</u> and your online course materials. Take a few minutes to review some of the common keyboard shortcuts (see table 2-1), and then practice them the next time you are working at your computer.

You can also customize keyboard shortcuts for functions that you commonly repeat that may not be standard for the Microsoft Windows operating system. Additionally, many of these same keyboard shortcuts are functional on Macintosh computers as well.

TABLE 2-1	Keyboard shortcuts for computers with Microsoft Windows*	
Key Combinations	**Function**
ALT + TAB	Switches through the active applications you are using. For example, allowing you to quickly move from one Internet search to another.
CTRL + n	New document in Microsoft Word or new browser window in Microsoft Internet Explorer or Netscape Navigator
CTRL+ a	Select all (most Windows applications)
CTRL+ c	Copy (most Windows applications)
CTRL+ END	Moves cursor to the bottom of the document (most Windows applications)
CTRL+ ESC	Same as clicking on the "start button" (most Windows applications)
CTRL+ HOME	Moves cursor to the top of the document (most Windows applications)
CTRL+ p	Print (most Windows applications)
CTRL+ s	Save (most Windows applications)
CTRL+ v	Paste (most Windows applications)
CTRL+ x	Cut (most Windows applications)
CTRL+ y	Does the last action again (most Windows applications)
CTRL+ z	Undoes the last action (most Windows applications)

*For parallel functions use the Apple key instead of CTRL on Macintosh computers.

Exploit the right click.   The typical computer mouse will have one or more buttons that can be pressed by your fingers as you move the mouse (as well as the pointer on the screen). Most of us are most familiar with the left mouse button since it is used to select software applications, open files, and do a variety of other functions with either single or double clicks. The right mouse button is, however, a useful timesaving tool that can be used effectively with little practice. Table 2-2 provides a list of sample functions that are available when you press the right mouse button in several software applications (for an Apple computer hold down Control when clicking).

TABLE 2-2 **Right-click functions for computers with Microsoft software**

Software Application	Sample functions available with right-click
Microsoft Windows desktop	Arrange Icons, Line Up Icons, Refresh, Paste, Rename, New Folder, New Shortcut, New File, Properties
Microsoft Word	Cut, Copy, Paste, Font, Paragraph, Bullets and Numbering, Synonyms, Hyperlinks, Table Features, Translations, as well as Spelling and Grammar check recommendations for indicated text
Microsoft Internet Explorer	Back, Forward, Save Image, Save Background, Set Wallpaper, Select All, Paste, Create Shortcut, Add to Favorites, View HTML Source, Print, Refresh, Properties

Accessibility Tips

For all students, both those with disabilities and those without, creating a functional computer environment is essential for success in online coursework. From tools for turning text to speech, to improving the contrast of colors on your computer screen, there are a variety of tools that can be used to improve the accessibility of information on your computer. You should take a few minutes before the semester begins to explore the accessibility options available on your computer; using these tools may enhance the efficiency of your studies when you are spending long hours at the computer completing your coursework.

Hot *Capitalize on the tools of the <u>operating system</u>.* The Windows' Control Panel (accessed by clicking on the Start button and then selecting the Settings <u>menu</u>) can be used to increase the accessibility of information in your computer. These features are not only useful for those with learning or physical disabilities; they can also be very helpful for anyone spending long hours at the computer completing online coursework.

Accessibility Options

▶ Add visual notifications for sounds produced by the Windows <u>operating system</u> (for example, a visual alert that accompanies the sound associated with closing an application).

▶ Select high contrast screen colors.

▶ Turn off the mouse and use only the keyboard.

▶ Select alternative input devices other than the keyboard and mouse.

Display Options

▶ Set the appearance to have high contrast colors for application <u>windows</u>, <u>menus</u>, and other features.

▶ Use the settings tab to enlarge or reduce the size of images displayed on the monitor.

▶ Select the use of larger icons on the <u>desktop</u>.

Keyboard Options

▶ Increase or decrease the sensitivity of the keyboard.

Mouse Options

▶ Select the mouse to be orientated for left or right handed use.

▶ Vary the speed of double-clicks with the mouse.

▶ Increase the size of the pointer image that is controlled by the mouse.

▶ Increase or decrease the speed of the pointer as it travels across the screen.

▶ Add a trail to the pointer image to increase visibility.

Advance your use of software applications. Individual software applications also typically have a variety of resources that can be used to expand accessibility.

Web Browsers (such as Microsoft Internet Explorer and Netscape Navigator)

▶ <u>Web browsers</u> allow you to enlarge or reduce the text font size for <u>Webpages</u> that you select to view. You can typically make these adjustments from the "view" <u>menu</u>.

▶ Text-to-speech is also available to assist those who are visually impaired. These software applications typically work with most <u>Web browser</u> applications.

▶ The TAB key can be used to advance through options (such at text <u>fields</u> in an online survey) available on many <u>Webpages</u>.

▶ If provided by the <u>Webpage</u> developer, <u>Web browsers</u> can be set to provide text descriptions of online images.

Hot

Word Processing

▶ Text-based tips can be viewed to provide descriptions of <u>icon</u> <u>menu</u> options.

▶ To increase the visibility of text when using a <u>word processing</u> software application, you can improve the visibility of the document by increasing the font size or the zoom. Increasing the font size will increase the size of each letter (or character) in the document both on the screen as well as when the document is printed. Increasing the zoom (for example, from 75% to 100% or 120%) will improve the visibility only while the document is on the computer screen.

▸ Text-to-speech is also available to assist those who are visually impaired. These software applications typically work with most <u>word processing</u> applications including Microsoft Word and Corel WordPerfect.

▸ Sounds can be added for many <u>menu</u> options.

Magnifier Application

▸ The typical installation of Microsoft Windows will include the Magnifier application (accessed by clicking on the Start button and then selecting the Programs <u>menu</u> and the Accessories and Accessibility sub-<u>menus</u>). The Magnifier application allows you to enlarge any portion of the Windows screen for greater visibility.

Additional Information

▸ Microsoft also provides a variety of assistive technologies, tips, and tools that are available online at <**http://www.microsoft .com/enable/default.htm**>. Likewise, Macintosh provides an assortment of accessibility features, tips, and resources available at <**http://www.apple. com/disability/easyaccess.html**>. These include guides for specific physical disabilities, information on using a keyboard with one hand or finger, and other resources that can improve the accessibility of computer resources.

ACTIVITY 2-1   Have you missed something?

As a review, answer the following questions by marking the correct response.

1. Which key would you press in conjunction with the control (<u>CTRL</u>) to copy information that is highlighted?
   a. The "x" key.
   b. The "c" key.
   c. The "v" key.

2. Which key would you press to move from one <u>field</u> to another (e.g., name to address, or phone number to fax number) in a data form available on the World Wide Web?
   a. The "shift" key.
   b. The "tab" key.
   c. The "alt" key.

3. Which of the following functions is *not* available when you right-click in Microsoft Word?
   a. Change the font size, color, format, etc.
   b. Copy-and-paste.
   c. Print.

Tips for Managing Your Files

Keeping track of the many files that you will create throughout college will be an overwhelming burden if you don't set a strategy for staying organized from the first semester.

Create a <u>folder</u> structure.   Before you add any new files to your computer you will want to develop a strategy for organizing the many files that will be created over the semester. To do this you will want to construct a hierarchy of file <u>folders</u> in which you can store your many files. Putting a little thought into the structure of these <u>folders</u> before you begin classes can save you lots of time later in the semester.

#2

#4

A strategy that many students find useful is to first create a <u>folder</u> for each semester they are in college. Then within the appropriate semester they create another level of <u>folders</u>; one <u>folder</u> for each course they are taking. All files related to the individual course will then have a specific location where they should be saved. In a similar manner, for courses with a large number of assignments or activities, a third level of <u>folders</u> may be used to organize files by assignment or activity.

No matter the <u>folder</u> structure that you select for organizing your files, you should go about creating the empty file <u>folders</u> at the beginning of each semester. This way the <u>folder</u> structure will be in place and you will be able to quickly identify which files should be saved in which <u>folders</u> throughout the semester.

> **STUDENT-TO-STUDENT TIP**
>
> Each online class generates a lot of files so, to keep track of them, I create a folder for each new class and within that class folder I create a folder for major assignments and then save corresponding files into those folders.

Develop a file naming strategy.   When you create a new file (whether it is Microsoft Word document, a PowerPoint presentation, or a MP3 music file) you should have a naming strategy that will help you identify the files later on. Useful naming strategies will include essential information for identifying the contents of the file, including course name or number, assignment name or number, date of the file, or other information that will be useful when you later search for a desired file. In most <u>operating system</u>s you cannot, however, include the following characters in a <u>file name</u>: " ' | \ / [ ] , ? * < >

By developing a file naming strategy early on in your college experience you will be less likely to lose valuable information, distribute the wrong files to classmates, or submit erroneous files to your professors for grading (see table 2-3).

Don't change the file extensions.   The <u>file name</u> you provide for documents that you create only provides part of the information necessary for you to access the file. Added to the end of each <u>file name</u> is a three or four character extension (after the last period) that identifies the computer application that should be used to open (or run) the selected file (see table 2-4).

TABLE 2-3   Examples of effective naming strategies

Ineffective File Names	Effective File Names
History1.doc	HIS101-assign1-draft3.doc
Termpaper.doc	EDU101 term paper 10-12-05.doc
Johns presentation.ppt	Assign2 John Reynolds.ppt
Music mix.mp3	Alternative Mix 4-10-05.mp3

TABLE 2-4   Common file extensions

File Extension	Common Use of File	Commonly Associated Software
.doc	Word processing file	Microsoft Word
.wpd	Word processing file	Corel Word Perfect
.pdf (portable document file)	Document sharing file	Adobe Acrobat PDF Reader Adobe Acrobat PDF Distiller
.rtf (rich text format)	Word processing file	Most any text or word processing software for Macintosh or Windows operating systems
.txt, .text (ASCII or Simple Text format)	Word processing file	Most any text or word processing software for Macintosh or Windows operating systems
.au	Audio file	Most any audio software including Microsoft Media Player and RealNetworks Player
.avi	Movie file	Most any video software including Microsoft Media Player and RealNetworks Player
.bmp	Graphics file	Most any graphics viewer including Microsoft Internet Explorer, Word, and Microsoft PowerPoint

Table 2-4   Common file extensions *(continued)*

.gif	Graphics file	Most any graphics viewer including Microsoft Internet Explorer, Word, and Microsoft PowerPoint
.jpg, .jpeg	Graphics file	Most any graphics viewer including Microsoft Internet Explorer, Word, and Microsoft PowerPoint
.mov, .qt	Audio and video formats	Apple QuickTime
.mpg, .mpeg	Audio and video formats	Most any audio or video software including Microsoft Media Player and RealNetworks Player
.ra, .ram	Audio and video formats	Real Audio Player
.tif, .tiff	Graphics file	Most any graphics viewer including Microsoft Internet Explorer, Word, and Microsoft PowerPoint
.wav, .wave	Audio file	Most any audio software including Microsoft Media Player and Real-Networks Player
.ppt	Slideshow presentation	Microsoft PowerPoint (or the free Microsoft PowerPoint Viewer)
.shw	Slideshow presentation	Corel Presentations
.exe	Executable file (starts a software application)	Window operating system
.zip	File compression	WinZip. StuffIt, and PKZip software
.htm, .html (HyperText Markup Language)	Interactive files available on the World Wide Web	Microsoft Internet Explorer and Netscape Navigator

For example, at the end of the Microsoft Word file it will typically have the extension ".doc" to indicate that the file can be opened with Microsoft Word or another application that supports Microsoft Word files.

The inclusion of the extension to the <u>file name</u> is essential in managing your files. Without the accurate extension the computer is not able to automatically open the file using the appropriate software application, thus causing the computer to request that you select the fitting application to open the file (which you may or may not remember later in the semester). As a result you should not change or delete the file extension on files that you create or rename.

File extensions will also provide you with essential information when other students or instructors share files with you from their computer. By reading the file extension you will be able to identify whether or not you have suitable software for opening a file. For example, if your professor <u>email</u>s you a copy of the course syllabus in a file named "Geo 101-3 syllabus.pdf" you would be able to determine that the <u>Adobe Acrobat PDF</u> software application was required for viewing the contents of that file.

Use the tools for finding files.   Microsoft Windows offers three primary tools for finding files after you have saved them to your computer's hard drive: Find Files or Folders, Windows Explorer, and My Computer. When you make use of each tool will depend on your file structure and how much you remember in locating the desired file.

My Computer: This tool for accessing the file structure is most useful when you have a good idea about where the desired file is located. It will allow you to quickly move through file <u>folder</u>s (in a single or in multiple <u>window</u>s) until you have located the file. My Computer does not, however, illustrate the <u>folder</u>s structure in the viewable <u>window</u>. My computer is accessible from the Windows desktop.

Windows Explorer: This tool for finding files is useful when you are less sure of the location of a desired file. Windows Explorer allows you to navigate the contents of file <u>folder</u>s quickly in a single <u>window</u> format that simultaneously shows both the hierarchy of the <u>folder</u> structure as well as the contents of individual <u>folder</u>s. Windows Explorer is accessible from the "Start" button menus.

Find Files or <u>Folder</u>s: The Find feature is accessible from the Start button in Microsoft Windows and facilitates the search for files or <u>folder</u>s when you do not know how to locate a desired file. The Find Files or Folders option will allow you to select the hard drive (such as your "C:" drive), floppy disk, CD, or DVD in which you would like to begin the search. From here you can also narrow the search to a particular <u>folder</u> (i.e., <u>file directory</u>).

The Find Files or Folders application will then search for the desired file based on the search parameters you provide. For example, if you know that the file should have the course number included in its name, then you could search for "Bio 101" and the Find application would locate all files whose name includes "Bio 101" with the specified <u>folder</u> (i.e., <u>file directory</u>). You can also search for files by their file extension. For example, if you know that the desired file is a Microsoft PowerPoint presentation that should be located in the <u>folder</u> that contains all of the files from the fall of your first year in college, then you could search for all PowerPoint files within that <u>folder</u> by using the <u>asterisk</u> to represent the name of any file (e.g., *.ppt) and followed by a period and the file extension. Other search examples could include *.doc for any Microsoft Word document or *.ram for any Real Audio Player file.

Back-up your files every week.   In order to keep up with the organization and management of your files you will want to back-up your course files on a floppy disk, recordable CD or DVD, or other data storage device each week throughout the semester. Though memory failures such as hard drives freezing or CD-ROMs losing their data are less common with today's technologies, you do not want to risk losing the valuable files you are creating in completing your college coursework. Take a few minutes each week to back-up your course files to a recordable CD or DVD (or to another back-up system like a shared server, secondary hard drive, or even a floppy disk).

ACTIVITY 2-2   Have you missed something?

As a review, mark the correct word or phrase that completes the following statements.

1. The file extension for a file that is available on the World Wide Web and viewable using a <u>Web browser</u> is…

   a. .exe.

   b. .ppt.

   c. .html.

2. The Find Files or <u>Folders</u> function is accessed by first…

   a. clicking on the "My Computer" icon.

   b. clicking on the "Start" button.

   c. using a right-click.

3. In most <u>operating systems</u>, this character can be included in the name of file.

   a. \

   b. -

   c. *

Tips for Using the World Wide Web

Know some of the Web basics.   The World Wide Web offers an assortment of resources that will be essential to your college education. From accessing course materials that professors make available in <u>educational portals</u> to conducting library research from home, the World Wide Web will provide you the critical information for being successful while providing you with access to that information 24 hours a day. However, you will often find that you can access information faster if you use the World Wide Web in the morning before 11:00 A.M. or after 10:00 P.M., since the number of users is typically lower during those hours.

The basic function of the World Wide Web is to provide the connection between millions of computers that share information. Individuals or organizations that want to offer information on the World Wide Web simply make the information available on a specialized computer called a server, which is then linked to the network of computers around the world. Distinct files can then be added to the server and made available to all of those that are connected to this world-wide network; these files are what we call Web-pages. (When multiple pages are linked together through hypertext, they are called Websites.)

Given that there are millions of Webpages available everyday on the World Wide Web, uniform resource locators (URLs) are used to provide an address for Webpages so users of the network can locate desired files. The URL has four primary components that provide computers with the network address for desired files, see the figure below.

| Protocol | Web Server | Directory | File |

http://collegesurvival.college.hmco.com/students/index.html

Protocol: The protocol provides the computer with a set of rules for exchanging information across the World Wide Web. The hypertext transfer protocol (HTTP) and file transfer protocol (FTP) will likely be the ones you use most often as a student. As their names suggest, the first is for the transfer of Webpages (which are typically hypertext files with the extension .html or .htm) while the latter is for the transfer of files from one computer to another.

Web server: The Web server name provides the computer with information regarding the location of the computer that hosts the desired Webpage. Though you will typically use a textual description for the desired Web server (such as <http://www.youruniversity.edu>), this will actually be converted into a numeric Internet address that is used to determine the location of the Web server using a Domain Name System (DNS). When an individual or organization purchases the rights to use a URL name (such as <http://www.youruniversity.edu>), the name is registered with an organization that assigns a numeric address to the URL name.

Directory: When your computer has identified the address of the Web server that contains the files you desire, you will frequently then provide additional information that identifies the folder location of the specific file you want to view. The same organizational structure used in your personal computer, files stored in <u>folders</u>, is also used in <u>Web servers</u>. The <u>file directory</u> location indicates the <u>folder</u> location of the desired file.

File: The <u>file name</u> and extension provide the computer with specific information regarding the name and type of file that is stored in the <u>file directory</u> on the <u>Web server</u>. Most commonly the files you view on the World Wide Web are hypertext markup language (<u>HTML</u> or HTM) files. If you do not know the specific file that you want to access when you enter a <u>Web server</u> and <u>file directory</u>, then by default the file that will be accessed is index.html.

Use your institution's *educational portal*.   <u>Educational portals</u> are a specialized type of <u>Internet</u> portal used by colleges and universities to provide a variety of resources (such as synchronous <u>chat</u> rooms, <u>discussion boards</u>, <u>email</u>, technical support, etc.) through a single <u>Website</u> that can be easily accessed by students and instructors. The most common <u>educational portals</u> at colleges and universities are WebCT and Blackboard. You should be familiar with the variety of resources that can be accessed through your institutions <u>educational portal</u> before you are required to use it in one of your courses.

#23

#30

Download *additional tools and resources that may be useful*.   <u>Downloading</u> software applications from the World Wide Web can add useful tools and resources to your computer. From adding software that will compress files so they take up less space on your computer to accessing tools for improving the search capabilities of your <u>Web browser</u>, you should become familiar with the procedures for <u>downloading</u> and installing software from the World Wide Web. This will allow you to expand your use of the computer as a tool for learning.

There are five primary types of software that you are likely to <u>download</u> from the World Wide Web as a student:

- ❥ **Updates.** Companies often provide files that you can <u>download</u> and install in your computer to improve the performance of software you have already purchased.

- ❥ **Plug-Ins.** These software applications are directly tied to <u>Web browsers</u> and once installed they will automatically activate themselves when required.

- ❥ **Trials.** Since potential clients often want the opportunity to try-out software that they may later purchase, many software developers offer 30-, 60-, and even 90-day trials of their software that you can <u>download</u> for free.

- ❥ **Shareware.** Individual software developers commonly make software applications they develop available on the World Wide Web for anyone to <u>download</u> and install. Shareware developers commonly request a small payment ($5 - $20) for their product, but no mandatory fee is charged.

▶ **Freeware**. Individual software developers may also make the software applications they develop available to the public without charge (or expectation of payment).

When you have selected and clicked on the link to a file that you would like to <u>download</u>, the <u>Web browser</u> will take you through the necessary steps for moving the file from the <u>Web server</u> to your personal computer. You should be sure to note the file <u>folder</u> in which you are <u>download</u>ing the desired file to your computer. This is important since after the file has been <u>download</u>ed you will then have to identify the location of the file on your computer in order to install or open it.

If you are <u>download</u>ing a file that contains a software application (i.e., with a file extension of .exe) then you will want to double-click on the file to start the installation process. The installation file will guide you through the necessary steps to install the software application in your computer.

Listed in table 2-5 are several practical tools and resources you may want to <u>download</u> and install from the World Wide Web at no cost.

Have a strategy for searching the Web. In order to find more of what you want on the World Wide Web you will want to develop multiple strategies that can be used in searching for information. Depending on what information you want to find, the detail of the information you require, and how much you already know about the topic, you will want to use distinctive search strategies to locate useful information most efficiently.

▶ Be specific in your search. For example, if you are looking for information regarding the history of the Seminole Indians during the Civil War, you will likely find more information that is of value to your coursework if you search for "Seminole Indians Civil War History" rather than simply "Seminole Indians"

▶ Many <u>search engines</u> allow you to limit your search to <u>Websites</u> that provide specific types of information or files (such as, news, shopping, pictures, audio, etc.). Use these features to reduce your search time; they can be accessed by buttons provided on the <u>search engine</u> <u>Webpage</u>.

▶ Use the plus "+" and/or minus "-" signs to include or exclude terms from your search. For example, if you are looking for information on the members of the United State's congress in 1970 you would want to search for "congress +members +1970". Likewise, if you wanted to search specifically for those members of congress in 1970 that were not in congress in 1975 you would want to search for "congress + members +1970 -1975".

▶ If you want to locate information on the World Wide Web that is a phrase (such as, "MTV music awards") then you should use quotation marks to indicate that only instances where the multiple terms are used in a specific order should be identified.

▶ Boolean search commands (such as, "and", "or", "not", etc.) can be used with most <u>search engines</u> to provide additional information for

Software Application	Use	Available for download from...
Adobe Acrobat Reader	Allows you to view PDF files	<www.adobe.com>
WinZip	Allows you to compress (or decompress) large files	<www.winzip.com>
Eudora	Allows you to send, organize, and store email	<www.qualcomm.com>
NetZero	Allows you to access the Internet with no monthly fee	<www.netzero.com>
ICQ	Allows you to send and receive instant messages with others using the same software	<www.icq.com>
QuickTime	Allows you to view audio and video files that are created in the Apple QuickTime format	<www.apple.com>
RealOne Player	Allows you to view audio and video files that are created in the RealPlayer format	<www.realnetworks.com>
Shockwave Player	Allows you to view online animations created in the Shockwave format	<www.macromedia.com>
Flash Player	Allows you to view online animations created in the Flash format	<www.macromedia.com>

TABLE 2-5   Free software applications that you can download

the search. For example, if you are looking for information on the European "Axis" powers during World War II, then you would want to search for "War and Germany or Italy not Japan".

▶ When searching for information that you know is contained on a specific Web server (such as, <www.nasa.gov>) you can limit your search only to those files found on the specific Web server by using "site:" or "host:". For example, if you were looking for information on NASA programs regarding Jupiter, then you would want to search for "site:www.nasa.gov +jupiter". (AltaVista.com uses "host:", while Excite.com, Google.com, and Yahoo.com use "site:".)

▶ You can also use the "site:" or "host:" commands to limit your search to a specific type of Web server (such as, .edu for educational institutions or .com for private organizations). For example, if you wanted to restrict your search for information on Jupiter to only sites maintained by government agencies you would search for "Jupiter +host:gov".

▶ Many search engines also have additional software that you can download to improve your search capabilities as plug-ins for your Web browser. These software applications typically add search features to your Web browser that permit you to conduct searches limited to the pages within the Website you are viewing without having to leave the Website.

▶ Don't be fooled into believing that if a Webpage comes up at the top of the list it is necessarily the most useful Webpage for finding the information you desire. Most search engines provide placement within search results based on advertising revenue provided by Webpage owners. For example, if you want to market a product you can pay many search engines to show your Webpage near the top of the list when people search for similar products.

▶ If you have found a Webpage that provides useful information and you believe that additional information may be contained elsewhere on the Website (i.e., Web server) then you can "back search" by removing first the file name from the URL, and then (if necessary) elements of the directory (see the URL figure on page 36). The process of "back searching" will provide you access to other files available within the same file directory as the file you initially found in your search. For example, if you were searching for information on strategies for using search engines you may locate the Webpage <http://searchenginewatch.com/reports/seindex.html>. If you would like more information on search engines you would not have to conduct another search, rather you could "back search" by removing the file name and extension (i.e., seindex.html) from the URL and hitting enter. This would leave you with <http://searchenginewatch.com/reports/>.

> **STUDENT-TO-STUDENT TIP**
>
> Search engines are powerful tools, but relying simply on the basic search for advanced searches is not very useful. Each search engine has its own set of "rules," so it is a good idea to actually read the online directions for using and getting the most out of the search engine's capabilities.

Know which search engines to use.   There are three primary types of search engines that you can use depending on your search requirements. You will want to practice using each type of search engine so you can later evaluate which ones will be the most effective and efficient tools for finding the information you desire on the World Wide Web. Determine which is your personal favorite in each category and keep those <u>bookmarked</u> in your <u>Web browser</u>.

Basic Key Word Searches: Key word <u>search engines</u> are the most commonly used. These <u>search engines</u> review the key words contained on millions of <u>Webpages</u> to provide you with a list of <u>Webpages</u> that may be useful in providing you with the information you desire. These <u>search engines</u> are most valuable when you want to conduct a general search for information and have few leads as to where this information may be found on the World Wide Web. Disadvantages to key word <u>search engines</u> include the large number of useless <u>Webpages</u> they provide in their search results.

Examples of <u>search engines</u> of this variety include: Altavista.com, Google.com, Hotbot.com, Directhit.com, Lycos.com, Excite.com, and Fastsearch.com.

Web Directories: Web directories are the "yellow pages" of the World Wide Web. They can assist you in quickly identifying <u>Webpages</u> that may be useful resources by providing you access to millions of pages that have been classified into categories by topic. Web directories are most useful when you can categorize the information you are searching for into broad categories (such as, government agencies, history, baseball, etc.) since they will commonly provide you with a larger percentage of useful <u>Webpages</u> than other types of <u>search engines</u>.

Examples of <u>search engines</u> of this variety include: Yahoo.com, About.com, and Looksmart.com.

Meta Searches: <u>Search engines</u> that provide a meta search utilize the resources of many other <u>search engines</u> to provide you with a list of <u>Webpages</u> that are most likely to meet your search requirements. By using other <u>search engines</u> to provide information, meta searches are most useful when you have had little success with your favorite <u>search engine</u>. Results from multiple <u>search engines</u> can be used to locate resources that may not be found by any single search. Like with key word searches, however, the percentage of useful <u>Webpages</u> may be low with meta <u>search engines</u>.

Examples of <u>search engines</u> of this variety include: Dogpile.com, Metacrawler.com, and Savvysearch.com.

Tips from <http://www.findspot.com>

AltaVista.com Tips

❑ *You can enter up to 200 characters (15 to 20 words) into this search box.*

❑ *To reduce the number of documents retrieved by your search, try combining multiple terms with the search operators. Example:* +*"mountain climbing" +photos -tours finds pages containing the phrase mountain climbing and the word photos, but not the word tours.*

(continued)

Dogpile.com Tips

❑ *If your search uses the NOT operator, note that when your search is forwarded to search indexes that don't support its use, the operator and the word that follows will be removed from the search statement.*

❑ *Dogpile will also use the NEAR operator for indexes that support it (AltaVista, InfoSeek). Entering the search: cat NEAR dog will match documents where these words are in close proximity to each other. For search engines that do not support NEAR, Dogpile will substitute the AND operator.*

Google.com Tips

❑ *Google is not case sensitive. All searches are processed as lower case.*

❑ *Google doesn't perform word stemming. A search for "cat" will not retrieve documents containing the word "cats."*

❑ *Google ignores common words ("and," "is," etc) and single characters and digits in its searches. To force Google to include a common word, single character or digit in a search, precede it with a + sign.*

Yahoo.com Tips

❑ *Documents matching more of the search terms appear before those matching fewer.*

❑ *Matches to words in the Yahoo category tree are sorted higher than matches in Web documents.*

❑ *If there are multiple matches within the Yahoo category tree a higher placement is given to the broader, less specific category.*

❑ *Matches to words in the titles of Webpages will appear before matches to words in the body text of Webpages.*

Evaluating Online Resources

Both accurate and inaccurate information is readily available on the Internet and World Wide Web. As a student you will want to develop the critical thinking skills for determining which information that you find online is of value and should be included as a resource for your online coursework. Consequently, evaluating online resources will be an essential skill for your success. Unfortunately there is no formula for sifting out useful and reliable sources of information on the Internet from those that you would not want to use in college coursework. What follows are guidelines and suggestions for assessing the reliability, quality, and usefulness of online (as well as traditional print-based) resources. You should review these tips before, during, and after you conduct any research using the Internet to ensure that you have selected only the information sources that will lead to your success.[1]

Source Reliability

The reliability of the information you have available to include when writing your term papers, reviewing for exams, making references in position papers, and so forth will be an essential ingredient to your success in college. While there is no simple formula for assessing reliability, by following the steps below you can better ensure the reliability of your sources.

▶ **Contact information.** Check to determine if the author's contact information is available for the selected information. This information should include name of author, title, organizational affiliation, as well as postal or email addresses.

Hot

▶ **Author's credentials.** The credibility of an author is often related to their credentials. Review the biographical information provided about the author to determine if he or she is a reliable source of information. For example, have they published several scholarly articles on the topic in the research journals of their field or have they been recognized by professional organizations for their contributions to their field of study.

▶ **Publication's reputation.** Publications (journals, magazines, Websites, etc.) build their reputation with a field of study by publishing reliable and useful information for readers. You should become familiar with the reputations of various publications within your field of study as you begin your research. You can always ask your professor to make recommendations on the reputations of various publications.

▶ **Sponsoring organization(s).** Many publications (journals, magazines, Websites, etc.) are sponsored by organizations such as professional societies, non-profit organizations, and other entities with a mission behind the publications they sponsor. Reviewing the mission of the organization that funds any Website, journal, or other publication can provide you with information regarding potential biases or perspectives that may shape the reliability of the information.

E-learning Experiences

While teaching a course on educational technologies a few years ago I had a student that came across a <u>Webpage</u> that he thought would be a valuable resource for an upcoming course assignment. The <u>Webpage</u> title was "Parents of Nasal Learners Demand Odor-Based Curriculum." The article went on to say that parents of nasal learners, backed by olfactory-education experts, were demanding that U.S. public schools provide odor-based curricula for their academically struggling children.[2]

While most students would quickly notice the humor as they read the story on the <u>Webpage,</u> in a hurry to finish his course assignment this student eagerly wrote about the injustices of an educational system that would not equally support students with less-known learning disabilities. If he had taken the time to review the <u>Website</u> for the organization that initially published the article (<http://www.theonion.com>), he would have promptly discovered that the organization provides daily satire on news stories from around the world and commonly makes up false stories with a humorous twist.

Accordingly, don't be fooled by everything you see or read on the World Wide Web. Some information is intentionally misleading, while some is inaccurate by accident.

▶ **Blind peer review.** The most reliable publications are typically viewed as those that are "blind peer reviewed." Many, but not all, scholarly journals provide for a blind peer review process where scholars in the field assess articles submitted for publication before the articles are published. You should determine which publications in your field of study use a blind peer review process since these will often be the most reliable sources of information (this information is often located in the introductory materials on the primary <u>Website</u> or in the front pages of a printed journal).

▶ **Write the author.** Although the information that you find posted to public bulletin boards and other discussion forums should rarely be viewed as reliable information for use in your college courses, these resources can often provide you with useful leads to reliable information. When you find information that may be useful, write to the author of the posting to determine if they can provide you with additional references or resources where you can find reliable information for use in your assignments or activities.

Information Quality

The quality and accuracy of information you use in college coursework is critical. Inaccurate or misleading information may end up costing you points toward your grade; consequently taking the time to examine potential resources for indicators of accuracy is always worth it.

‣ **Broad generalizations.** Inaccurate information is commonly detectable when an author uses broad (i.e., sweeping or vague) generalizations about the subject. As a result, statements like "All students . . .," "Everyone must . . .," or "Athletes always . . ." can be identified as indicators that over-generalizations are being made by the author and the accuracy of the statements should be questioned. This isn't to say that all generalizations are inaccurate, but rather that generalizations are often used when the accuracy of information should be questioned.

‣ **Dates.** Check on the date of publication, as well as dates of references, statistics, and other resources used by the author. The timeliness of information can often impact on its accuracy in the current context. For example, you would not want to quote statistics from 1990 about the number of single mothers enrolled in college courses since these numbers have grown steadily in the last decade.

‣ **Consistency of facts.** Examine the facts (especially the statistics) to see if there is consistency. Inaccurate information is often unintentionally added to publications (journal articles, magazines, Webpages, etc.) when an author who is not familiar with the relationships of statistical values discusses a variety of statistics. For example, on one page the author may state that 250 subjects participated in a study, but then during the data analysis the author may inadvertently use data from only 200 participants. Inconsistencies like these can indicate imprecise conclusions on the part of the author.

‣ **Grammar and spelling.** Numerous errors in grammar and spelling are often indicators that information may not be of a quality that you want to include in your college coursework.

‣ **Online databases.** Online databases are generally excellent resources for finding quality information, though each individual database should be evaluated using standards similar to those that you would use to assess the quality of information in an academic journal or other resource.

‣ **Biases.** If the author presents only one side of a debate or an issue, it is often an indicator that information is not from an objective source. You should look for signs of partiality in the terms and phrases used by the author. For example, proponents of uniform testing refer to exams as "standardized tests" while opponents refer to them as "high-risks testing." By examining the words the author chooses to use when describing a topic you can often identify potential biases.

‣ **Comprehensive review.** Most of the scholarly resources that will provide you with quality information for your college coursework present a comprehensive review of the literature supporting the many viewpoints regarding an issue. Single perspectives on an issue or topic are typically of less use to students, since there is greater potential of bias.

▶ **Citations and references.** An author's ability to provide accurate and complete citations and references for the information they extract from the other resources is a good indicator of the quality of information contained within their work. If quotes, statistics, and other excerpts have inaccurate citations or incomplete references, then you should examine the information with keen scrutiny.

▶ **Original source.** If you want to use a quote or specific fact from an earlier publication that is referenced in your current resources, you should always go back to the original source (i.e., the referenced article or book) to verify that the current author's interpretation of the quote or fact is consistent with that of the original author. When original source documents are not available then you should cite those resources appropriately (for example, "Stevenson, 1966 as cited in Voung, 2003").

▶ **Support.** Quality information is rarely presented without corroboration. Authors should provide adequate support from additional journals, books, and other resources that substantiate their position and/or facts.

Information Usefulness

Lastly, you will want to evaluate potential resources for information based on their usefulness to your specific course assignment or activity. The unfortunate reality of research is that very few of the potential resources you will review when searching for useful information will be of assistance in completing your college coursework. To help reduce the amount of time and energy you spend reviewing resources that will not be useful in your assignment or activity, you will want to develop strategies for quickly assessing the potential utility of resources such as Webpages, journal article, books, and online databases.

▶ **Relate to goals.** Whether it is a Webpage or academic journal article, you will want to determine if (and how) each potential source of information relates to the goals of your course assignment or activity. Spending time to locate and read through sources of information that are not useful to your coursework is not a strategy for success in college.

▶ **Outline before writing or researching.** One of the best ways to know what information will be the most useful in your coursework is to outline your assignments or activities before you start to write about or research a topic. While outlining your assignment or activity you should be able to identify the types of information that will be most useful when you construct the submission. For example, when outlining an essay on the influence of affirmative action programs on the admissions policies of colleges, you would identify several locations in the paper where supporting statistical facts would be useful. Then in your search for useful resources you would know what types of statistical facts would later be useful when you compose your essay.

▶ **Audience level.** Typically, sources of information that are written for an audience that is either below or above your level of expertise do not turn out to be the ideal resources for college coursework. Just as a high school chemistry book will not likely provide you with the information you require for college courses, an engineer's guide to chemical reactions may provide you with information that is beyond your current level of understanding and that is of little use as well.

▶ **Level of detail.** Depending on the characteristics of your course assignments or activities, the level of detail you are looking for in resources will help you narrow your search for useful resources. If you are required to write a one-page position paper on a current event topic, searching through statistical databases for obscure relationships and supporting data is not likely to be an effective use of your time.

ACTIVITY 2-3   Have you missed something?

As a review, match the following word, phrase, or acronym with the correct definition.

_____ **1.** Google.com

a. An example of a <u>search engine</u> that uses a directory to search for information on the World Wide Web

_____ **2.** and

b. An example of a <u>search engine</u> that uses key words to search for information on the World Wide Web

_____ **3.** site:

c. A Boolean search command that can be used with most <u>search engines</u> to provide additional information for the search

_____ **4.** Yahoo.com

d. Can be used to limit a search of the World Wide Web to a specific phrase

_____ **5.** parentheses

e. Can be used to limit a search of the World Wide Web to only those <u>Webpages</u> found on a specific <u>Web server</u>

Tips for Using Your <u>Web Browser</u>

Effectively using the many resources that are available on the World Wide Web requires that you learn to utilize the features and tools available in your <u>Web browser</u>. Below are several suggestions for taking advantage of these browser capabilities.

❏ <u>Download</u> the most recently available **plug-ins** for your <u>Web browser</u> before the semester begins. You do not want to find out that you do not have the latest release of a plug-in required for accessing course materials the day an online assignment is due.

❏ Creating **bookmarks (or favorites)** for <u>Webpages</u> you find useful can help you find the resources you want, when you want them. It is also useful to create <u>folders</u> within the <u>bookmarks</u> (or favorites) directory for keeping valuable <u>Webpages</u> organized.

❏ When you locate your college's <u>educational portal</u> on the World Wide Web (or other course <u>Websites</u> that you plan to use often) you should **create a <u>shortcut</u>** to the page that appears as an <u>icon</u> on your computer's <u>desktop</u>. By clicking on this <u>shortcut</u> the computer will automatically open a <u>Web browser</u> and locate the specific page you have selected.

❏ When you have selected a link to another <u>Webpage</u> that you would like to view, you can open that link in a new <u>Web browser</u> <u>window</u> by selecting the **"open in new <u>window</u>"** option when you right-click on the link. As a result you will not have to hit the "back" to return to the initial <u>Webpage</u>. This is also useful if you want to conduct multiple searches for the same information using more than one <u>search engine</u>.

❏ When printing <u>Webpages</u> that are contained within a frame (i.e., a smaller <u>window</u> appears within a larger <u>window</u> that commonly contains <u>menu</u> options) you can **print the contents of the frame** without printing the entire page. By right-clicking on the area of the <u>Webpage</u> that you want to print, you can select the print option and only print the contents of that <u>window</u>.

❏ When you post information to a <u>Webpage</u> (such as on a <u>discussion board</u>) the information you post may not automatically appear on the screen. If this is the case, then you should hit the **refresh** (or reload) button on the <u>Web browser</u>'s <u>menu bar</u> to retrieve an updated copy of the <u>Webpage</u>.

❏ <u>Web browsers</u> typically read <u>Webpages</u> that are written in the hypertext markup language. These files should have file extensions of either .html or .htm in order to be viewed properly. If you have entered an <u>URL</u> with one of the two file extension (for example, .html) and the file does not open, you should try entering the same <u>URL</u> with the alternative file extension (in this case, .htm).

❏ <u>Cookies</u> are typically small files that some <u>Webpages</u> will automatically <u>download</u> to your computer in order to remember information about you (such as, shopping preferences, mailing address, credit card information, etc.). By adjusting the **security control features** of your <u>Web browser</u> you can open or deny <u>Webpages</u> access for storing <u>cookies</u> on your computer. <u>Cookies</u> can be good or bad depending on their use and your desired level of privacy. You should decide what level of privacy fits best with your use of the World Wide Web and review the help <u>menu</u> of your <u>Web browser</u> for directions on setting the appropriate level of security.

Tips for Using <u>Email</u>

While you have likely developed many useful strategies for using <u>email</u>, the following list of tips can provide you with some additional technical skills for making the best use of the many features that most <u>email</u> software applications and Web-based <u>email</u> systems offer for students.

❏ Most colleges and universities will provide students with access to individual student <u>email</u> accounts through the World Wide Web (commonly referred to as Webmail and often included in <u>educational</u> <u>portals</u>). Using these **online <u>email</u> systems** to manage your <u>email</u> does provide you with access to your <u>email</u> from any computer linked to the World Wide Web, and many features of <u>email</u> programs that are not Web-based are typically included in Webmail. However, you can only access these features when you are connected to the <u>Internet</u>.

HOW TO TUTORIAL
#19

HOW TO TUTORIAL
#26

As an alternative you may want to <u>download</u> and install an <u>email</u> application (such as Microsoft Outlook or Qualcomm Eudora) to your personal computer for managing your <u>email</u>. These software applications allow you to view, create, and edit <u>email</u> messages even when your computer is not linked to the <u>Internet</u>. They also offer many features for organizing and managing the numerous <u>emails</u> you will receive as a college student (for example, a common feature of <u>email</u> software applications allows you to conduct key word searches through past <u>emails</u> that you have either sent or received).

❏ Use the **<u>email</u> account** provided by your college or university for all of your coursework. The college or university is responsible for maintaining your access to only that account. If you are using a private <u>email</u> account through another service and it stops functioning properly, professors are less likely to be lenient in accepting late assignments. Most often if the college or university <u>email</u> system fails to function properly, instructors will take delays resulting from the failure into account since it is a resource maintained by the institution.

Hot

#19

#26

❏ In college courses you will frequently be required to **attach files** (such as Microsoft Word documents or Adobe Acrobat PDF files) to emails you are sending to your professor or fellow students. Practice attaching files to your emails prior to the start of classes to verify that this feature works with your current email software (for example, send yourself an email with an attached file).

Many Web portals and email software applications require that you first identify the file you want to include as an attachment, often done by clicking on a "browse" button, and then attach the file in a second step by clicking on the "attach" button.

❏ When you receive an email with a file attached, **be cautious.** Files that are attached to email that you receive can contain files with computer viruses. If you do not know the sender of the email or if you are not expecting an attached file from an instructor or classmate, do not immediately open it. Take the time to email the sender of the email in order to verify that they did intend for you to receive the file and that the file does not contain a computer virus. It is worth the extra time to be cautious since a computer virus can wipe away months of your work in just a few minutes.

❏ Whether it is an email software application that you have installed on your computer or a Web-based email system, you will want to create an **address book** that organizes the email addresses of your many classmates and instructors in college. Using the address book will save you time and can help avoid potential problems that occur (such as, missing periods or reversed letters) when you type in email addresses. When creating your address book it is recommended that you cut-and-paste email addresses from previous emails into the book rather than manually typing in each address, this will again save you time and avoid potential errors in spelling and punctuation.

❏ Most email software applications and Web-based email systems allow you to create a **signature** that will appear at the end of each email message you send. This can be useful since you do not want to send email messages without important contact information for the recipient to use when replying to your message. Your signature file should be concise and only provide essential information for contacting you in reply to the email message (for example, do not include long quotes, jokes, or other extraneous text messages with your signature).

❏ To be successful in college you will want to remain organized, and this includes managing your numerous email messages. Do not plan to store all of your email messages in your email "inbox". By **creating folders** (much like you would on your computer hard drive) you can organize your emails based on a structure that you determine to be effective. Typically, having email folders for each college course is recommended since it will allow you to quickly access the email messages related to course assignments and activities without a prolonged search.

❑ When you want to **share a URL** (i.e., Website address) with your fellow students or instructor, you should insert the URL between a "less-than" character (<) and a "greater-than" character (>). This technique will clearly indicate for the recipient what marks the beginning and the end of a URL. For example, <http://collegesurvival.college.hmco .com/ students>.

In addition, as with email addresses, you will want to cut-and-paste URL information into the message rather than typing in each character. This will reduce the likelihood of mistakes in spelling or punctuation.

Tips for Using Microsoft Word

Like many of today's software applications, Microsoft Word has far too many useful features to be listed in this companion. The following list of tips for using Microsoft Word highlights a few of the more useful functions for students completing online course assignments and activities.

❑ You will want to set Microsoft Word to **automatically save** any document you are working on every 3-5 minutes. By setting this in the options menu you will be able to ensure that recent changes to your document are saved even if power is lost to the computer or other technology failures trouble you. To set the time interval for automatic saving of your document, go to the "options" menu located under "tools" in Microsoft Word.

❑ The first time you save a Microsoft Word document you will be asked to name the file and select the folder location where the file will be stored. You may also select the **file format** in which you wish the file to be saved if you prefer an alternative to the default, which is the version of Microsoft Word you have installed (for example, Microsoft Word 2000 or XP). Often you will want to back save files to earlier versions of Microsoft Word since your classmates or instructors may not use the most recently released version that you have.

❑ When searching for specific words or phrases within a Microsoft Word document you can use the find feature **(CTRL + f)** to quickly locate all instances when the word or phrase are used in the document. You can even select to have the word or phrase replaced with an alternative each time it is identified.

❑ If you have created a Microsoft Word document that extends onto the following page by just a few lines, you can use the **shrink-to-fit** feature of Microsoft Word to automatically format the document so that no text is left at the top of the last page. The shrink-to-fit feature can be accessed through the "print preview" option.

#5

❏ When working with other students in the development of a Microsoft Word document, you can activate the **"track changes"** feature through the "tools" <u>menu</u>. This feature will monitor the additions, deletions, and comments of each student who edits the document, allowing others to later accept or reject their changes.

❏ In Microsoft Word you can **format** a word (such as, make it **bold**, <u>underlined</u>, or *italics*) by moving the cursor anywhere inside the word and selecting the desired format. You do not have to highlight the entire word by dragging your mouse pointer over the entire word in order to change the format.

❏ You can construct creative tables in Microsoft Word by using the **"table auto-format"** feature found in the "table" <u>menu</u>. The "table auto-format" feature provides a long list of table formatting options that, when selected, are automatically applied in your document

❏ If you are searching for just the right word and your cursor is anywhere inside the word you can access the Microsoft Word **thesaurus** by holding down "Shift" and also hitting "F7" on your keyboard.

❏ In the "file" <u>menu</u> of Microsoft Word you can quickly **open files** that you have recently created or edited in the past. In the "options" feature found in the "tools" <u>menu</u> of Microsoft Word, you can select the number of recently used files that are viewable, up to 9.

❏ By using the **right-click** function of your mouse you can quickly correct spelling and grammatical errors identified by Microsoft Word. Spelling and grammatical errors are indicated in Microsoft Word by red or green underlines respectively, as a result you can simply right-click on the underlined text to select a suggested revision.

❏ The Microsoft Word **ruler** can be used to create consistent indents, tabs, and margins for any documents. This is far more efficient than using the Tab key and can be accessed through the "view" <u>menu</u>.

❏ All Microsoft Word documents that you create should include **page numbers.** By selecting "page numbering" from the "format" <u>menu</u> you can quickly add page numbers to your documents. If page numbering is not sequential in the document you are creating, then you can use "section breaks" to vary page numbering (see the Microsoft Word help <u>menu</u> for more information on using section breaks).

❏ Additional information regarding the document can be added to the top or bottom of each page by using a **<u>header</u> or <u>footer</u>** in Microsoft Word. Inserting the titles, chapter names, and dates can be useful when you are creating many Microsoft Word documents for a course. You can add "header and footer" information through the "view" <u>menu</u>.

❏ Microsoft Word will automatically count the **number of words** in any document. You can access this information through the "tools" <u>menu</u>.

❑ **Comments** can be added to Microsoft Word documents that will appear for others that may review the file. Adding such comments can be useful when you are reviewing the work of other students or having others review your work before submitting it to the instructor since these comments can be hidden later on.

#6

❑ When using Microsoft Word you can insert **footnotes and endnotes** into the document to add additional information that may be useful to the reader but is not necessary within the main text. Both footnotes and endnotes are numbered and organized by Microsoft Word, making this an easy feature to add to your college coursework.

> **STUDENT-TO-STUDENT TIP**
>
> I would copy-and-paste class readings into Microsoft Word and use the highlighter and comment functions to make notes in my online reading. I would also copy my citation information into Microsoft Word before I started to read an article or other information so I could easily take the highlighted information and have the citation ready.

Technology Support Tips

Before starting online coursework it can be beneficial to become familiar with the online support services offered to you as a student. From technology support provided by the institution offering the course to support provided by manufacturers of hardware and software, you will want to be familiar with available support services since problems always arise at the worst times when you are taking any course.

Online Technology Assistance

Your college or university will typically offer a variety of technology support services for students. For students taking courses that require online coursework these services will be of great value, since at some point during your college education you will likely have many questions regarding technology. With a little planning and time spent getting to know the support services available to you as a student, inevitable problems with technology won't keep you from success.

Starting on the first day of classes you should take the time to explore your school's Website to determine what resources are available to you. Often technology support services will be divided among various operations within the institution. One support group will provide assistance when the school's Internet portal does not respond, while another group will help out when your email account stops sending messages.

> **STUDENT-TO-STUDENT TIP**
>
> The worst situation that you can be in is to want advice or assistance and not know where or how to go and get it. I found that by understanding the student support system, most of the issues that I had could be resolved in very short order.

We recommend that students maintain a list (on the back cover of this companion) with contact information and service hours for the technology support units that are responsible for providing support for each of the technologies you may use in completing their online course requirements. This list should include support units for the school's <u>Internet</u> portal (for example, Blackboard, WebCT), <u>email</u> accounts, computer labs on campus that you may use, as well as <u>Internet</u> connections that you may have available in your dorm. Having this information handy will be useful at some point, and getting timely assistance can make the difference between success and failure.

Manufacturer (Hardware or Software) Customer Support

If you do purchase a computer or other technology (for example, digital camera, scanner, etc.) in order to meet the requirements of a college course, then the support services available from the manufacturing company will often provide you limited services 24 hours a day. These can be invaluable when your <u>operating system</u> freezes up at midnight while you are preparing for your class presentation the next day or when your <u>Internet</u> connection fails while you are searching the college's online library for resources. Often these support services provided by the manufacturer will also provide you with trouble shooting guidelines for errors that may not be linked directly to their products, so don't be afraid to ask them a variety of questions.

Like with the technology support services provided by the college, keeping a list (including contact information with phone numbers and <u>email</u> addresses, as well as hours of operation) for the services available to you by the manufacturer is a good idea. The last thing you want to worry about at midnight before a class presentation is going through a year's worth of old receipts trying to find the toll-free number for your laptop.

ACTIVITY 2-4   **Have you missed something?**

As a review, match the following word, phrase, or acronym with the correct definition.

_____ **1.** shortcut   a. Keyboard short cut for access of the Microsoft Word thesaurus.

_____ **2.** address book   b. A feature in <u>email</u> software applications to organize <u>email</u> addresses.

(continued)

ACTIVITY 2-4   **Have you missed something?**

_____ **3.** bookmarks

c. An icon that can be created on your computer desktop to provide quick access to a specific file, folder, or <u>Webpage</u>.

_____ **4.** shift + F7

d. Keyboard short cut for Microsoft Word to quickly locate specific words or phrases used within a document.

_____ **5.** CTRL + f

e. A link in a <u>Web browser</u> to provide quick access to specific <u>Webpages</u> available on the World Wide Web.

Developing a Technology Contingency Plan

Computers and other online technologies will inevitably fail to work from time to time during your college experience. And unfortunately, these failures will most commonly happen when you can least afford it; such as when an assignment is due the next day. Knowing that these failures will happen, however, is to your advantage. Creating a technology contingency plan is an essential skill for students who are going to be successful in college. Contingency plans merely outline what resources you have available if (and when) the technology you normally use fails to function properly. Here are a few tips for outlining your technology contingency plans:

> **STUDENT-TO-STUDENT TIP**
>
> Make sure you have at least limited access to one additional computer with an <u>Internet</u> connection in case the computer you primarily use malfunctions. Find out if your local library has computers for public use, or if you could use the computer lab at a local high school, community college, YMCA, or other education facility, just in case.

❑ Identify **alternative on-campus computer labs** that you could use at anytime throughout the semester. Most college and university campuses will have a limited number of computer labs that are open 24 hours a day. If necessary, you may have to make arrangements at the beginning of the semester for access to the lab and its resources.

❑ Since going to campus is not always an option, identify a **classmate** that you can contact if you lose access to your computer or the World Wide Web. They can provide you with updated information on assignments as well as contact the instructor to let them know of the technology problems.

❑ Establish a **secondary <u>email</u> account** that can be used in case the <u>email</u> account provided by your college is temporarily out of service.

There are free <u>email</u> accounts provided by a variety of <u>Websites</u> (such as, <http://www.mail.com>, <http://mail.yahoo.com>, <http://www.hotmail.com>, etc.).

❏ Have the **contact information for your professor** (including office phone and fax numbers) written down in case you can't access your computer or the World Wide Web during a technology failure.

❏ Have the **contact information for the technology support services** written down on the back cover of this book in case you can't access your computer or the World Wide Web during a technology failure.

❏ **Back up** your course files every week. As a result, even in the event that you cannot access your computer, you will continue to have access to the course files you require.

❏ If power failures are common in your home, you may want to invest in a **power back up system** that supplies your computer with energy through a battery when the power goes out.

#1

#3

ACTIVITY 2-5   Are you prepared?

Given that problems with technology typically occur when you can least afford to be slowed-down in your studies, it is essential for your success in college that you are prepared with all of the essential information for solving a problem quickly. Take a few minutes now to complete the Important Contact Information page on the back cover of this book. Your college's <u>Website</u> should provide you with the contact information for technology support services, on-campus computer labs, and library services. For contact information from your <u>Internet</u> Service Provider and computer manufacturer, you should review their <u>Websites</u> and/or other documentation they provided at the time of purchase.

By keeping this information with you whenever you are completing online coursework, you will have the necessary contact information for getting help quickly and getting back to your studies when technology problems do occur.

CHAPTER SUMMARY

Taking advantage of the many tools and resources that are available to you when you are using the computer and <u>Internet</u> to complete your course assignments and activities requires that you become familiar with the functions of a variety of software applications, including your <u>operating system</u> and <u>word processing</u> software, as well as your <u>Web browser</u>. By learning more about the available options, you will be able to improve both the efficiency and quality of your studies in college. Periodically review the technology tips provided in this chapter and throughout the book, since you will likely forget to use these techniques and strategies as your college courses start to demand more of your time.

CHAPTER TWO   EXERCISE

To begin the exercise you will want to access your Web-based course materials (i.e., <u>educational portal</u>) using a <u>Web browser</u> (such as, Netscape Navigator or Microsoft Internet Explorer, etc.). In addition, you will want to open a new document in a <u>word processing</u> program (for example, Microsoft Word).

Though each <u>Web portal</u> (or <u>educational portal</u>) used for online coursework will likely be a little different, the following steps should provide you with an activity that you can complete within most Web-based course programs. If the buttons and links described in the activity are slightly different from those within the <u>educational portal</u> you use for online coursework, be flexible and try a few until you click on one that seems to provide the functionality described in the activity. If you have any problems identifying appropriate button links or completing any of the steps below, be sure to use the Help option provided within the Web-based course software program.

STEP ONE: Using the <u>Web browser</u> software, locate two <u>search engine</u>s, one that uses basic key words (for example, <http://www.google.com> or <http://www.altavista.com>) and a second that uses Web directory format (for example, <http://www.about.com> or <http://www.yahoo.com>).

#18

STEP TWO: Using both of the <u>search engine</u>s you have selected, complete a search to identify at least three <u>Website</u>s that provide useful tips for improving your writing skills (for example, search for "college writing skills").

#25

STEP THREE: Based on the information included on the three <u>Websites</u> you have identified through your search, select five writing skills tips that you believe will be useful in improving your writing skills in college.

STEP FOUR: Using your <u>word processing</u> software, create a list of the five tips that you identified for improving your writing skills. Save this document to your computer's hard disk with the title "writing skills" and place it in a <u>folder</u> where you will be able to find it later.

STEP FIVE: Log into the <u>email</u> account provided by your college (for example, <myname@mycollege.edu>). Use the college's <u>Web portal</u> or the <u>email</u> software to access your <u>email</u> account.

STEP SIX: Create a new message and include your <u>email</u> address in the recipient <u>field</u> (i.e., <myname@mycollege.edu>).

STEP SEVEN: Using the <u>email</u> <u>attachment</u> feature, attach the "writing skills" file that you created in step four. Depending on the <u>email</u> software that you use to access your <u>email</u>, you may have to "browse" the list of files that you have stored on your computer's hard disk drive in order to locate the "writing skills" file that you saved. When you have located and selected the file, you will typically click on "ok" to attach the file to your <u>email</u>.

STEP EIGHT: Send the <u>email</u>, along with the <u>attachment</u>, to yourself. When you receive the <u>email</u>, open the attached "writing skills" file to verify that it arrived without any changes to the content.

CHAPTER TWO SKILLS CHECKLIST

After completing this chapter you should be able to do the following. If there are skills below that you may not be able to do, take a few minutes to review the chapter, focusing on those areas that you may have missed the first time through.

❑ I can utilize keyboard short cuts in order to save time.

❑ I am able to use the right-click features to more efficiently access software features.

❑ I am able to improve the accessibility of my computer.

❑ I have the skills to manage the files I create on a computer.

❑ I can find files that are located on a CD-ROM, floppy disk, or my computer's hard disk.

❑ I am able to efficiently and effectively search the World Wide Web for useful information.

❑ I can select an appropriate <u>search engine</u> to search for the information I want to find.

❑ I am able to take advantage of features included in my <u>Web browser</u> software.

❑ I am able to take advantage of features included in my <u>email</u> software.

❑ I am able to take advantage of features included in Microsoft Word software.

❑ I have the information readily available to contact appropriate technical support services.

❑ I have a technology contingency plan in case I have technical problems.

❑ I have completed the chapter 2 activities.

ADDITIONAL RESOURCES

Additional resources on topics covered in this chapter are available on the <u>Website</u>: **<http://collegesurvival.college.hmco.com/students>**.

NOTES

1. See http://www.virtualsalt.com/evalu8it.htm
2. See http://www.radford.edu/~thompson/obias.html
   or http://www.runet.edu/~thompson/obias.html

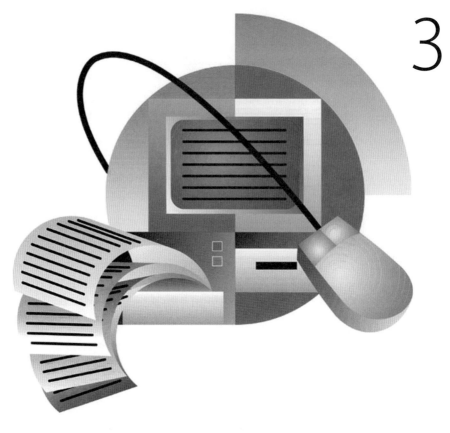

3

Selecting the Right Opportunities for Success

ost all of us enjoy movies that take us on a journey with someone as they struggle to overcome obstacles or challenges in pursuit of their goals and ambitions. Some of the stories are of athletes who were challenged by the prejudices of society, while others are about writers who struggle with the inner obstacles of adding meaning to their words. But it is neither the character nor the context of the story that is most often central to providing us with inspiration. It is the struggle, the struggle to overcome the obstacles that others and we have placed in our path toward success.

Even though the journey to success in college is filled with many challenges for all students, to be a successful student you don't necessarily have to overcome as many obstacles as you might think. For most of us, through our decisions we frequently make the path of success much more of a challenge than it has to be; while successful students make decisions to ensure that the path toward success in school is not made more difficult by obstacles that they can control.

Often we try to do too much and regularly each of us selects the wrong opportunities; or we select the right opportunities but at the wrong times. No matter the circumstances or the reasons, throughout the E-learning Companion we will focus our attention on making decisions that will provide us with the best opportunities for being successful in our studies.

Increasing the Odds of Your Success

Too often in life we put ourselves in situations where the odds of being successful are not in our favor. We do this by taking too many courses in a given semester, by enrolling in courses for which we have not mastered the prerequisite skills, by signing up for more than one challenging course in the same semester, or by committing to many outside activities in the weeks leading up to final exams, and the list could go on for pages.

There are few opportunities in college (or life) where success is guaranteed, so each of us must learn to play the odds. We will want to make decisions that put us in situations where all of the support necessary for our success is in place. Although there will be obstacles to our success, we can make decisions that minimize the barriers and increase our chances of achieving our academic goals.

We want to avoid anything less than success whenever possible, as a result we will work on making better decisions about what courses to take and when; balancing our academic, personal, and work commitments. This way we can enter each semester with the best possible odds at being successful.

> **STUDENT-TO-STUDENT TIP**
>
> Start out with your comfort zone and then branch out into unknown content territory after you have learned how to use the online learning tools.

E-learning Experiences

It wasn't until my junior year in college that the importance of selecting the right opportunities became very clear to me. At most universities, and in most majors, students commonly agree that a particular course (often with a particular professor) is used to "weed-out" those students that are destined to graduate in the major from those who will have to search elsewhere for a career. For my major that course was Calculus and passing Calculus was one of my barriers to success.

Given my course of studies within my major I had mistakenly decided, without the input of my academic advisor, to enroll in Calculus during the fall semester of my junior year. Now to me this seemed like a great time to

(continued)

take this course that I knew would be a challenge; after all I had already passed a few other courses in my major. But when you go to a university with a top football program, and each weekend brings family and friends to town for the games, the fall semester is not the best time to take your most challenging courses. By the fourth week of the semester our football team was on a winning streak, but I was falling behind in my studies as fast as they scored touchdowns. At the end of the semester my less than ideal study habits were matched by my less than passing grade. Though I did go on to pass Calculus the following semester, the lesson I learned about taking courses when you are most likely to succeed has stayed with me much longer than any of the mathematical formulas.

Now for you the distractions of college life may not be related to athletics and they may not be confined to a single semester, but for each of us there are always many distractions that can lead us away from success in our courses. Making decisions about what opportunities to take, and when, will however be essential in your success in college. Courses that require online study, whether for a completely online course or for additional activities in an on-campus course, require the same careful analysis as any other college course. Don't be fooled; just because you have the opportunity to complete some or all of your assignments using online tools doesn't necessarily mean that the course will require any less time, concentration, or effort.

In selecting the opportunities that offer you the best prospects for success you not only want to consider the amount of time a course requires, but also the timing of the course with your other obligations. It is essential for success to keep these two elements of your time in balance. Nonetheless, we often only think of the first. Being able to negotiate stability across these two elements of time is typically the critical factor determining the success of a student.

Be Realistic with Your Time

Hot

The time necessary to complete the requirements of online coursework (for example, class time, time working on assignments, time discussing topics with the instructor and other students, time studying for exams, etc.) will be roughly equal to the time that you would spend on traditional classroom assignments and activities. But when and where you will spend that time will likely be dramatically different.

In the conventional course the majority of the discussion concerning course topics and concepts takes place two or three times a week in the lecture hall, lab, or classroom. However, with online coursework it is more typical that you will be expected to discuss the course materials in small chunks of time throughout each week of the semester. This often means that you will be online posting messages and responding to <u>email</u>s every day, or every other day, throughout the semester.

Of course you may be online for only a few minutes each day. Yet by the end of the semester you will have spent approximately the same amount of course time as you would in a traditional classroom course. And while this may sound like a small change with little impact on your study habits, the shift from concentrating on a particular course for an hour on Tuesday and Thursday afternoons to being actively involved in class discussions each day of the week for the entire semester can be a major obstacle to success.

Although online courses and coursework will typically require about the same amount of your time as a conventional classroom course, the flexibility of online coursework does offer many advantages (and some disadvantages) that should be considered when selecting the courses in which you are most likely to be successful.

For example, if you are planning to take an overload (typically more than 12 to 15 credit hours in a given semester) and also participate in extracurricular activities (a theatre production, fraternity or sorority events, intramural athletics, etc.) then the flexibility of a course that offers opportunities for the coursework to be done online could be to your advantage. However, if you already have trouble staying on task and maintaining your motivation throughout the semester, then the flexibility of online coursework may be dangerous since there is often no set schedule for you to follow like there is in conventional classroom courses.

There is, unfortunately, no easy formula to give you for determining whether or not you have the time for successfully completing all the requirements of any college course. Throughout this book we will, however, provide you with several tools for assessing your unique situation and selecting the opportunities that offer you the best odds for being successful.

A Little History: Carnegie Units

So how do colleges and universities decide on how much time you should spend studying for each of your courses? Here is a little background information that can help explain. In 1909, while defining what constitutes a course in order to assess college professor pension, the Carnegie Foundation for the Advancement of Teaching established a standardized measure of academic equivalency. This definition established a measurement of work based on time in the classroom. According to the Board's definition, a standard of 750 minutes with a qualified instructor was equivalent to one hour

(continued)

of academic credit or Carnegie Unit. This unit of measurement has since be-come a standard throughout American education and is the reason why the typical 3 credit hour on-campus course meets three times a week for 50 min-utes each time, over a semester of approximately 15 weeks. This gives stu-dents 2,250 minutes of time with a qualified instructor for each 3 credit hour course.

Of course, professors typically add to this the expectation that you will study two to three hours on your own for each hour you spend in the class-room; thereby requiring roughly 4,500–6,750 minutes (or 75–112 hours) of studying for each 3 credit hour course. In courses requiring online course-work, however, you won't typically interact with the instructor or other stu-dents during three prescribed time periods in each week. Rather, many of your 75–112 hours will be spent watching, listening to, or reading lecture materials provided by the instructor, discussing course topics with other stu-dents online, completing online activities, and/or doing other course assign-ments that can be facilitated using online technologies.

ACTIVITY 3–1   Analyze your time.

Complete the following table based on your experiences in the last 6 months. Although there are no *correct* answers to the questions, by examin-ing your response to each question you can evaluate the effectiveness of your current study habits as you develop new learning skills for online coursework.

	Never	Some of the time	Most of the time	Always
1. Do you keep up with course readings even when there are no required deadlines, quizzes, or assignments?	o	o	o	o
2. Do you say "no" to friends when you have coursework to be done?	o	o	o	o
3. Do you study effectively after 10:00 P.M.?	o	o	o	o
4. Do you have time set aside each day (outside of class) for your studies?	o	o	o	o

(continued)

	Never	Some of the time	Most of the time	Always
5. Do you typically procrastinate on completing coursework until the day before it is due?	o	o	o	o
6. Do your friends and family support your efforts to be successful in your courses?	o	o	o	o
7. Do your friends and family keep you so busy on weekends that you don't have time to study?	o	o	o	o
8. Do you schedule your personal commitments around your course commitments?	o	o	o	o
9. Do you plan to study and then find other things to do?	o	o	o	o
10. Do you often feel like you have committed yourself to too many activities?	o	o	o	o

Consider the Timing

Closely related to assessing whether or not there is enough time in your day to complete all of the requirements for your courses is comparing the timing of your college courses to that of your other commitments. For each of us there are a variety of events that add meaning to our lives beyond the boundaries of our studies (for example, artistic expressions, music, athletics, etc.). And yet their impact on your success in school, both positive and negative, cannot be underestimated. In deciding upon the best opportunities for your success you will want to consider the timing of courses (as well as specific activities, assignments, projects, exams, and so forth) in relation to these other events.

Developing a timeline of courses that you plan to enroll in over the next two to three semesters is an essential step for comparing the timing of courses. Based on the requirements for graduation at your college or university (and the advice of your academic advisor and other successful students) you should create a list of what courses you plan to take in future semesters. In making the timeline be sure to consider which courses should be taken during the same semester, any pre-requisite requirements, and what outside events may distract you from your studies. Also include any other personal variables that you may consider important.

The idea behind viewing your schedule of courses over several semesters is to negotiate a balance of commitments between your studies, friends, family, work, and other obligations each semester. For example, if you are interested in auditioning for a college theatre production of *Hamlet* in the spring, it may not be an ideal time to also enroll in two of the more difficult courses required for your major. Maybe one of the more challenging courses can be taken the following summer. You can also add some flexibility to your schedule for the spring semester by taking an elective course that meets only once a week and that uses online technologies for the other coursework requirements.

Planning in advance can help ensure that you are selecting the course opportunities where you are most likely to be successful. Knowing your commitments and your ability to manage (i.e., balance or negotiate) your commitments will be essential. Two primary categories of commitments that you likely have in addition to your academic commitments are work commitments and personal commitments. Both of these will have substantial influence on selecting the right opportunities for your success in college.

Balance Your Academic and Work Commitments

For most students, the increasing cost of a college education requires the negotiating of course demands with the commitment to work full or part time.[1] For many students it is this requirement for flexibility in scheduling around work commitments that persuades them to look for courses that either utilize online technologies to supplement the classroom experiences or even to investigate courses that are offered completely online. Without this flexibility, in fact, a college education would be beyond the reach of many students currently attending colleges and universities.

In selecting the opportunities that offer the greatest likelihood of success one of the major variables that you should consider is the balancing of your educational and work commitments. Depending on your specific situation you may or may not have these competing demands on your time, but whatever your situation, the competing requirements for your time and attention do not have be a barrier to success. By understanding the conflicting demands for your time you can make a decision that puts you in the best possible situation to be successful.

A few of the variables you will want to identify and consider in planning your course of studies include:

❏ Does your work schedule remain the same throughout the semester?

❏ When during the semester will your courses require the most attention (for example, midterms, finals, major assignments)?

❏ Do you have access to the <u>Internet</u> at work?

❏ Can you complete online coursework at your workplace when you have completed your work requirements?

❏ How can online activities and assignments that add flexibility to your course demands be used to ensure that you can meet your work commitments?

❏ How many hours will you have committed to work and school if you add together the time required for studying and the number of hours you are planning to work?

❏ Knowing your past success and study habits, is it realistic to attempt to study and work each week throughout the semester?

Clearly you may not have all the information for answering each of these questions at this time. But by taking the time to talk with instructors of the courses that you are considering for next semester, along with your employer, you can make better informed decisions and increase the likelihood of your success.

Balance Your Academic and Personal Commitments

As a college student, a primary distracter from your studies will more than likely be your many personal commitments. Whether they are plans for a ski vacation with friends, dinner with co-workers, or a sorority/fraternity social event, the personal commitments to friends and family will take time away from studies throughout any semester. And while these social activities are important to your success in college, they too must be balanced with the requirements of your coursework.

In negotiating your study times with your other personal obligations, the flexibility and individual control of online coursework will likely be attractive, although the total number of hours spent studying for each course should be about the same as a traditional course. The advantages (and disadvantages) that are inherent with individual control and flexi-

> **STUDENT-TO-STUDENT TIP**
>
> Set a specific time at least three to four days a week to do your regular communications such as discussion forums, emails, and instant messaging.

bility should also be considered as you select the right courses and extracurricular opportunities for a successful college experience. Finding this equilibrium does, nevertheless, require that you carefully assess your learning skills and study habits. Without knowing your strengths and weaknesses, making decisions about how to manage your time in college is next to impossible.

ACTIVITY 3–2   Plan with your commitments in mind.

Complete the following table for the next three semesters with the best estimates that you can make at this time.

	Academic commitments		Personal commitments		Work commitments	
	Course	Hours/week	Commitment	Hours/week	Commitment	Hours/week
Fall						
Spring						
Summer						

Get Your Feet Wet: Take an Online Course of Personal Interest

Today there are a variety of Internet sites that offer a diverse array of online learning experiences that you can participate in for free. From wine tasting to the chemistry of the human brain, these free courses can provide you with an assortment of experiences while allowing you to develop some basic learning skills and study habits for being successful in online coursework. At the same time they can help you assess your readiness for further courses that utilize online technologies. Typically these courses are short (five to six weeks) and can be taken at a variety of times throughout the year, including summer.

By building on your experiences with online technologies outside the classroom, you can be better equipped for success when your college course requires that you use technology. Online sources for free courses include:

<http://www.bn.com>

<http://www.free-ed.net/catalog>

<http://www.docnmail.com>

<http://www.word2word.com/course.html>

<http://www.thirdage.com/learning>

<http://www.fathom.com>

Review Prerequisite Requirements

Most college and university courses will require that you have a range of prerequisite skills and knowledge. These requirements are typically identified by the instructor in the course syllabus and are often included as a component of the course registration system. Prerequisite requirements, both those related to previous courses as well as technical skills, should be considered when making your decision about what courses to take and when to take them (for example, having mastered college algebra requirements prior to taking chemistry or being able to send <u>email</u> with an <u>attachment</u> prior to taking a course that uses online technology).

Prerequisite requirements are selected by professors to help students gauge their preparedness for success in a college course, therefore you will want to check the prerequisite requirements for any course in which you are considering enrolling (especially those courses that may require that you use online technology). Not having even one of the required skills greatly reduces the likelihood of your success. Particularly for courses in your major, you will want to contact the professor prior to enrolling in the course to ensure that you have met the prerequisite requirements.

> **STUDENT-TO-STUDENT TIP**
>
> Making sure that you are grounded in the prerequisites is absolutely essential to having an enjoyable and successful experience. Once the prerequisites are satisfied you can concentrate all of your efforts on the task at hand versus having to expend extra energy in getting prepared for the learning experience.

Verify Your Support Services

`Hot`

While success in college rests primarily on your shoulders, without adequate support services from the institution, achieving your goals will be much more difficult than it has to be. From offering librarians that work with students online, to technology support and financial aid, the support systems of the institution should be examined carefully to ensure that you are making the best use of the resources available to you.

College Computer Labs

Most colleges provide computer labs that are available to students. On many campuses different computers feature specialized software for students that most often use that particular lab. For example, a computer lab located near the Statistics department will commonly feature specialized software for making statistical calculations while a computer lab in the main campus library may only provide access to a limited range of software applications used for searching databases and locating resources. Campus computer labs will also routinely offer differing hours of operations, some being open 24 hours a day while others close in the early evening. You should become familiar with the variety of computer labs available to you as a student and verify the software available in each lab that you may use throughout the semester. The technical support provided at most computer labs is limited, though the staff is often more than willing, to the best of their ability, to help you resolve any technology problems you may have.

Online Library Services

Colleges and universities today typically offer a range of online services through their libraries. These services are designed to help you manage your time and get the most from the library resources. You will most likely have to contact your institution's library to find out the range of services available; though descriptions of the services are often available on the World Wide Web or through your dormitory.

Services available without having to go on campus typically include online searchable databases for identifying resources without leaving your apartment or dorm, as well as completely online journals, newspapers, and magazines. Although all of the resources you will require in college will not be available online, you will still have to go to the library. Many libraries will even offer orientation sessions for students where an information specialist will help you identify and utilize both the online and on-campus services offered by the library.

Technical Support

Your college or university will commonly offer a variety of technology support services that you should take advantage of while registered as a student (also discussed in chapter 2). From helping you trouble shoot why your <u>email</u> account is not working to providing you with access to virus scan software, most institutions typically offer many technology support services to students. When taking a course that requires use of online tools (for example, <u>chat</u> rooms, <u>discussion boards</u>, online readings, etc.) the likelihood of the availability of these services goes up. And since these services are typically included in your tuition,

> **STUDENT-TO-STUDENT TIP**
>
> Being able to contact the institution for assistance and support on any problems that come up can make all the difference, leading to a positive learning experience and success for the student.

you should not look for outside technical support that may cost you hundreds of dollars.

When you first enroll in a course that uses technology you should contact the college or university technology support services to identify all of the resources available to you. Make a list of essential phone numbers and office hours that you can keep next to your computer. When a technology crisis happens the last thing you want to spend your time doing is chasing down the phone number of the right person to contact.

Student Training Courses

As a student you may be able to enroll in many of the training courses offered by the college. These courses will typically provide you with foundational skills for using a specific software program (such as Microsoft Word or Microsoft Excel) and are often as short as two to three hours. These training courses can provide you with an excellent opportunity to practice many of the skills that you will later be required to use in completing your online coursework. It is often worth your time to contact your college's technical support services to see what training courses are available to students and when.

Career Counseling

Many institutions now offer both on-campus and online career counseling services. From conducting job searches to getting feedback on your resume, these support services are often very useful (yet under-utilized). By visiting the career counseling center's Website, which most college and universities now have available, you should be able to identify the spectrum of services available to you as a student.

Financial Aid

As the price of a college education has increased, financial assistance has become a common requirement for most students. Though applying for and receiving financial assistance may still require your presence on campus, many institutions now offer some limited services through the Internet or automated phone systems. Before going to the financial aid office at your institution it is likely worth your time to first visit their Internet site, or call them on the phone, to determine what time saving services they may now offer through technology.

Special Needs Accommodations

Hot

Accommodating the requirements of special needs students is required under federal law for colleges and universities. These accommodations are not however limited to the conventional classroom. Online resources must also meet a standard for accessibility for special needs students (including accommodations for sight and/or hearing impairments, learning disabilities, and other factors that may add to the burden of the student). Your college or university will be able to provide you with specific guidelines for applying for accommodations and ensuring that you are aware of the services available to you as a student.

Writing and Mathematics Labs

Support for students taking writing and mathematics courses is a standard support service provided at most institutions. Today, these services will typically provide you with a range of support including technology support on using software that is required for coursework. Although less common than other support services, many institutions now offer some online services through their writing and mathematics labs. From reviews of draft term papers to answering questions about college algebra, these services can be useful to students when there is no time to visit the offices on campus. Since these services are typically limited you should contact the writing and math labs at your institution to identify what types of support are available to you.

ACTIVITY 3–3 **Have you missed something?**

As a review, answer the following questions by circling True or False for each statement.

1. True–False   Colleges are required by law to provide special accommodations for disabled students even when courses are delivered using online technologies.

2. True–False   When doing research for course assignments and activities, you should always start by going to the on-campus library.

3. True–False   The prerequisite skill requirements for a course provide guidelines on what you should be able to do before enrolling in that course.

4. True–False   Online databases available through most college libraries have access to online full-text copies of all journals available at the campus library.

5. True–False   Enrolling in courses where you are most likely to be successful requires more than just knowing which courses are being offered for the upcoming semester.

CHAPTER SUMMARY

Success in college requires that you choose your opportunities wisely. When planning for college experiences and scheduling courses each semester you will want to consider a variety of factors that may impact on the likelihood of your success. From personal commitments that may interfere with your study times to prerequisite skill requirements outlined by the instructor, selecting only the right opportunities for your success is a critical skill for college students.

CHAPTER THREE   EXERCISE

To begin the exercise you will want to have access to the World Wide Web using a Web browser (such as, Netscape Navigator or Microsoft Internet Explorer, etc.).

STEP ONE: Identify and locate the Web portal for information regarding the services of your college or university. This is not typically the educational portal where you would find links to real-time chats, discussion boards, and course syllabi, but rather the Website where you can locate information on the academic degree programs, faculty and staff, the library, as well as the other support services provided to students.

STEP TWO: Locate and select the link to the Webpage for the college's library. When you have identified the Webpage for the college's library determine the appropriate librarian (or library services department) that should be contacted with regards to the online services offered by the library.

STEP THREE: Contact, by email or phone, the librarian (or library services department) that provides the online services offered by the library. In your email (or phone call) request information on online tutorials, as well as any on-campus training that is available from the library on using the online library resources.

STEP FOUR: Locate and select the link to the Webpage for the college's *student technical support services*. When you have identified the Webpage for the college's technical support for students, determine the appropriate department that should be contacted to access this support (for example, a "student help desk").

STEP FIVE: Contact, by email or phone, the department that provides technical support for students. In your email (or phone call) request information on online tutorials, on-campus training, hot-line phone numbers, and other resources available for students from technical support.

CHAPTER THREE   SKILLS CHECKLIST

After completing this chapter you should be able to do the following. If there are skills below that you may not be able to do, take a few minutes to review the chapter, focusing on those areas that you may have missed the first time through.

❏ I have created a timeline of courses I plan to enroll in for at least the next two to three semesters based on the college or university requirements for graduation.

❏ I have a list of my personal commitments that will impact on my time for studying.

❏ I have considered my work commitments in selecting only those course opportunities where I have the best odds of being successful.

❏ I have identified at least two activities each week that can be combined with other commitments in order to reduce the demands on my time.

❏ I have identified and contacted the library, technology, and other support services available at my college or university.

❏ I have completed the chapter 3 activities.

ADDITIONAL RESOURCES

Additional resources on topics covered in this chapter are available on the Website: <u>Website</u>: **<http://collegesurvival.college.hmco.com/students>**.

NOTES

1. See http://nces.ed.gov/pubs98/condition98/c9852a01.html

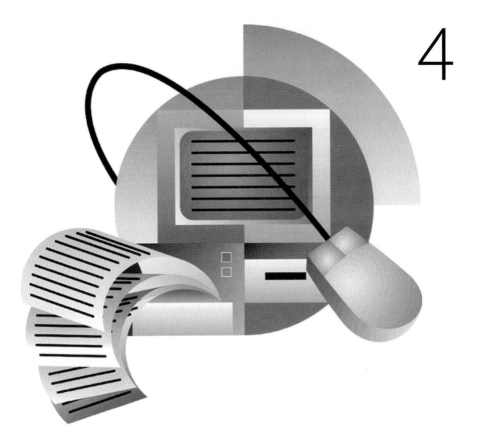

4

Create a Plan and Follow It

oger Maris, a famous baseball player, once said *"You win not by chance, but by preparation."*[1] The same is true for success in college; you succeed not by chance, but by preparation. Planning for success is a significant step toward accomplishing your goals in your college courses. From visualizing your achievements to scheduling your time and creating a helpful studying environment, planning is much more than just stating that you want to be successful.

You must follow through with your plans in order to accomplish the results you want to achieve. Merely developing plans will not be enough to ensure your success. Acting upon your plans is what moves good intentions to positive achievements.

Whether in the traditional classroom or in the online classroom, creating and following through on your plans will lead you to the success you want to have in your college courses. While this may sound fairly simple and straightforward, unfortunately it is not for most of us. In this chapter we will discuss many strategies, tips, tools, techniques, suggestions, and rec-ommendations for setting goals that you can accomplish, making plans that will lead to success, creating environments that support your success, and achieving your goals by following through with your plans.

Planning for Online Success

The flexibility of college courses that utilize online technologies can be a double-edged sword for most students. The opportunities to complete as-signments or activities at times that are convenient for you can be mislead-ing, swaying you to procrastinate or encouraging you to attempt the course without a well thought-out plan for your success. As a result, the impor-tance of planning for success is by no means diminished when you have the opportunity to complete your coursework using online tools.

Not only must you set out a clear plan of activities that will lead to your eventual success in the course, you must also ensure that you keep to your plans. From setting time aside each day for accessing online materials to creating a study environment with few distractions, all during the course you should stick to your plans for success. As you find out more about the course requirements, the requirements of individual instructors, the goals of your fellow students, and even your preferred study habits, you will likely want to alter your plans somewhat. Always, however, remain true to your initial decisions regarding your plans for being successful in your studies.

Developing and revising your plans for success with regards to any on-line coursework involves just a few minutes each week. Starting on the first day of the course you will want to define a clear statement of what you want to accomplish. Not just the grade you want to receive, but what knowledge and skills you would like to have when the course is complete as well. It could be to gain specific skills such a mastering the calculations re-quired for algebra or it could be to create a short story that will hopefully be published someday.

No matter what the specific goals you may set, by planning for success you can make an initial estimate of how much time the course will require, what types of study environments will be best for ensuring that you reach your goals, and decide how you can balance your academic, work, and per-sonal commitments. Making these and other decisions will be essential to your success. From this initial assessment a plan will be conceived that out-lines many of the major action steps that you will have to take in order to accomplish your goals for the course.

Yet no matter how good the plan we create, many times during a course each of us will likely want to depart from our plans; maintaining good study habits can be difficult as other interesting distractions come our way. Athletic events, homecoming events, trips home to visit family and friends, all will compete for your attention. But by staying with your initial plans, you have the best opportunities for success in the course and can es-tablish habits that will ensure your success in later endeavors as well.

Short-Term and Long-Term Goals

Achieving success in college requires that you can both visualize and plan for your success in the long-term as well as the short-term. By linking together what is required for long-term success (in this instance, the goals you have set with regards to your performance throughout your college experience) with the more immediate requirements (such as, which assignments must be completed today) you will ensure that you have a holistic plan that is capable of guiding you on the path toward success.

However, neither long-term planning nor short-term planning in isolation from the other is effective. Long-term plans that do not define what must be accomplished today and throughout the week are inadequate since long-standing achievements, like your success in college, are built on a foundation of interim accomplishments,

> **STUDENT-TO-STUDENT TIP**
>
> I still take online classes and always set as my goal what I want to take away from this class that will help me in my profession.

such as getting an "A" on your creative writing assignment. Likewise, short-term plans alone are ineffectual since they do not have the means to continuously support the motivation required during semester long courses (let alone two- or four-year degree programs). Only by establishing an integrated plan that includes short-term and long-term plans can you better ensure your success.

☐ Plan for success in college.

`Hot`

Although a college education is merely a stepping-stone toward many life-long ambitions, to keep our focus in this book we will want to limit our vision of long-term success to your college experience. This long-term perspective of what is required for you to be satisfied with your performance in college will establish the standard for the personal expectations and goals you set each semester.

Planning for success in college requires that you first define what it will take for you to consider yourself successful at the end of your college experience. For many, graduation will define success, while for others their Grade Point Average (GPA) within their major may be at the heart of what they consider success. Leaving college with a high paying job may be part of your definition as well as acceptance into graduate school. No matter how you define success, you should take the time now to write down your definition of success on paper. Merely the act of writing down what it will take for you to consider yourself successful will greatly improve the odds that your vision will be realized.

☐ Plan for success this semester.

Success in college typically has as its foundation your accomplishments across several semesters. Not meeting your aspirations during one or more semesters can greatly reduce the chances of meeting your overall goals for college. For example, it is much more difficult to improve a low GPA from your first year in college than it is to damage a higher GPA once it is established. For that reason you will want to plan for your success semester by semester, course by course, setting goals for each semester that will lead to your long-term success in college.

❏ Plan for success this week.

While plans for success at the semester level will provide more details than you had when you defined *success in college*, the comprehensive plans for being successful in the weekly assignments and activities of your courses are crucial if long-term goals are to be realized. Creating and following through on weekly plans will not only help you align your short-term and long-term planning, but it will also help you manage your time, keep track of course assignments, evaluate your course performance, schedule events with other students, plan your daily tasks, and even find time to relax.

Unlike the long-term plans that you have set for the semester and throughout college, your weekly plans will likely require more frequent revisions. For example, imagine that one of your goals for this week is to collect four journal articles as references for a paper you are writing for your sociology course. However, after searching your college or university's online databases you realize that the articles you want will require that you go to an off campus library. Revising your weekly plan (as well as your daily plans) will be necessary since you won't be able to complete this research until next week. Revising weekly plans is common, and as long as you keep the weekly plans aligned with semester and daily plans you should be on target to accomplish your long-term goals.

❏ Plan for success today.

`Hot`

Daily planning is at the core of the short-term successes that lead to long-term accomplishments. Each day you will want to determine what goals you must achieve in order to provide a foundation for weekly and semester accomplishments. You will want to write down a daily list of tasks you should complete and goals you want to accomplish. Each morning you should create your list and each evening you should review your list to evaluate your success. By evaluating and tracking your progress on a daily basis you can better ensure that your daily accomplishments lead to your weekly, semester, and long-term success in college.

ACTIVITY 4-1   Daily to do list.

Complete a table like the following, with *To do lists* for each day of the upcoming week. Each day should have at least three activities, which can be academic, personal, or work-related.

To Do List

Sunday	Monday	Tuesday	Wednesday	Thursday	Friday	Saturday
1.	1.	1.	1.	1.	1.	1.
2.	2.	2.	2.	2.	2.	2.
3.	3.	3.	3.	3.	3.	3.

Setting Realistic Expectations of Online Coursework

Establishing realistic expectations of online coursework can provide a practical foundation for planning your success. The pre-conceived ideas you may have about online technologies and online learning (for example, the quality of instructional materials, the amount of interaction with the instructor and other students, the value of online readings, etc.) will often define how you participate in online coursework as well as affect your achievements in the online classroom. Yet, for better or for worse, most of these *accepted wisdoms* about online coursework are not based on the realities of the course or courses you are currently taking. Since each course at each college or university will utilize online technologies in their own unique way, you should build your expectations based on what you know about the current course. Although finding accurate information about what you should expect with regards to the use of online technologies within your particular course may not be easy to uncover, you should start your search by asking the course instructor.

Here are a few questions you may want to **ask your instructor** in order to better define your expectations about online coursework in the class:

❏ Will I be expected to participate in a synchronous <u>chat</u> each week?

❏ Will my participation grade be determined by the number and quality of postings you make to the <u>discussion board</u>?

❏ Do you require online readings or traditional textbooks or both?

❏ What types of online support services are offered by the college or university?

❑ Should I expect to receive replies from you to my <u>emails</u> within 24 hours?

❑ Will there be a requirement for online group activities in the course?

❑ How does student performance in online coursework compare with student performance in on-campus coursework provided by the instructor?

❑ What suggestions do you have for being successful in the online coursework?

Common Misconceptions of Online Coursework

Nevertheless, most of us will enroll in courses with several mistaken ideas about what an online learning experience is really like. Below are several misconceptions students commonly have about online coursework:

Courses that use online technologies require less time than traditional on-campus courses.   Unfortunately the opposite is actually true for most students. The requirements of online coursework are typically new to students and the primarily text-based methods for communicating online slow down the learning pace for many students. When completing online coursework you should ordinarily anticipate spending more time reading and writing than you would in most conventional on-campus courses.

Hot **Hot** ***Not having to go to class means I can wait until the last minute to participate.*** Unlike in the traditional lecture course where your participation is commonly required only once or twice a week during a scheduled time, online course more often than not takes place 24 hours a day, 7 days a week. This isn't to say that you will be expected to participate every day throughout the semester, but waiting until the last minute to participate in online discussions is not a strategy for success in online coursework. In general, you will want to participate in online discussions and coursework at least three or four days each week.

Online instructors are always online.   You should never wait until the day before the assignment is due to <u>email</u> your professor with a question or request feedback on a draft term paper. Online instructors are not always online, nor will your message necessarily be at the top of the priority list in responding to <u>emails</u>. Many times students have the expectation that if they are awake at midnight working on an activity for class, then the instructor will also be awake and answering their <u>email</u> (or, the instructor will answer <u>email</u> questions at 8:00 A.M.). This is however a misconception. Teaching courses is just one of the many duties your instructors will have at the college or university, so you should plan ahead to ensure that there is adequate time for the instructor to reply to your questions or requests before assignments are due.

You can't make friends in an online course.   Strong friendships can be, and often are, built online. Many students actually find that it is easier to create friendships online since the online environment doesn't have many of the social pressures that are common in the classroom (e.g., body image, physical disabilities, or social cliques). In fact, so many people believe that friendships and other relationships can be developed online that during a single month in 2002 more than 18 million people visited online dating Websites.[2]

Little feedback is given on online assignments and activities.   Like in the conventional classroom, the level of feedback you receive on your assignments and activities done online will vary by the instructor delivering the course. Many professors that use online technologies will use the tools and resources available to provide feedback to students sooner than the long-established 5 or 7 days that many on-campus instructors have between class meetings, while other faculty members may take days before answering your email questions.

If I don't like to participate in class then online courses are better for me.   Learning, either online or in the classroom, is an active pursuit. Your success in college will depend on your dynamic involvement in your coursework. From reading required textbooks to discussing ideas with study partners, the more you can be involved in the learning experience the greater the likelihood that you will be successful.

For those students that do not like to participate in class due to a possible disability or social fear, then the online learning environment can offer shelter from many of the social pressures that are common in the classroom. Your active participation is, however, still required for learning to take place.

Online materials are always available.   Although online course materials are typically available to you 24 hours a day, you do not want to wait until the last minute to access the resources required to complete any college activity or assignment. Often professors will turn off the students' access to course materials for a given week, module, or lesson after the related activities or assignments are complete. And, of course, critical technology failures can (and will) happen at unexpected and inopportune times. As a result you should plan ahead to ensure that you have all of the online materials you will require (such as online readings, assignment descriptions, submission guidelines, online library resources, etc.) well before an online course assignment or activity is due.

ACTIVITY 4-2   Have you missed something?

As a review, mark the correct phrase that completes the following statements.

1. Goals for your success in college should focus on ...
   a. the long-term (for example, your grade point average at graduation).
   b. the short-term (for example, your grade on the mid-term).
   c. both the long-term and short-term aligned together.

2. For most college students, courses that use online resources typically require ...
   a. about the same amount of time as traditional classroom courses.
   b. significantly less time than traditional classroom courses.
   c. almost no time since they are easier than traditional classroom courses.

3. When emailing a question to a college professor you should expect a response ...
   a. within 12 hours.
   b. within 2–3 days.
   c. within a week.

Clarifying Personal Expectations and Setting Goals

Once you have swept away any misconceptions or inaccurate perceptions you may have had concerning online coursework, it is time to establish some realistic personal expectations for the course. Your expectations for any college course should be based on realistic prospects given your past performance; grades in courses with similar content, performance in similar semesters given other work, personal, or academic commitments, as well as performance in classes that require similar use of online technologies.

If you have few experiences with college level courses, the basis for your expectations will have to rely even more heavily on the recommendations of your academic advisor, course instructor, and fellow students. Performance in high school courses, though of some value, rarely predicts success in college level courses that utilize online technologies. Not only has the learning environment shifted away from fifty-minute class meetings five times a week, the expectations for independent learning have also increased with your move to college level courses. It is essential, therefore, that you discuss your expectations and plan for success with your academic advisor and/or professor. They will be able to offer you guidance and assistance in preparing your path toward success.

Since your expectations regarding the course will provide a foundation for your course goals, here are a few questions you will want to consider when establishing course expectations:

- ❑ Does this course require that I apply skills or knowledge that I have not applied recently (e.g., was my last course in Math three years ago)?

- ❑ Am I familiar with the online technologies that I will be required to use in completing the course?

- ❑ Is this course required for my major?

- ❑ Given the assignments and activities required in the course, how have I performed in the past when other classes had similar requirements?

- ❑ Will other courses I am enrolled in this semester divert my attention away from my studies for this course?

- ❑ Is the topic of the course of great interest to me, or will I struggle to remain motivated?

- ❑ Have I developed the necessary learning skills and study habits to be successful in this course?

Based on your expectations of each course, you will want to set independent goals related to each course you are taking. These goals will provide you with operational definitions of *success* for each course. In other words, by achieving these goals you will be achieving *success* in your studies.

`Hot`

These definitions of success that you establish through your goals for each course are individual and specific to your college experience, so you shouldn't feel pressure based on the goals others have set for themselves. They are your standards and when you have accomplished them you should consider yourself successful. Everyone will set their own goals, and thereby their own definitions of success, but the only classifications of success that really matter are those defined by you. Meeting the expectations of others just isn't practical; after all, they have come to different answers when analyzing their expectations for the course.

Course goals should include the final grade you would like to receive (when appropriate) as well as the knowledge and skills you want to take away from the experience. Though these goals may be linked, this is not always the case. Typically, in some courses you will want to focus more on the course grade (especially in courses within your major), while in other courses your interests may be more about developing or applying skills (for example, many college students will take art courses as electives, though their majors may be in the social sciences like psychology or education).

For goals to be effective tools they should have the following character-istics:

✔ They should be specific to each course. Although you will have goals for your overall college experience (e.g., overall GPA) you will want to set more specific goals for each course.

✔ They should be measurable. Define what it takes to be successful and you will know when you are successful.

✔ They should be challenging, yet realistic. Goals should push you to do your best while remaining consistent with the expectations you have established for the course.

Below are a few examples of course goals that you may establish:

▶ I will have an average score of 85 or higher on the four exams I am required to take for Algebra 101.

▶ My participation grade will be 40 out of 40 points in Public Speaking 200.

▶ I will score no lower than an 80 on each of my mid-term exams this semester.

Building Comprehension Skills

You should build into your plan for success the time and resources neces-sary for developing your comprehension skills. Research has shown that students who have built skills for comprehending greater amounts of infor-mation from readings and discussions are more likely to have higher acad-emic achievement.[3]

By improving your comprehension skills in four areas (reading, listen-ing, conversation, and feedback) you can be successful in all of your college coursework.

Reading Comprehension: Even with the enormous growth of tech-nology use in education, reading proficiency and comprehension remains a foundational skill for success in the college classroom, whether online or on-campus. Improving your reading comprehension starts by becoming an active reader: previewing readings, taking notes, asking questions, an-ticipating materials, and summarizing what you have learned. While most of the strategies for successful reading that apply to printed works are appropriate for online readings as well, often you will want to use the resources of online technologies to improve your skills and build on these habits. In chapter 7 you will find many strategies and techniques for im-proving your reading proficiency and comprehension when course read-ings are online.

Listening Comprehension: Often daydreams or other distracters in the classroom will keep us from gaining a full grasp of all the materials covered by a professor during a lecture. Increasing your listening compre-

Hot Hot

hension requires that you become an active listener; asking questions, taking notes, anticipating forthcoming topics, and so forth. Listening comprehension is an essential skill for online coursework that requires listening to or watching lectures that have been recorded. Though you may not be able to receive immediate responses to questions, keeping a list of questions to email your instructor or study partners is a good technique to increase your listening comprehension (as well as to manage your time since you will not have to review the lecture in order to clarify questions).

Conversation Comprehension: By and large most of us are not great conversationalists. During our conversations with other students we commonly find ourselves so eager to make our next comment or ask our next question that we fail to listen to the other people that are in the conversation with us. Or at the end of the conversation we realize too late that we have not clarified our expectations nor do we really understand what we are supposed to do next. The same failures to comprehend the valuable information contained in any conversation are also common in online conversation (such as in a chat with your study group members or in a discussion board conversation with your instructor). In order to increase your comprehension in all of your conversation (online or in-person) you want to be an active participant.

The ratio of two ears to only one mouth is important to conversation comprehension; ideally you should listen two-thirds of the time and speak one-third. Neither dominating nor failing to participate in a conversation is an effective strategy online or in the classroom. For example, during an online synchronous chat you should not feel pressure to respond to every line posted by other students or your instructor. Take your time to reflect upon what is being discussed, ask specific questions for clarification, and post well thought-out items that add value to the discussion. If you are continuously attempting to respond to every posting in the discussion you will comprehend little of the conversation and only manage to tire out your fingers.

Feedback Comprehension: A lack of meaningful feedback in previous course experiences (for example, only getting a letter grade from an instructor on a 10 page paper) has produced for many of us an unconscious reflex that reduces our comprehension when others are giving us feedback on our work. We are so familiar with negative or worthless feedback, that we have learned to hear, but not listen to, the feedback others offer. Although you will most likely still receive meaningless feedback in some of your college courses, increasing your attentiveness to feedback and potential valuable lessons that may be contained within each statement is a hallmark of successful college students. By comprehending and applying the feedback offered by other students and your instructors, you can improve your learning skills and study habits and increase the odds of your long-term and short-term success.

HOW TO TUTORIAL
#24

HOW TO TUTORIAL
#31

Establishing Study Times

An essential element of any plan for success in online coursework is scheduling your study time. Dedicated study times are both an issue of time management (as discussed in chapter 5) as well as a matter of effective planning. Developing a flexible plan for success that will keep you on task throughout the semester is the goal when creating a schedule that you can follow. You should try to balance expectations that are compatible with the goals you have for the course with realistic time frames given your other personal and professional commitments.

Setting aside consistent blocks of times each week for working on online course assignments and activities is one strategy for developing a regular flow to your online studies. Though it will likely be tempting to designate differing times each week for your online coursework, a familiar pattern of study times each week throughout a semester can help you avoid procrastination and manage your time. Too often online activities will be postponed from Monday to Tuesday, and then Tuesday to Wednesday, until the assignments are overdue and your success in the course is jeopardized.

Establishing a study schedule (for example, completing online coursework on Monday and Wednesday nights from 8:00 to 10:00 P.M., as well as on Saturday afternoons from 1:00 to 2:30 P.M.) for your courses will also help you develop the types of learning skills that make for success in college courses. While a certain amount of flexibility will be required to meet all of your academic, personal, and work commitments, adhering to your established study schedule can provide consistency in your study habits, help you manage your time, and improve the odds that you will stay with your plan for success until the goal is accomplished.

STUDENT-TO-STUDENT TIP

It is extremely important to schedule your time to work on online course assignments and activities. Be realistic in your plans to be able to complete assignments. Always assume that something will interrupt you and/or that something may not work as you had planned and, therefore, delay you.

For most of us it will be important to prepare our study schedule for the entire course at the beginning of the semester to ensure that we don't have conflicts. For example, you wouldn't want to inadvertently plan a weekend at the beach before a critical research paper is due. By planning for the entire semester you can visualize when potential conflicts may occur and plan your study times accordingly. That way, you can complete the research paper and still be able to enjoy a weekend at the beach.

ACTIVITY 4-3   **Have you missed something?**

As a review, read the following statements, then circle *True* or *False* for each one.

1. **True–False**   Listening comprehension skills are not necessary for success in online coursework.

2. **True–False**   Short-term goals for each course should be specific and measurable.

3. **True–False**   Conversation comprehension is improved when we are active participants in the conversation, whether online or in-person.

4. **True–False**   You should establish regular study times that you can stay with throughout the semester.

5. **True–False**   Most strategies used to improve comprehension when reading a newspaper or book are not effective when reading online.

Creating an Effective Study Environment

Your study environment should be a component of your plan for success. In the conventional classroom much of the study environment was created for you (for example, rooms with few distractions, resources for communicating with other students, etc.). In the online classroom, however, you will typically have the ability to create an individualized study environment (including both the physical environment of the room in which you access online materials as well as the online course environment that you establish on your computer). In both cases, developing a study environment that facilitates your success by minimizing your distractions will be the goal of your plan.

Physical Studying Environment

Where you study plays an critical role in your success in online coursework. Depending on the computer you use to access the <u>Internet</u> (i.e., laptop or desktop) you can have varying levels of flexibility with your physical study environment when completing online coursework.

Here are several tips for creating a positive studying environment:

☐ Find a place with adequate access to the <u>Internet</u> and electrical power.

A functional study environment for today's college student requires both access to electrical power as well as the <u>Internet</u>. Although college students do still use traditional paper, pencils, and pens in completing some assignments, the vast majority of coursework in college today requires the use of computers; from making mathematical calculations to writing term papers, the tools of success are typically functions of the personal computer. And while not all college assignments and activities will require that you utilize <u>Internet</u> resources, the availability of reference materials and other online assets can help ensure that you have all of the resources you require to be successful. Some examples are the online dictionary available at <http://education.yahoo.com/reference/dictionary> or the online thesaurus found at <http://www.thesaurus.com>.

❏ Find a quiet place where you can concentrate.

Most of us can concentrate better on our studies when there is not high volume conversation, music, or television in the same room. For some students however, depending on your preferences and the potential for sporadic noises, some low volume background music may be good for your concentration. If you find that this is true for you, then you should select music that is consistent (for example, a music CD is probably a better choice than the radio since there are fewer interruptions and unpredictable shifts from music to commercials to announcers) and keep it at a low volume so you do not end up listening to the music instead of comprehending what you are reading.

`Hot` `Hot` ### ❏ Limit the number of potential distractions.

We can typically plan for most of the distractions that will interrupt our studies. For example, if friends like to come by your dorm room to talk, close the door before you begin to study. Don't be tempted to have a television that you can view from your desk, and turn off your cell phone (and/or the ringer on your home phone). Reducing the number of potential distractions from your studies is a relatively easy step you can take on your path toward college success.

❏ Take study breaks.

Long uninterrupted periods of studying may seem like the most efficient use of your study times, but in actuality study breaks will help sustain your comprehension as well as provide your eyes, fingers, and brain with the necessary rest to avert exhaustion. Depending on your study environment (for example, the comfort of your desk and chair) and the length of time that you have been studying, the frequency and duration of your study breaks should vary. While a 3 to 5 minute break every 45 minutes may be enough when you first sit down to study, a 6 to 8 minute break every 30 minutes may be required after several hours of studying.

Study breaks should involve leaving the computer or study desk to stretch your arms, legs, and back (as well as rest your eyes). Simply moving from completing your homework at the computer to <u>surfing</u> the World Wide Web will not provide your body and mind with the necessary intermission from studying.

❑ Don't forget to drink water and to eat nutritional snacks during study breaks.

Your body, including your brain, requires water and nutritional snacks to function properly and maintain the heightened levels of concentration required for effective studying. Although you may not want to have these right next to your computer (to avoid distractions and possible spilling), keeping them close by (such as in your backpack, dorm refrigerator, or kitchen) can be helpful so study breaks do not have to be extended while you go out for water and a nutritional snack.

You will also want to avoid beverages or snacks that have a good amount of processed sugars in them (for example, candy bars, sodas, chocolates, etc.) since the energy from the sugar is quickly used up and the "sugar hangover" that follows will only reduce your ability to study.

❑ Find your "ideal" room temperature.

The ideal temperature for studying is generally an individual preference. Typically, however, it is better to study in a room that is a little cooler than a room that is too warm. If you are going to study in a room where you do not have control over the temperature (for example, the library, study lounge, or a friend's apartment) then you should dress in layers. This will offer you the flexibility to find the ideal comfort level for studying.

❑ Select a good computer desk and chair.

Long hours of studying at your computer can be tiring, and potentially harmful, for your body. Before studying, ensure that the computer desk and chair are at the correct height for your body size. Ideally your keyboard will be at approximately elbow height allowing the hands, wrists, and forearms to be in a straight line that is approximately parallel to the floor. For extended periods of studying, a computer with a detachable keyboard that can tilt at a slight angle can be invaluable for reducing the effort required of your fingers, wrists, and forearms. While most laptop computers only offer a flat keyboard, additional keyboards can commonly be added to the laptop when you are planning to study for longer periods (see your laptop computer's manual for instructions on attaching a second keyboard for temporary use).

A high quality chair with adequate lumbar support for your lower back, as well as an adjustable height control for your keyboard to ensure that hands, wrists, and forearms are parallel to the floor can increase the duration and comfort of your study times.

❑ Have essential resources close at hand.

The last kind of interruptions that you want to have to your study time are those that you can plan for and avoid. By keeping the necessary resources for completing your assignments and activities close at hand (such as, books, articles, pens, printer paper, etc.) you can reduce the number of these distractions from your studies. If you are studying in your dorm or apartment then having these resources close by shouldn't be a problem; keep them in or around your desk. However, if you regularly study in the library, student lounge, or in other locations away from your desk then you will want to keep a variety of these resources in your book bag, backpack, or computer case so they will be available whenever necessary. Remember, being prepared will lead to your success.

❑ Study where there is proper lighting.

Since computer monitors do not provide adequate lighting for your studies, your study environment should also include top lighting that illuminates the keyboard, books, papers, and other studying resources you will require to complete your online assignments. Lights should not, however, glare or reflect strongly on the computer screen and natural light is preferred by many students. Additional lighting will not only help reduce the strain on your eyes, but research suggests that lighting may also influence a student's attitude as well as their academic achievement.[4]

Online Studying Environment

Like the physical study environment, the online study environment you create for completing your coursework will be critical to your success. In planning for success you will want to create an ideal online study environment that can aid in reducing distractions and increase your comprehension of essential course information.

❑ Don't have a cluttered or disorderly computer.

Although maintaining a strategy for organizing all of the course-related documents, software applications, and other files in your computer will require some planning, the benefits of being able to locate and access files that you want to use, when you want to use them, is essential for being successful in online coursework.

Organize your computer so that each course has its own file <u>folder</u> in which you keep all files related to the assignments and activities for that particular course. Each semester you should start with an empty <u>folder</u> for each course for which you are enrolled. In addition, you should use sub-<u>folders</u> for organizing assignments, keeping notes on online readings, organizing feedback you have received on draft documents, and so forth. By including dates in the files names (for example, "assignment two 10-13-04.pdf") you can further classify which files have been submitted for grading and which are earlier drafts.

❑ Eliminate online distractions.

When studying or completing any type of online coursework you will want to reduce the number of possible online distracters that will diminish your comprehension or keep you from your studies altogether. Just like in the physical study environment, the online environment offers a variety of potential distracters that you can avoid. For example, turn off the <u>email</u> and <u>instant messenger</u> software applications you may have running on your computer. <u>Emails</u> or instant messages from family or friends are common distracters since most of us can't help but read these messages when they first arrive.

Surfing the Web, like television, is another distraction that most of us have a difficult time avoiding. Relatively few of us can <u>surf</u> the World Wide Web for just a few minutes and then go back to our effective study habits. Instead, 5 minutes of looking for interesting <u>Website</u> quickly becomes 45 minutes of looking at <u>Websites</u> that are of little interest (having an effect similar to that of flipping through numerous television channels finding nothing to watch).

❑ One assignment or activity at a time.

Hot

Sustaining your concentration and comprehension commonly requires that you do not jump back-and-forth between various online assignments and activities. Attempting to complete your biology homework while at the same time doing research for a history paper will usually reduce the amount you get done on either project. Most often you will want to close all of the files and software applications that are not required for the current online coursework. This will help you stay focused on the task at hand.

❑ Make a plan for <u>backing up</u> your files.

You should have a plan and schedule for making <u>back-up</u> copies of all the files on your computer each semester. In addition, you should also plan to <u>back up</u> the assignments and activities for your current courses each week throughout the semester. Burning copies to CD-ROM or DVD, saving copies to a floppy disk, or moving copies to a shared <u>server</u> space can all be effective techniques for ensuring that you do not lose essential files.

> **STUDENT-TO-STUDENT TIP**
>
> Many students don't think of backing up their files until they lose them the first time!

❑ Install and maintain an <u>antivirus</u> software application.

Viruses are software programs that are created to disrupt your use of the computer and they can cause many of your course-related files to stop functioning. These virus programs can be sent to your computer by <u>email</u> or through <u>Websites</u>, because of this you will want to have the most recent virus protection software available. Many colleges and universities have site licenses for <u>antivirus</u> software that you can install and maintain free of charge as long as you are a student. By contacting the technical support services at your college or university you should be able to find out more about what <u>antivirus</u> software applications they offer and support.

❏ **Install any required software at the beginning of the semester.**

When planning for the semester you should identify and install any software that you may be required to use in completing your coursework. This will give you time to ensure that the software is running properly before you must start work on an assignment or activity. If there are problems with the software or questions about how to use the software, having installed it at the beginning of the semester will give you the opportunity to troubleshoot or contact technical support well before any coursework will be due.

`Hot` ❏ **Don't plan to install unnecessary software during the semester.**

When you have the software required for your coursework installed at the beginning of the semester it typically isn't a good idea to risk installing new software unless necessary. Though the likelihood that one software application will disrupt the functionality of another is not always high, it typically will not be worth the risk since inevitably any troubles will come at a time when you can least afford to have computer problems.

Planning with Learning or Physical Disabilities in Mind

Planning for success in online coursework, like success in the classroom, requires some additional attention for students with learning or physical disabilities. While all colleges and universities are required to provide reasonable accommodations that support students with a variety of learning or physical disabilities, the implementation of these accommodations is not always as obvious in the online classroom. Nevertheless, there is an ever-growing variety of assistive technologies (as well as software accessibility features discussed in chapter 2) that can be used to ensure that you have the resources required for online success. Below are descriptions of just a few assistive technologies that may be useful in preparing for success with online coursework:

Text-To-Speech can read text at the desired speed and voice, while recording it into a variety of file formats. A user can listen to email, Webpages, eBooks, and other documents on the computer or a portable MP3 player.

Talking Word Processor is a word processing software program that has built in text-to-speech features providing auditory feedback of letters (characters), words, sentences, or whole paragraphs.

Voice Recognition allows a user to use his/her voice as an input device. Voice recognition may be used to dictate text into the computer or to give commands to the computer (such as opening application programs, pulling down menus, or saving work).

Talking Web browsers are Web browsers that use plug-ins to add text-to-speech capabilities.[5]

For more information on the accommodations and assistive technologies available at your college or university you should contact your academic advisor or institution's student services department. At many institutions, however, you are required to provide confidential documentation of your learning or physical disability in order to receive accommodations. Even if you don't anticipate requiring accommodations during your college experience, it is worth your time to document your disability once you are enrolled with your college or university to ensure that there will be minimal delays if you decide later on that accommodations would be helpful.

Familiarizing Yourself with the Course Design

Planning for success in a college course is difficult when you have little information about what to expect. Most often, course syllabi (as well as access to online course resources) are provided to students on the first day of classes. When you first have access to the course syllabus and other materials that outline the structure of a course, it is important that you note the dates on which assignments are due, as well as submission requirements, test dates and formats, and other critical information regarding online technologies for planning your success.

Here are few tips of what to highlight in each course syllabus:

✔ What is the instructor's email (and phone number)?

✔ When are the instructor's office hours (these may also include online office hours when the instructor is available for synchronous chat discussions)?

✔ When are assignments and activities due?

✔ How should assignments, activities, and exams be submitted for grading?

✔ What are the course policies regarding attendance (including online participation)?

✔ How can online resources be accessed (passwords or logins)?

✔ Is group work required? If so, how will teams be formed and facilitated?

✔ Which textbooks are required? Are there online resources that accompany these books?

✔ Is specialized software required for the course?

✔ What technical support is provided for online coursework?

✔ Will feedback and grades be provided online?

Staying in Touch

Even the best of us fall short of keeping with their plans from time to time. Unfortunately, at some point during your college experience an unexpected event that disrupts your plans, such as a computer failure or an illness, will likely occur. Therefore staying in contact with your instructor, or online project group members, is essential for your success.

When unexpected events do occur, let the instructor know immediately. Typically alternative arrangements can be made when unforeseen events disrupt your studies; although if you wait until after assignments are due or exams are taken, there are typically fewer options available for the professor.

When contacting your instructor about an unexpected event that is impacting your studies, the following guidelines may be useful:

Hot

✔ While you will not typically be asked to provide personal information (for example, the nature of the illness) you should be prepared to **provide specific information** regarding the impact of the event on your studies. Such as, "On Wednesday April 22nd my dorm room was broken into and my personal computer was stolen."

✔ In your conversation (online or in person) with your professor **include specific dates** related to the impact of the unintended event. For example, "I have not been able to participate in the online course discussions since last Friday (November 3rd) but I should be able to resume my participation tomorrow (November 5th)."

✔ **Offer to provide supporting documentation** for the expected event (such as, a note from the emergency, a receipt for the replacement of a broken computer hard-drive, documentation from an Internet service provider that services were not available after an ice storm, etc.).

✔ **Include a proposed plan of action** that includes reasonable suggestions or alternatives for getting back on track toward success in the course.

✔ Since unexpected events commonly influence our performance for several weeks, let instructors know that you will **keep in contact** with them throughout the remainder of the semester.

Creating an Effective Plan

By familiarizing yourself with the course structure and integrating that information into your goals and schedules you will be better able to plan for your success. Below are several steps for developing a successful plan for online coursework.

1. Define success for yourself. Identify your long-term goals for your college experience (including each semester). You should do this once now and then review your progress at the end of each semester.

2. Define how you will determine if you are successful in the short-term. Define short-term goals for each course and each week of the semester. This will have to be done each semester.

3. After reviewing your course syllabi for the semester establish an appropriate study schedule for the semester. Set consistent study times for each week, taking into account holidays, breaks, and other interruptions to your regular study times.

> **STUDENT-TO-STUDENT TIP**
>
> Instructors give us a syllabus for a reason; remember that an online class typically isn't a work-any-time class. Check your due dates, set your work times, and go.

4. Arrange for required software to be installed in your computer (as necessary). After installing the necessary software for the semester, don't install superfluous software since you don't want to have conflicts or problems.

5. Determine the ideal physical study environment for each course assignment or activity. Depending on what is required, your physical study environment may change to ensure that you have the proper resources for success.

6. Create a model online environment for your success. Turn off possible distracters from your computer (such as <u>instant messengers</u>) and devise a plan for organizing your course files.

7. Visit online resources (for example, <u>Internet</u> portals such Blackboard or WebCT) to make certain that you have access when it is necessary. Include in your study times additional time for reviewing online resources.

8. Develop strategies for increasing your reading, listening, conversation, and feedback comprehension throughout the semester.

9. Identify potential assistive technologies that you may require for the course.

10. Contact your instructor if any unexpected events hinder you from achieving the goals you have established for the semester.

ACTIVITY 4-4 — Have you missed something?

As a review, match the following word, phrase, or acronym with the correct definition.

_____ **1.** instant messenger   a. Should be studied when planning for success in any course.

_____ **2.** success   b. Should be organized and structured to improve accessibility.

_____ **3.** installing software   c. Should be turned off to prevent possible distractions while studying.

_____ **4.** files   d. Should **not** be done unless necessary during the semester.

_____ **5.** course syllabuse.   e. Should be defined as your first step in planning.

CHAPTER SUMMARY

Success in college requires that you not only create a useful plan, but that you also follow through on that plan throughout each semester. From aligning your long-term and short-term goals to establishing an effective online study environment, achieving the success you want in college courses is within your reach. By taking the time to plan for success you can greatly improve the odds that you will accomplish all of your goals.

CHAPTER FOUR EXERCISE

To begin the exercise you will want to access your Web-based course materials (i.e., educational portal) using a Web browser (such as, Netscape Navigator or Microsoft Internet Explorer, etc.). In addition, you will want to open a new document in a word processing program (for example, Microsoft Word).

STEP ONE: Locate an online copy of a syllabus for a course in which you are currently enrolled or plan to enroll. (If an online copy is not available then you can use a paper syllabus provided by an instructor.)

STEP TWO: Review the course syllabus to determine which assignments and activities will be graded during the semester. In your <u>word processing</u> document list in a table (four columns wide) the assignments and activities that will be graded, along with the number of possible points for each and the date it is due.

STEP THREE: For each graded assignment and activity determine a goal for your grade. These goals should be based on your experiences and expectations, and be aligned with your long-term goals for college success. In the fourth column of your <u>word processing</u> document you should insert your goal for each assignment and activity.

STEP FOUR: Below the table that contains the assignments and activities for the course (along with your goals), identify five changes you will have to make to your learning strategies and study habits in order to achieve success. These can include changes to your online study environment or study schedule, competing commitments, and other topics that have been discussed up to this point.

CHAPTER FOUR   SKILLS CHECKLIST

After completing this chapter you should be able to do the following. If there are skills below that you may not be able to do, take a few minutes to review the chapter, focusing on those areas that you have missed the first time through.

❏ I have established long-terms goals for my success in college.

❏ I have established short-term goals that are aligned with my long-term goals.

❏ I have measurable goals for each of my courses this semester.

❏ I have realistic expectations of online coursework.

❏ I am able to avoid misconceptions about online coursework.

❏ I can improve my listening comprehension.

❏ I can improve my reading comprehension.

❏ I can improve my conversation comprehension.

❏ I can improve my feedback comprehension.

❏ I have a good online study environment.

❏ I have a good physical study environment.

❏ I know who to contact if I have a learning or physical disability.

❏ I am able to create an effective for plan my success in college courses.

❏ I have completed the chapter 4 activities.

ADDITIONAL RESOURCES

Additional resources on topics covered in this chapter are available on the Website: <u>Website</u>: **<http://collegesurvival.college.hmco.com/students>.**

NOTES

1. http://www.najaco.com/literature/quotes/planning.htm
2. http://www.msnbc.com/news/806278.asp
3. http://chronicle.com/free/2002/06/2002061001u.htm, *Chronicle of Higher Education,* June 10, 2002
4. Dunn, R. Krimsky, J.S., Murray, J.B. & Quinn, P.J. (1985). Light Up Their Lives: A research on the effects of lighting on children's achievement and behavior. *The Reading Teacher,* 38(19), 863-869.
5. Based on http://www.nsnet.org/atc/tools/

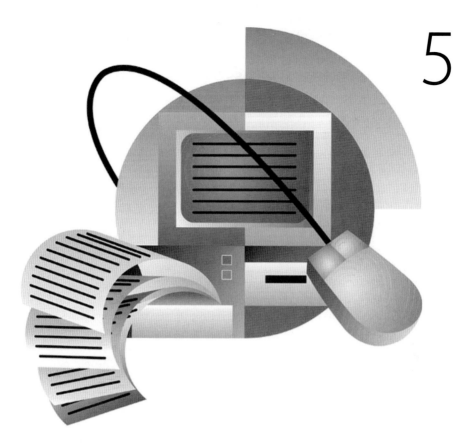

5

Time Management Strategies

anaging your time as a college student is essentially your responsibility. From making arrangements to arrive to your classes on
time each week to ensuring that personal commitments do not
interfere with your academic success, staying organized and
managing your time is a task that only you can supervise. Fortunately
there is a diverse assortment of technologies that can assist you in managing your time more effectively. At the same time, many of the tried-and-
true strategies for managing your time remain effective even when your
courses require online participation.

Time Management Success Strategy One: Don't Procrastinate

Hot **Hot** Sounds simple doesn't it? Unfortunately, avoiding procrastination is rarely as easily accomplished as it is said. Overcoming the temptations that lead to procrastination will be an essential component to your success in college. One useful technique to steer clear of procrastination is to break your course assignments into smaller chunks that you can accomplish prior to the due date for the entire assignment.

> **STUDENT-TO-STUDENT TIP**
>
> The best advice I can give to you is to keep up with your assignments. You can get your work done at the last minute, however, it will be a lot less stressful and you will be able to process the information more effectively if you keep up. Do not procrastinate!!

To illustrate this concept, imagine that your chemistry professor requires that you know the molecular structure of elements defined in the periodic table. You know that merely memorizing the elements of the table the weekend before the exam will not be enough to ensure your success. Therefore, you decide to divide the periodic table so that you have a week to study the molecular composition of the elements in each row. By sticking to this timeline you can evade the temptations of procrastination and still find plenty of time throughout the semester to focus on your other courses.

The same principle can be applied to any of your course activities or assignments. If you are required to make a presentation to the class at the end of the semester, set interim deadlines for yourself including a deadline for selecting a topic, finishing your research, writing a first draft of the slides and handouts that you will use, and giving a practice presentation to your friends for feedback. By breaking down any assignment into smaller assignments that you can do more easily, you can avoid procrastination.

> **STUDENT-TO-STUDENT TIP**
>
> Treat each assignment as a project. Plan for each and every component, allowing plenty of time for review and revision.

Another useful technique to help avoid procrastination is to tell a variety of people about both the deadlines you have set for yourself as well as those set by the professor. Ask roommates, sorority sisters, lab partners, and others to remind you of your commitments or to ask you about your progress. And don't limit this to your roommate or best friends, ask the other students in your class to keep in touch with you as well. They can send you emails or contact you using instant messenger to inquire about your progress. This not only keeps you on task, but it helps keep them on task as well. After all, peer pressure doesn't have to be seen only as a negative tool. You can use it to your advantage as well.

Time Management Success Strategy Two: Don't Wait for Perfection

It has been said that "anything worth doing is worth doing poorly . . . at least at first."

Upon first reading the above quote you may not find it to be all that insightful, nor of much use in being successful in your online coursework. Yet while the implications of the quote may be subtle, the value of the perspective it brings is priceless. In trying to live up to the expectations and pressures of college, too often you will want to strive for the perfect term paper, the flawless class presentation, or even the ideal procedures for calculating a formula. Although each is a laudable goal, the reality is that the amount of time and energy put into attempting to achieve perfection is rarely the best approach to being successful.

Managing your time requires that you negotiate a balance that makes it possible for you to do high quality work that will accomplish your goals, while at the same time accomplishing similar goals in your other college courses, work obligations, and personal commitments. With only 24 hours in the day and more to do than simply fixate on any one assignment, finding this balance will require that you turn in many assignments and activities that are not perfect, but good enough to receive the grade you desire.

Hot

Continuing to revise and revisit the same assignment until it reaches a level of perfection isn't practical for students who want to be successful. Find a balance for yourself, where you can accomplish all of your goals without sacrificing one in attempting to achieve perfection in another.

Time Management Success Strategy Three: Combine Activities

Most all of us, from time to time, will over-commit to too many projects, activities, courses, and so forth. And as you take on more responsibilities, through personal and professional commitments, the pressures to get more done in less time will only continue to grow. One of the best survival techniques to apply is finding out how to meet the requirements of several obligations through the same activity. For example, if you are required to write a term paper for your English course and you also have to fulfill university requirements for volunteer work in the community, try to find a way to combine these two activities so that you can do your research for the term paper while assisting a local social services agency in doing their work.

ACTIVITY 5-1

In the table below write five course-related activities or assignments that you will be completing over the next two weeks (such as, writing a reaction paper to a chapter in your Sociology text book, studying for an exam in Biology, searching online for information regarding an upcoming term paper in History, etc.). When you have identified five upcoming course activities or assignments, connect the activity or assignment with another task that you will also be working on this semester. You should attempt to determine at least three activities from this list that you can combine with other activities during the semester.

Time Management

Course Activity or Assignment	To be combined with ...
Example: Library research for English paper due next week	Example: Research for a class presentation in my Communications course
1.	
2.	
3.	
4.	
5.	

Time Management Success Strategy Four: Don't Expect Your Instructor to Always Be Online

Do not wait until the day before an assignment is due to email your instructor with questions concerning the assignment requirements or asking for feedback on your first draft. Professors are typically busy with much more than just teaching courses; being online to answer your questions is not something they do 24 hours a day.

You should plan your time wisely, so here are a few tips:

✔ Email questions as soon as possible after an assignment is given.

✔ Schedule at least 48 hours in advance to meet online with your instructor.

✔ Include with your email any draft documents and other files that may be useful for your instructor to review in answering your question.

✔ Keep a copy of any <u>email</u> correspondence you have with your instructor and fellow students; documenting the conversation can be useful later on.

✔ Don't wait until the last minute to start your assignments; inevitably you will have questions, so plan accordingly.

Time Management Success Strategy Five: Keep to a Schedule

For the majority of courses you will take in college the pace of assignments, tests, group projects, and other coursework will increase throughout the semester. As a result the only way you can keep up and be successful is to be organized. Writing down all of your assignments and other commitments will be essential for staying on task and not falling behind.

Keep the schedules for your various academic, work, and personal commitments all in one place. Whether you use an online calendar, <u>personal digital assistant</u>, or a paper calendar on your desk, write down everything that you are supposed to do as soon as you commit to doing it. By having all of your commitments in one calendar you can effectively manage your time and ensure that you are not obligated to be in two places at the same time.

Based on your consolidated calendar of commitments, each day you should write down a daily *To do list*. Your daily list will help you to plan your time effectively and avoid procrastination.

Hot

> **STUDENT-TO-STUDENT TIP**
>
> Set aside a time to work each day, time to read, write, and post. Keep it the same time and stick to it. Before long, that work time simply becomes part of the fabric of your life. I actually discovered free time by keeping myself on a schedule.

Time Management Success Strategy Six: Use Your Free Time Wisely

Though you will often feel like there just isn't enough time in the day to get all of your school responsibilities done, you can recapture some of that time by using your free time wisely. Maybe it is 15 minutes between classes or 5 minutes waiting for group members to show up for a class project meeting; in either situation (or any of the thousands of other situations in which each of us finds ourselves) there is typically some free time each day that we cannot afford to waste.

Hot

To use this time effectively you have to be prepared. Carry note cards with you so you are always prepared to review key definitions or formulas when you have a few minutes without other things to do; keep your calendar with you when you are riding the bus so that you can update your daily *To do list;* bring a textbook with you when you go to a doctor's appointment; or keep a pen and paper handy so you can take down some notes for an upcoming assignment as you wait for the bus. Your time is a valued commodity and you shouldn't let any of it go to waste when you have so much to do.

ACTIVITY 5-2   Find your free time.

For a typical week during the semester complete the following table estimating the number of hours you spend doing each of the following activities.

Finding Your Free Time

	Mon.	Tues.	Weds.	Thurs.	Fri.	Sat.	Sun.
Completing home work							
Reading for school							
Working on the computer for coursework							
In class							
Traveling to and from school or work							
Waiting between classes							
Cooking and eating							
Watching television							
Playing video games							
Leisure activities (sports, movies, parties, etc.)							
Community service							
Family activities							
Club or association activities							

Time Management Success Strategy Seven: Learn to Say "No"

In the book *The One Minute Manager Meets the Monkey* the author explores how many of us fail to be successful in our work when we take on the responsibilities of others.[1] Monkeys, within the context of the book, are the challenges and responsibilities that each of us carries on our backs every day. For you, your monkeys may include course assignments, responsibilities to your fraternity or sorority, a commitment to the marching band or drama club, family obligations, and the like. And everyone you know will also carry numerous monkeys on their backs as well.

These monkeys can, however, limit your success in college when people start passing their monkeys off to you. For example, though you may be up late studying for a quiz, your roommate may decide to pass one of her monkeys on to you. Maybe it is her responsibility to make signs advertising the new positions available at the college radio station, but she also wants to go to the movies with friends tonight. So she may try to pass this monkey along to you by asking if you could do her a big favor.

We all know people who are continually asking others to take a monkey off their back. And sometimes we do want to offer them our support. But most often we each have enough monkeys of our own to keep ourselves busy.

Don't get burdened with other people's monkeys, they will only slow you down on your way to success. By saying "no," you can escape the additional weight of carrying other people's monkeys along with your own.

Time Management Success Strategy Eight: Make Use of Technology

In recent years there have been many technological advancements that can help you better manage your time. Successful students take advantage of these new technologies and use them effectively (and efficiently) to stay organized, to make use of their time, to communicate with fellow students and instructors, as well as to cope with competing demands for their time. Below is a short list of technologies (many of these are defined in more detail in the next chapter) and a description of how you can use them to help manage your time. You can likely think of other tools and their uses, and you should use those as well to become a successful student.

Personal Digital Assistant (PDA)

Personal Digital Assistants (for example, Palm, PocketPC, etc.) are common devices typically used for scheduling events and keeping an electronic calendar that can be linked to your personal computer. PDA devices also can help you manage your time by giving you access to personal notes and other documents that you would otherwise have to carry with you on paper. Most of these devices allow you to create and read <u>email</u> messages that you have <u>download</u>ed from your computer, and newer services allow you to use the PDA to access the <u>Internet</u> from any location through cell phone services.

In addition, many online courses will have information from the course that you can <u>download</u> directly to PDA, providing you with access to course calendars, instructor lectures, and other information at any time. This feature allows you to use your free time to catch up on coursework, take notes for upcoming assignments, <u>email</u> fellow students about assignments, and even review past lectures when preparing for tests.

Online Calendars and <u>Groupware</u>

Keeping your own schedule is typically enough of a challenge, but when your courses require that you work with other students to complete group projects, then the additional task of coordinating the schedules of several people can be a real burden. To be successful students today have got to use the technology available to them, and online calendars and <u>groupware</u> should not be overlooked. These online programs, often available free of charge, allow you to create group areas online where you can contribute to a common calendar for scheduling meetings and other events. You can also post files for others in the group to review and respond to, organize project related tasks, and do many of the other project management related tasks that must be accomplished in order for the group to be successful.

Though many of these services are available throughout the <u>Internet</u>, here are a few <u>Websites</u>:

<http://www.fecg.net/pims.asp>   <http://calendar.yahoo.com>
<http://www.caliday.com>   <http://www.calendars.net>
<http://www.appoint.net>   <http://www.huntcal.com>
<http://www.e2do.com>   <http://www.groove.com>
<http://www.iexpect.com>   <http://www.gawpus.com>
<http://www.akapa.com>   <http://www.flex7.com>

<u>Email</u> and <u>Instant Messengers</u>

Although <u>email</u> and other online technologies that assist you in becoming a successful student will be discussed in more detail in the next chapter, it should be noted here that these tools can also be used to help you manage your time. From sending files to professors instead of taking the time to walk across campus, to preparing for a mid-term with a partner who lives out of town, online technologies can save you time and ensure that you are utilizing effective study techniques even when you are outside of the classroom or library.

Cell Phones

While most colleges and universities don't permit the use of cell phones in the classroom, your cell phone can still be a useful tool in managing your time. With your cell phone you can keep in touch with members of your study group even when you are not in your dorm room; change meeting times, let them know about the new reference you found in the library, or even participate in a three-way call instead of meeting after class.

The flexibility and freedom of cell phones can be a tool for your success, though it can also lead to your failure if you allow it to be a distraction from your studies.

Time Management Success Strategy Nine: Know Your Studying Prime Times

Finding the hours when you can gain the most from your studies is essential for managing your time. If you can complete a required assignment in just two hours of studying in the early afternoon rather than four hours of studying late at night, then why would you want to procrastinate? Not only do you want to manage your time so that you can effectively manage your way to success, but you also want to consider the efficiency of your studies as well.

A word of caution, however, don't fool yourself in believing that your personal prime time for studying is at the odd hours that surround the times of your other personal activities. Though many college students might say that they can study effectively at 1:00 A.M., the truth is that for most of us the peak hours for staying focused on our work and effectively learning new skills is during the day or early evening. So you must be honest with yourself . . . your success in college depends on it.

ACTIVITY 5-3   Prime times

To help determine what time of day is your studying *prime time,* answer the following questions.

1. When the alarm goes off in the morning do you ...?
   a. throw it against the wall
   b. immediately get out of bed
   c. hit snooze at least 3 times

(continued)

ACTIVITY 5-3   **Prime times**

2. An hour after you get out of bed are you ...?
   a. somewhat asleep and little dazed
   b. unmotivated to get things done
   c. wide awake and ready to get the day started

3. Around noon are you ...?
   a. so focused on your work that you have to be reminded of lunch
   b. not able to concentrate because you are hungry
   c. daydreaming about what you are going to do that evening

4. At mid-afternoon are you ...?
   a. still dazed from your lunch
   b. focused on your work
   c. wondering what is happening on television soap operas

5. At dinner time are you ...?
   a. not able to concentrate because you are hungry
   b. distracted by activities with family and friends
   c. able to concentrate on what you are reading

6. In the early evening hours are you ...?
   a. distracted by television or activities with friends
   b. able to concentrate on what you read on the Internet
   c. too tired to keep your eyes open

7. Around midnight are you ...?
   a. energetic and able to focus on what you are reading
   b. sleepy and your eyes keep drifting shut
   c. busy flipping through all of the channels on television

8. Write one to two sentences that complete the following statement by summarizing when you can study most effectively:

   My studying *prime times* are . . .

CHAPTER SUMMARY

Though there are only 24 hours in each day, by applying time management strategies you can get more done each day than you likely believe possible. Managing time, instead of letting time manage you, is an essential skill for being successful in college. Technology offers us many tools and resources for managing our time, but building those into your daily and weekly study habits does take some practice. Adopt the time management strategies provided in this chapter over the next several weeks; using these to improve the effectiveness and efficiency of your time will not only improve your productivity at college but will also give you more free time to spend with friends and family.

CHAPTER FIVE   EXERCISE

Creating a family calendar can be a useful activity that gives you the opportunity to explore the features available through any online calendar while at the same time developing a practical tool for your family. To begin the exercise you will want to have access to the World Wide Web using a <u>Web browser</u> (such as, Netscape Navigator or Microsoft Internet Explorer, etc.). After completing the exercise take a few minutes to consider how you can effectively use online tools to facilitate group meetings throughout your college experience.

STEP ONE: Locate the calendar tool of your college's <u>educational portal</u> or select one of the online calendar sites listed previously in this chapter. If you select a calendar tool outside of your college's <u>educational portal</u> follow the unique instructions for registering a new account with the online calendar site. Since these companies may add you to <u>email</u> lists for advertising purposes you may not want to use your primary <u>email</u> account. Many students find it useful to establish a secondary <u>email</u> account through a free service (for example, <http://www.hotmail.com>, <http://mail.yahoo.com>, <http://www.mail.com>, etc.) that you can use when you would like to divert possible advertising <u>emails</u>.

STEP TWO: When you have registered for the calendar service you selected, create a new calendar. Include in the calendar your birthday, as well as the birthdays for your parents, spouse, children, and/or siblings.

STEP THREE: Add to the calendar the assignments for at least one of the courses you are currently enrolled in. If available through the online calendar service you selected, include an <u>email</u> reminder for the next assignment that will be due for at least one of the courses you are currently enrolled in.

STEP FOUR: Make your calendar available for at least one friend, family member, or another student in the class. This feature is available with most online calendars, though you may have to provide the person with information regarding the calendar site so they can also register for an account.

CHAPTER FIVE   SKILLS CHECKLIST

After completing this chapter you should be able to do the following. If there are skills below that you may not be able to do, take a few minutes to review the chapter, focusing on those areas that you may have missed the first time through.

❏ I can combine my activities to save time.

❏ I know that every assignment and activity doesn't have to be perfect for me to turn it in.

❏ I am able to say "no" to friends and family when I have to get my coursework done.

❏ I have several strategies for avoiding procrastination.

❏ I know to contact my instructors early since I realize that they will not be online at all times.

❏ I keep a daily schedule and "to do" list.

❏ I use technology to manage my time.

❏ I have identified my studying *prime times*.

❏ I have completed the chapter 5 activities.

ADDITIONAL RESOURCES

Additional resources on topics covered in this chapter are available on the Website: **<http://collegesurvival.college.hmco.com/students>**.

NOTES

1. Blanchard, 1989.

6

Developing Positive
Online Relationships

The social life of an online student can be an active and stimulating one, but it doesn't happen without some directed effort. From reviewing draft term papers for other students to social <u>chats</u> about which instructors to take and which to avoid, the online communities that can be developed through online technologies both parallel and support many of those that you are likely more familiar with from the conventional classroom. In the past we have seen students become close friends with online classmates and at the same time seen students struggle in their online coursework because they were not able to build the social structures that were necessary for their success.

The extent to which an online social life is necessary for your success in online coursework is somewhat dependent on your learning and studying preferences. Some students prefer to discuss ideas before starting to put anything on paper, while others don't even want to have draft manuscripts reviewed by fellow students. But to some extent, most students do better when they are involved with other students, whether it is an on-campus social life or an online social life.

The opportunity to get friendly feedback on using the correct formula in chemistry before submitting it to the instructor can be the difference between an outstanding grade and merely a passing grade. Although an online study group the week before an exam may not be ideal for your studying style, it can better ensure that you are adequately prepared for whatever questions the instructor may ask. Yet, beyond the value of study groups and peer feedback, the relationships that students can develop with other students transform what could be a lonely or isolating course experience into one that is interesting, motivating, and even enjoyable.

Most often you can't rely on your instructor to push your online relationships forward. The talents of the instructor to develop activities and assignments that engage students as a learning community will vary and can only go so far. It remains up to the individual students to devise a plan, and follow through with that plan, in order to create a supportive network of fellow students that will make for an attention-grabbing and note-worthy learning experience.

> **STUDENT-TO-STUDENT TIP**
>
> Be bold and ask questions. Give positive comments and praise in the class work. There is sometimes more of an opportunity for this in the online environment than in a face-to-face learning situation. Some people tend to be more constrained face-to-face.

Online Relationships

The skills for developing positive online relationships are not necessarily unique to the online environment. Often you will want to adapt the same skills for creating a positive relationship that you use when you are in the classroom, the library, the student lounge, or anywhere else. And sometimes you will want to adopt new skills. However, most of us don't normally recognize the skills we are applying when building relationships with other students or our professors (for example, eye contact, body language, first impressions). Therefore we have to pay extra attention to these skills when we are attempting to develop useful online relationships. The limited types of communications available to you when using online technologies, typically synchronous or <u>asynchronous</u> text communications, only further require that you examine how you can go about building positive relationships with other students online.

E-learning Experiences

A few years ago I was teaching a course delivered completely online with students from around the world, many of who were in their last semester of their master's degree. And like in any class, online or on-campus, I had some students who were active participants in every discussion and others that preferred to primarily listen and only interject when necessary. Two students in the class were both the former, active participants in every discussion and very involved in a team project in which they happened to be paired together. Levonnie was a spirited elementary school teacher who lived in southern Georgia while Emily was just establishing her own consulting company in Las Vegas to develop online training courses for real estate agents. As you can imagine both had an assortment of exciting stories to share with each new discussion topic, from stories of life growing up in rural Georgia to the exhilarating chronicles of life in "Sin City."

During the semester Levonnie and Emily became close friends and both spoke impatiently about finally meeting each other for cocktails after graduation at the end of the semester. Unfortunately at the last minute Emily wasn't able to attend graduation due to a health problem in the family. Even if the story ended there the support and friendship that Levonnie and Emily built that semester would be an excellent example of how online relationships can develop and how those support networks can be used to ensure that everyone is successful in their online coursework. But the story doesn't end there. Weeks after graduation I got an email that Levonnie and Emily were headed to New York City for a "girl's weekend out" and to finally meet in person; building on a friendship and supportive relationship that they developed initially online.

The development of an active social life within online coursework does however require some purposeful effort. I am confident that neither Levonnie nor Emily would have been as successful in my course if they had not developed a relationship beyond the all-too-common short emails asking when the next assignment was due. Nor would they have had the opportunity to create within the online course a comfortable environment where they, and other students, felt that they could learn among friends.

Making a Good First Impression Online

Online relationships with your fellow students will be very similar to those that you will have in the conventional classroom. And just like in the traditional classroom, first impressions can make all of the difference online as well. In order to establish good working relationships with your classmates even the wording of your emails is of critical importance in developing a good first impression that can pave the path for your success.

Here are a few steps that you can use to ensure that you make the right first impression in your online communications:

❏ **Take a few extra minutes** in your initial <u>emails</u> to your fellow students to make sure that they are grammatically correct and that the spelling is checked.

❏ Take time to **personalize** your <u>emails</u> to your fellow students. Just as in the classroom when you may ask them first how their day has been before asking to borrow their notes on a previous lecture, online you should do the same. Making a good first impression typically requires a personal touch.

❏ Provide fellow students with your **contact information** (i.e., the <u>email</u> account you want them to use, your <u>instant messenger</u> name, or even your phone number if you want them to call you). Being able to contact other students is a first step in developing positive relations.

❏ Take into account that when you are talking with a fellow student online (either through <u>email</u>, <u>chat</u>, or <u>instant messenger</u>) that the **non-verbal** clues that you may rely on for building a successful relationship in person may not be available. Later in this chapter we will provide more information on how non-verbal communication skills can be transferred to online discussions.

❏ Include specific information regarding **what should happen next** (for example, when you will contact them again, a proposal for the next steps to be taken, questions you would like for them to answer). It is often best to propose what you believe should happen next, and then ask for feedback to make sure that your proposed schedule is workable in their schedule.

STUDENT-TO-STUDENT TIP

Do not take yourself or any course too seriously! You can't learn if you are not having fun. Keep an open mind! Learn from the vast experiences and knowledge that everyone brings to the table.

ACTIVITY 6-1   **First impressions Case Study**

Situation: Today is your first day of class in the Introduction to Early American Literature 101 course at your college or university. Though you are somewhat disappointed that the instructor is a doctoral student and not a full-time fac-

(continued)

ACTIVITY 6-1   *First impressions Case Study*

ulty member, the reading list for the course does seem appealing to you. The course assignments will however require that you work with a student part-ner in developing a critique on a novel of your choice from the genre, as well as a presentation at the end of the semester for other students in the class. When the instructor assigns partners, however, you find out that your part-ner, Samuel, lives an hour away from campus and that his work schedule will keep him from meeting with you on campus for the project. After your short discussion at the end of class you decide to work on the project together using online technologies like email and instant messenger.

Activity: On a piece of paper (or on a computer) write an initial email to your partner for the project. Write an email in which you lay the groundwork that will lead to later success. Do this before reading on.

Feedback: Below is an example of what your first email may include when attempting to make a positive first impression. There is no "perfect" ini-tial email, but this example contains many elements of a successful first im-pression. Review your initial email for similar characteristics with this example.

Samuel,

After our brief meeting in class yesterday I am excited about the opportunity to work with you on the course project for Early American Literature 101. Though this is only my second literature course at the university my experiences last se-mester in critiquing British literature should be helpful as we move ahead on our project.

I know that your commute to campus is long, and I agree that we can use email and instant messenger for most of our conversations regarding the project. My instant messenger contact information and my phone number are listed below. Also, if you could email me your contact information I would appreciate it.

By next Monday I will send you a list of possible novels that we could con-sider for the project. If you could create a list of your own that would be useful for comparison.

I hope that you have a good weekend and I will be back in touch with you on Monday.

Thanks,
Natasha
Natasha@mycollege.edu

Effective Email Communications

Though your first impression email will not be identical to the example above, there are several elements from the sample email you may want to include.

❑ The spelling and grammar have been checked for accuracy.

❑ The introduction includes a personal touch (for example, the fact that this was the second literature course the writer had taken at the university).

❑ The <u>email</u> confirms the agreement made in class to communicate using <u>email</u> and <u>instant messenger</u>; and gives the other party an opportunity to clarify whether or not this information was mutually understood.

❑ The communication includes contact information (for example, <u>instant messenger</u> contact information and a phone number).

❑ A plan of action is proposed concerning what steps will be taken next to complete the project.

❑ Feedback is requested on the proposed next steps to be taken.

❑ A date is given for the next communication.

❑ An informal and friendly ending to the message is included (for example, I hope that you have a good weekend...).

Staying Organized Online

While remaining organized with your online coursework is essential for your success in any class, keeping track of your academic and social relationships with other students is also critical. Sending a message to the wrong classmate cannot only be embarrassing, but it can also undermine your relationships with many other students. (Don't think that gossip is limited to the boundaries of the dorm.) Losing your copy of a group assignment can also lead to awkward relationships with your fellow students.

Here are several strategies for staying organized with your online coursework:

Hot

❑ Maintain a separate mailbox within your <u>email</u> for each course. Keep all of the <u>emails</u> you exchange with the instructor and other students in this one place so you can always come back to them later.

HOW TO TUTORIAL #2

❑ Create a <u>folder</u> for each of your courses in the <u>file directory</u> of file <u>folders</u> on your computer. Copies of all drafts and final documents related to course requirements should be kept in this <u>folder</u> for safekeeping. Even if other students are responsible for portions of a group project, keep your own copies of all files; if you want you can always delete them after the course is complete.

HOW TO TUTORIAL #4

❑ Be careful not to send <u>emails</u> to the wrong students. Check, and double check, to make sure that your <u>email</u>'s "To:," "Cc:," and "Bcc:" <u>fields</u> include only the addresses to which you want the <u>email</u> sent.

(Cc: stands for carbon copy and adds recipients to the <u>email</u>; Bcc: stand for blind carbon copy and also adds recipients to the <u>email</u> although these recipients will not see who else has been included as recipients of the <u>email</u>.)

❏ Separate <u>email</u> accounts may be useful to keep course-related <u>email</u> separate from other personal or work-related <u>emails</u> (for example, personal, school, work, etc.). Many colleges and universities will give you an <u>email</u> account while you are a student and there are a host of other free online <u>email</u> services (for example, <http://www.hotmail. com>, <http://mail.yahoo.com>, <http://www.mail.com>, etc.) also available to help you keep your many online communications organized.

❏ Include the date that you created the file in the name of the file. For example, if you are creating a file that will be the first draft of a history assignment on the Revolutionary War, then include in the title the date of the draft (for example, "history assignment 4-23-05.doc"). This will help you, and any other students you may have to share files with in group assignments, quickly know which file is the latest and which should be submitted for grading.

❏ When submitting files to your course instructor, double check to make sure you are submitting the file in the right format and in the correct manner. Course assignments will typically specify the <u>file format</u> requested by the instructor (for example, Microsoft Word or <u>Adobe Acrobat PDF</u>). Often professors will want you to <u>email</u> some assignments to their <u>email</u> accounts, while requesting that you up-load other assignments to specific <u>folders</u> with an <u>educational portal</u> (for example, WebCT or BlackBoard). Take a few extra minutes to check the required <u>file format</u> and method for submitting each assignment; on your road to success you don't want to lose points for files that didn't end up in the correct place for grading.

Adding a Personal Touch

Since most of us enjoy and perform better in a course when we have a mixture of academic and social relationships with our fellow students, it is often essential that you personalize your relationships with other students. This isn't to say that you have to divulge personal information about yourself, nor do you have to build life-long friendships, but you should attempt to create an environment where other students don't feel that you are merely using them to increase the odds of your success in the course. By adding a personal touch to your online communications you can make great strides in developing the type of social relationships that are the most useful for your success and theirs.

Below are four steps for personalizing your online communications:

❏ We are often tempted to save time and send the same <u>email</u> to everyone in the class, yet sending individual <u>email</u>s to each student (i.e., with their name at the top) can show that you are taking the time to write them specifically. It may sound like an unimportant and small detail, but you would be surprised how many students feel isolated from others in their courses. When time is tight, however, you can <u>cut-and-paste</u> the same core message into each <u>email</u> and then customize each <u>email</u> with a few unique and distinctive sentences for each recipient.

❏ If you do have to send a mass mailing to many students in your course, then use the Bcc: (i.e., blind carbon copy) <u>field</u> to add recipients to the <u>email</u>. This will send the <u>email</u> to each individual, while not indicating that other students are also receiving the exact same <u>email</u>. In many <u>email</u> applications you can include all recipients in the Bcc: <u>field</u> without having to include any individuals as To: or Cc: recipients.

❏ Add a unique question or comment to individual <u>email</u>s to let each student know that you are keeping in touch with them (for example, "How are things at your fraternity?," "Did you do well on the last quiz we studied for?," "Are you still planning to take Astronomy 200 next semester?"). Each individualized question or comment can help build a stronger relationship.

❏ Resist sending every <u>email</u> joke or chain letter you receive to others in your class. A quick joke every now and then is fun, but repeated messages that start with "forwarded" or "FWD:" can be a turn off.

Attachment Etiquette

Attaching files to an <u>email</u> or submitting files to online <u>discussion boards</u> can be an effective tool for communicating with other students as well as the instructor. But the last thing you want to do is frustrate others with files that they cannot find (or open) for one reason or another.

Two simple suggestions for avoiding disaster when sharing files are:

Don't change the extension included at the end of the file name. If you are using the Windows <u>operating system</u>, files are named with two elements, the title and the extension. The extension follows the last period in the name and is typically three letters long (for example, .doc for Word files, .pdf for <u>Adobe Acrobat PDF</u> files, .htm for files that can be read by <u>Internet</u> browsers). These extensions are critical since they indicate to the computer which software application to use to open the file. Thus, if you alter or remove the extension the computer does not know which software application to use in opening the file.

Extensions are automatically created when you save a file, but if you later change the name on the file the extension can be lost. Therefore you should be careful whenever you change the name of a file to ensure that you do not erase the extension.

Include in the <u>email</u> message or <u>discussion board</u> posting the name of the file and software application used to create the attached file. For example, if you are sending a classmate a draft of a chemistry assignment that was written in Microsoft Word (the XP version) then you would want to include in the <u>email</u> "The attached file, *chemistry assignment 10-4-04.doc*, is a Word XP file. Please let me know if you have any problems opening the file." If a classmate has any trouble finding or opening the file they now have adequate information for solving the problem.

Getting To Know Your Instructor

Even when you are not in the classroom you can develop a very positive relationship with your instructor and doing so is well worth the time and effort. Professors, whether online or in the classroom, are by and large passionate about the courses they teach and spend a good amount of their time each day communicating with students and others about their interests. Don't be shy about communicating with your instructor when you have questions or want an alternative perspective on a topic. After all, your instructor is the most valuable resource you have for being successful in college.

> **STUDENT-TO-STUDENT TIP**
>
> Communication is important in any relationship and even more in the online environment. Communication with the instructor in the online environment is a way for the instructor to "feel" your presence and a way for you, the student, to share in the learning experience and gain a sense of community in the class.

Don't wait until the end. Waiting for the last weeks of a course to make initial contact with your professor isn't likely going to do you that much good. Starting the first weeks of class be sure to take the time to get to know your instructor. Ask questions about homework assignments that may be confusing or request additional information on a topic covered in the lecture; regardless of the purpose of the contact it is good for the instructor to know you by name well before the midterm.

Find areas of common interest to start the conversation. Instructors are generally more than happy to develop mentoring relationships with their students; their goal is to help you be successful as well. They are typically very interested in the subject they are teaching and enjoy sharing their passion of the subject with others that are interested. It is often valuable to review your instructor's bio on the college's Website to find out more about their interests and to discover interests you may have in common. You can use this information later to start conversations with them.

#24

Ask for feedback throughout the course.   Many students find that receiving feedback throughout a course is useful for ensuring their success. Don't wait for the mid-term to find out if you are on target for success, ask about weekly quiz grades, exam scores, or participation points throughout the semester to make sure you are doing what is required to be successful.

#31

Creating a Supportive Online Learning Community

In most college courses success will come with much less effort if you take the time to develop a learning community in which you can freely share ideas, obtain peer feedback, and together discover what it takes to be successful. Developing a supportive learning community typically doesn't happen, however, without time and energy from you and other students.

Isolation is typically the most common obstacle to success in online coursework. Without a supportive community of other students it can be challenging to keep your motivation, find the feedback you have to be successful, and generally enjoy the learning experience. Building an online learning community requires that someone take a leadership role in organizing the community. Often the instructor will do this by assigning students to study groups or organizing "office hours" or other times when students can meet together online to discuss course related topics.

If these elements are not built into your course experience, then with a little effort you can build an online community yourself. Take the first step by emailing one or two other students to let them know that you would like to work with them throughout the semester; reviewing papers for each other, asking questions of each other about lecture materials, and so forth. These do not have to be formal events, but having a "study buddy" for online coursework can be very useful.

Support Functions of an Online Community

An online community can provide you with many resources that will be of value throughout the semester. Five of the primary functions for an online community are described below.

Motivation.   Life will interfere with your studies without regard, obstructing your path toward success. Staying motivated throughout a three- or four-month semester is a challenge even for the best students. Maintaining your motivation and keeping a positive attitude about your studies is essential, and having a few supportive friends online who can help you through those tough times can be valuable (see chapter 8).

Peer feedback. Peer feedback is likely the most helpful, yet under-utilized tool available to students who want to be successful. Waiting for your instructor's grade as the first feedback you get on your work isn't a strategy that will lead to your success. Get as much feedback as you can before submitting any assignment. Classmates, roommates, sorority sisters, friends from the marching band, or anyone else can often provide you with some initial feedback on your assignments.

It is worth the extra time and effort to have someone else review your work. From grammatical errors to inverted numbers in a formula, having an extra person or two look over your work can help avoid minor (as well as serious) mistakes that could reduce your grade. With email and other online technologies you can quickly share draft files without even leaving home. But don't wait until the last minute to build the online relationships that can be helpful in getting peer feedback, build your online support community from the first day of class.

> **STUDENT-TO-STUDENT TIP**
>
> When permitted, it is helpful to discuss your answers with someone else (either online or otherwise) before submitting your assignments. Often you will find that some part of your response does not come across in writing or have the emphasis you wish.

Technical support. Your college's technical support services may not always be the best place for you to go when you have questions or technology problems. Often your family, friends, co-workers, and online classmates can provide you with much of the technical assistance that you may require. Many of the people around you will have experience with technology, and often times they will have struggled with similar technology questions and problems at some point as well. Do not be afraid to ask questions or request help from those around you; with technology there truly are no dumb questions.

> **STUDENT-TO-STUDENT TIP**
>
> Take a survey of your family, friends, and co-workers to see what skills, abilities, and areas of knowledge they have. The fact that my husband is a programmer and could help me with technical difficulties was an enormous advantage.

Study groups. Study groups can be active online communities. From sharing notes to asking each other review questions using instant messenger, online technologies can help any study group function. For example, in preparing for exams at the end of each semester, trying to schedule a time for a study group to meet on campus can be difficult to say the least. But you can use email, chat, and instant messenger to reduce (or eliminate) the amount of time you have to meet together, allowing each study group member to add flexibility to their schedule.

Enjoyment.   Getting to know your fellow students online can also be exciting and fun. You may be surprised by how many interesting people you can meet, especially when they all don't have to be sitting with you in the same classroom for the conversation to get started. Students from around the world may end up being part of your course, or maybe just students from another major that you wouldn't likely see on campus. No matter the case, try to make some friends, share some interesting stories, and enjoy your learning experience.

ACTIVITY 6-2   **Have you missed something?**

As a review, read the following statements, then circle *True* or *False* for each one.

1. **True–False**   You should always include your name and contact information in an <u>email</u> to a classmate or instructor.

2. **True–False**   You can develop many positive friendships with other students without having to meet them in the classroom.

3. **True–False**   Checking for spelling and grammar errors in <u>email</u> messages related to your coursework is *not* necessary.

4. **True–False**   When you get funny <u>email</u> jokes you should share them with all the other students in the class to build friendly relationships.

5. **True–False**   You should take time before the mid-term each semester to make initial contact with your professor.

Five Strategies for Successful Online Communications

Communicating effectively is hard enough when you are in the same room with a person. But when the distances that separate you from other students are measured not only in the thousands of miles but by the cultural differences as well, effective communication in an online course can be a real challenge. Gaining the skills to communicate effectively online with a diverse group of fellow students will be a key to your success.

Below are five strategies that you can use to be more effective in your online communications:

Success Strategy One: Spell check and grammar check everything related to your coursework

Although your typical emails to friends and family may be informal and misspelled words may be common, when establishing good relationships with your classmates make sure that you spell check and grammar check all correspondence. Misspelled words or incorrect grammar may give the wrong impression about your abilities as a student, the priority the course has for you, your attention to detail, or other characteristics that would keep fellow students from wanting to work with you throughout the course.

Fortunately, most educational portals (for example, Blackboard) and email applications (for example, Microsoft Outlook, Qualcomm Eudora) will have spell check and grammar check options. If your email service doesn't have these features, then you should first write your message in a word processing program (for example, Microsoft Word) using the word processing program's spell check and grammar check features. Afterwards you can copy-and-paste the checked and corrected message into your email.

Success Strategy Two: Compensate for not having non-verbal communications

Online communications are predominantly text-based conversations. And while there are advantages to largely communicating through written text (for example, you can reflect on an email before sending it), the lack of non-verbal communication techniques can make on-line communications very frustrating. Researchers estimate that about 55% of what is communicated is actually passed on through non-verbal communications (for example, eye contact, body language, etc.).[1] Making up for the lack of non-verbal communication strategies is therefore an essential element for your success.

> **STUDENT-TO-STUDENT TIP**
>
> Without the non-verbal clues we receive in face-to-face interactions, it's difficult to gauge tone in emails and postings. Learn to put your personality as well as your intentions into words in order to create a better and clearer relationship.

- ❑ Use personal comments throughout your emails and online chats to indicate that your partner in the conversation has your full attention. This acts as a substitute for eye contact or body gestures that would traditionally indicate your continuing interest.

- ❑ Use the tools that the software may offer you. For example most instant messaging software applications allow you to add smiley faces and other illustrations of your emotions and reactions to text conversations.

❑ Express your reactions in text when possible (for example, "hmmmm," "wow," "great"). There are also a variety of acronyms that can help you express your reactions in a conversation without having to take the time to type each word (see table 6-1).

TABLE 6-1   Useful acronyms for communicating online[2]

Acronym	Meaning	Acronym	Meaning
AAMOF	as a matter of fact	IMHO	in my humble opinion
BFN	bye for now	IMO	in my opinion
BTW	by the way	IOW	in other words
BYKT	but you knew that	LOL	lots of luck *or* laughing out loud
CMIIW	correct me if I'm wrong	NRN	no reply necessary
EOL	end of lecture	OIC	oh, I see
FAQ	frequently asked question(s)	OTOH	on the other hand
FWIW	for what it's worth	ROF	rolling on the floor
FYI	for your information	TIA	thanks in advance
HTH	hope this helps	TIC	tongue in cheek
IAC	in any case	TTYL	talk to you later
IAE	in any event	TYVM	thank you very much
IMCO	in my considered opinion	<G>	grinning
WYSIWYG	what you see is what you get	<J>	joking
<Y>	yawning	<L>	laughing
		<S>	smiling

❑ Emoticons can also be used to convey voice inflections, facial expressions, and body gestures in a text conversation (see table 6-2). Since there are no standard definitions for emoticons, we have supplied their most typical meanings.

TABLE 6-2   Useful emoticons for communicating online[3]

Emoticon	Meaning
:) or :-)	Expresses happiness, sarcasm, or joke
:(or :-(	Expresses unhappiness
:] or :-]	Expresses jovial happiness
:[or :-[	Expresses despondent unhappiness
:D or :-D	Expresses jovial happiness or laughing
:e or :-e	Expresses disappointment
:l or :-l	Expresses indifference
:-/ or :-\	Indicates undecided, confused, or skeptical
:Q or :-Q	Expresses confusion
:S or :-S	Expresses incoherence or loss of words
:@ or :-@	Expresses shock or screaming
:O or :-O	Indicates surprise, yelling, or realization of an error ("uh oh!")

Success Strategy Three: Avoid miscommunications

Whenever you are communicating online you will want to actively look out for and avoid possible miscommunications with other students or the instructor. However, when using online communication tools for your college courses there will be times when there are miscommunications. While typically in conventional conversations you most often naturally pick up on clues of miscommunication (for example, a questioning gesture with a person's eye brows), in online discussion you will most likely have to work at searching out clues of possible miscommunications. This is true whether you are sending messages or receiving messages since both actions offer a variety of opportunities for miscommunications.

When you are sending a message:

▶ Review every message you intend to send out before hitting the "submit" or "send" button. On important communications even ask your roommate or friend to review the email just to make sure that you are communicating clearly.

- Don't try to be clever with your language; your goal should be clear and concise communications.

- Use the spelling and grammar checkers available in most software applications. If necessary, <u>cut-and-paste</u> the message into your <u>word processing</u> program to make use of its' spelling and grammar checker before sending the message.

- Important information should be near the top of the message, not somewhere down in the fifth or sixth paragraph. Remember, people often lose their concentration near the end of a message.

- If you are including copies of previous <u>emails</u> or other communications in with the current message, be sure to make a statement in the message that the reader should review the attached or enclosed messages for additional information. Add a few extra spaces after your name in the <u>email</u> to clearly indicate where the new message ends and the previous messages begin.

- Review the To:, Cc:, and Bcc: list of recipients before sending an <u>email</u>. To communicate effectively you should be aware of exactly who is receiving each <u>email</u>; an inadvertent <u>email</u> to your professor can be more than just embarrassing.

- Within the <u>email</u> ask the recipient questions to see if they are clear about the content of your message (for example, "does that make sense to you?," "are you OK with those plans?," "does that work for you?," etc.).

When you are receiving a message:

- Don't read too much into <u>emails</u> or <u>chat</u> discussions with other students or take comments too personally.

- Read the entire <u>email</u> (not just the first few lines of each paragraph).

- Review the message more than once to ensure that you did not accidentally skip over any important information. For important messages you may want to ask a friend or roommate to review it as well.

- Review any attached files or enclosed previous <u>emails</u> to provide the context for the message.

- If a message is upsetting do not respond to it for at least an hour or two. Take some time to cool down and collect your thoughts.

- Ask any questions you may have about the content of the message. <u>Cut-and-paste</u> specific quotes from the message into your questions if there may be confusion on precise words or sentences.

- Repeat back to the sender the essential details of the message to clarify your understanding (for example, "Meeting on next Wednesday at noon works well with my class schedule.").

- Never include in an online communication anything you wouldn't write on a postcard.

▶ Respect the copyright on materials that you reproduce (including items you find online).

▶ If you are forwarding or re-posting a message, do not change the wording of the original sender.

▶ Culture, slang, jargon, humor, idioms, and especially sarcasm are rarely effective communication strategies in online conversations.[4]

Success Strategy Four: Avoid writing in all capital letters

When expressing the emotions in online conversations it has become common for people to use all CAPITALIZED letters when they want to shout or express other argumentative positions. Writing in all CAPITAL letters is often referred to as "flaming" and is considered unacceptable in most academic or school related conversation.

You should avoid using all CAPITALIZED words in your emails whenever possible, shouting or other confrontational communications rarely accomplish any goals and typically shut down future opportunities for success. If you are frustrated or have other emotions you would like to share with others, try using the less aggressive tools like emoticons and acronyms provided previously.

> **STUDENT-TO-STUDENT TIP**
>
> Using emoticons or just clearly stating your intentions improves rapport and creates a foundation upon which to build relationships. Simply typing "hee hee!" portrays a friendly gesture and the receiver knows to accept the material in a light-hearted way.

Success Strategy Five: Be sure not to reply to everyone on the Listserv

Listservs, as discussed in chapter 2, are common tools used for communicating with a large number of students in a course. For example, your instructor may use a listserv of all students in the course to send out email messages announcing reading requirements for an upcoming test; this saves them the effort of sending the email to each student individually. To send an email to a listserv you simply address the "To:" area of the email with the listserv instead of an individual recipient (for example, Spanish101Section2@state.edu).

When replying to an email message that you received from a listserv you will want to make sure that the "To:" area of the reply message doesn't, however, go back to everyone signed up on the listserv. If you use the "reply all" option of your email software application that is exactly what will happen, and everyone in your course will receive the email that you intended only for the instructor. Take the time before sending a reply to a listserv message, or any message, to double check the fields that indicate who the recipients of the email should be; it is well worth the extra few seconds to avoid potential miscommunications.

Hot

ACTIVITY 6-3   **Have you missed something?**

As a review, match the following emoticons or acronyms with the correct definition.

_____ **1.** :-/ *or* :-\   a. Expresses laughter in an <u>email</u> or <u>chat</u>.

_____ **2.** :e *or* :-e   b. Expresses shock or screaming in an <u>email</u> or <u>chat</u>.

_____ **3.** :@ *or* :-@   c. Expresses disappointment in an <u>email</u> or <u>chat</u>.

_____ **4.** ROF   d. Expresses boredom or tiredness in an <u>email</u> or <u>chat</u>.

_____ **5.** <Y>   e. Indicates undecided, confused, or skeptical in an <u>email</u> or <u>chat</u>.

CHAPTER SUMMARY

Developing an online social life can help sustain your motivation throughout the semester by giving you the opportunity to communicate with others about what is happening in the course. College courses typically present a variety of obstacles for students, being able to discuss complex problems or formulas with other students (or even with your professor) can provide you with the necessary information and confidence to ensure your success. Take the time to get to know your online classmates and instructors; it will not only be of benefit to your academic success but it can also help you enjoy your college courses all the more.

CHAPTER SIX   EXERCISE

To begin the exercise you will want to have access to the World Wide Web using a <u>Web browser</u> (such as, Netscape Navigator or Microsoft Internet Explorer, etc.). In addition, you will want to open a new document in a <u>word processing</u> program (for example, Microsoft Word).

STEP ONE: Select an upcoming assignment or activity for the course you are taking and identify a student in that course that you have not met before. You can likely find a list of students in the class in the course's <u>educational portal</u> or <u>Webpage</u>. (If not you can ask the instructor for a list of student <u>email</u> addresses in order to create an online study group.)

STEP TWO: In a <u>word processing</u> document, write a three sentence introduction of yourself that you could send to the classmate you selected. Include your name, the course you are in with the classmate, and why you are motivated to be successful in the course.

STEP THREE: For the assignment or activity you have selected, identify three to five major tasks that must be accomplished in order for you to be successful (for example, select an appropriate topic for a research paper, understand the relationship of two mathematical formulas, learn to read the periodic table, etc.).

STEP FOUR: In the <u>word processing</u> document list the tasks that must be accomplished for the assignment or activity, as well as an explanation of at least one way that studying with another person would be useful in being successful in each task. For example, "since the assignment requires that we identify an appropriate topic for our research it would be useful for me to have someone review my list of possible topics to determine if any would work for the assignment."

STEP FIVE: For each task and rationale for studying with a partner, identify an online technology (see chapter 1) that may be useful in communicating online with the classmate. For example, you might identify the use of <u>email</u> to share <u>word processing</u> documents or <u>instant messenger</u> to share descriptions of how mathematical formulas relate to one another.

STEP SIX: In the <u>word processing</u> document combine your introduction (step two) with the rationale for working with other students on each of the required tasks (steps four) and the proposed online communication tools that could be used (step five). Though you do not have to <u>email</u> this message to your classmate at this time, you should keep the <u>word processing</u> file as a model for the time when you do want to form an online study group.

For example,

"Alexia,

Hello, my name is Mehadi and I am a student with you in Spanish101. Since my major is Political Science and I have to get at least a B in this course, I would like to form an online study group to ensure that we can all be successful.

As you know assignment two is due in three weeks, and in order to be successful in that assignment we have to complete the following tasks. For each task, I have included ideas about how we can have an online study group that will provide each of us with practice and feedback.

First we are to identify. . .

Please let me know if you would like to join the online study group.

Thanks,

Mehadi

Mehadi@mycollege.edu"

CHAPTER SIX   SKILLS CHECKLIST

After completing this chapter you should be able to do the following. If there are skills below that you may not be able to do, take a few minutes to review the chapter, focusing on those areas that you may have missed the first time through.

❏ I can make a good first impression through my online communications.

❏ I can use separate <u>folder</u>s and <u>email</u>s accounts to stay organized with my online relationships.

❏ I use spell the check and grammar check on all correspondence with other students and my instructors.

❏ I add information regarding the name and file type for any files I attach to <u>email</u>s or <u>discussion board</u> postings.

❏ I am energetically working to build online relationships and a supportive online community for my coursework.

❏ I have made initial online contact with my instructor.

❏ I compensate for the lack of non-verbal communication strategies available online by using <u>emoticon</u>s and acronyms.

❏ I add a personal touch to every message I send to help build online relationships.

❏ I actively look out for and avoid possible miscommunications in my online communications.

❏ I have completed the chapter 6 activities.

ADDITIONAL RESOURCES

Additional resources on topics covered in this chapter are available on the <u>Website</u>: **<http://collegesurvival.college.hmco.com/students>**.

NOTES

1. http://www.hspeople.com/archives/HSCareers/CareerPlanning/021102.asp
2. Based on http://www.pb.org/emoticon.html
3. Based on http://www.pb.org/emoticon.html
4. Based in part on Winograd and Moore, 2003.

7

Study Tips for Online Students

Whether we realize it or not, each of us has a set of learning skills and study habits we use to succeed in the conventional classroom. Many of these skills and habits will, however, have to be transformed in order for you to have the same levels of success in online coursework. For example, you have likely developed throughout your educational experiences a set of skills that you find useful when working on a group project with classmates. Maybe you start off by assigning roles for group members, followed by a discussion of what has to be accomplished and when for everyone to be successful. The same skills can also be applied when the group members are meeting together online, however instead of discussing the roles and responsibilities at a small desk you may be each sitting miles apart, each of you at your home computers. Communicating clearly and using the technologies to your benefit will be keys to your success in this new classroom environment.

That being the case, while many of the delivery tools in an online course will be different from those that you experienced in the traditional classroom (for example, verbal discussion being replaced by <u>Internet</u> <u>chat</u>), many of the learning skills and study habits you have already developed will provide an excellent foundation for your success. In this chapter we will examine how many of these learning skills and study habits you bring from traditional classroom experiences can be transformed for success in any online course.

E-learning Experiences

It wasn't until I taught my first completely online course that I realized how different my preparation has to be to ensure success. In the past I had taught the same course in a traditional classroom, and when I was asked to teach online I planned to move many of my classroom activities into our <u>Web portal</u> (i.e., WebCT). Then the night came for our first class meeting, scheduled to take place in a synchronous <u>chat</u> room. After arriving a few minutes early and reviewing the notes from my traditional first-day lecture in the classroom, I thought that I was well prepared for success. When one or two students had arrived in the <u>chat</u> room the introductions and discussions were moving smoothly. But within minutes there were more than 20 students joining me in the discussion; each one wanted to include a message letting the rest of us know they had arrived and how excited they were about the course.

Needless to say within minutes I was overwhelmed; the multitude of discussions between students, as well as between students and me, was devastating the structured conversations I was used to in the traditional classroom. The night was a disaster... but fortunately most of the students persevered through those first couple of <u>chats</u> and we finished the semester with many successful experiences. I learned that semester, however, that it wasn't that my activities were inappropriate for online coursework, but rather that the techniques and resources I used to prepare for the course had to change in order for the course to be successful.

How to Use this Chapter

In each of the sections that follow we provide tips, suggestions, guides, and recommendations for preparing to be successful before, during, and after participation in a variety of online coursework activities. It is impractical (and most likely not that useful) to memorize these tips; rather, keep this book close to your computer so you can come back to these tips and ideas when you are assigned coursework that requires your participation online. Highlight, underline, and write in the margins of this section to underscore the tips that you believe will be most useful to you.

Online Real-Time Chats

#21

Real-time (or synchronous) chats provide you with one of the few online experiences where you can receive immediate replies to your questions or comments, thus allowing for a conversation to develop quickly with your instructor or classmates. For that reason you will want to take advantage of these unique opportunities.

#28

Before the chat

❑ Prepare a list of questions.

Before the chat begins identify questions that you would like to ask and receive answers to during the chat. Write the questions in a document that you can cut-and-paste from during the discussion. This will save you the time of typing and editing the question, especially a long question, before sending it. This technique will also help you avoid grammatical and spelling errors.

❑ Send additional questions by email.

For questions to which the timeliness of the response is less important you should send those by email or asked in class if you meet on campus. If you have questions for which the timeliness of the response is less important, send them by email or, if you meet on campus, ask them in class.

❑ Visit the chat area the day before.

You should check to verify that you have access to the chat area the day before a scheduled chat. If you do not have access this will give you time to contact technical support. Also, many educational portals will have multiple chat areas so you want to confirm that you are accessing the correct chat area.

❑ Create a good study environment.

For example, turn off the television, ask your roommates not to interrupt you, turn off instant messenger programs, etc. (See chapter 4.)

#2

❑ Identify and organize any files.

Files that you may want to reference during the chat should be easily accessible so you can view them quickly during the discussion.

#4

❏ Verify access to chat transcripts.

Check with the instructor to find out if you will have access to the transcripts of the <u>chat</u> after it is complete.

❏ Review any rules, agenda, and/or etiquette guide.

Often instructors will provide guidelines for course <u>chats</u> in the syllabus or in class. These could include rules for indicating when you have a question, etiquette for discussing topics with other students, and so forth. If you are going to lead the <u>chat</u> discussion (such as for a group project conversation) then develop an agenda and a set of rules for the <u>chat</u>. These should be shared with the other <u>chat</u> members prior to the <u>chat</u> session.

> **STUDENT-TO-STUDENT TIP**
>
> Use the chat room for your group projects. It will help you formulate your plans and it will make your team more cohesive.

During the chat

❏ Arrive to the <u>chat</u> area at least 5 minutes before.

This will give you time to ensure that your computer and connection are working properly.

❏ Do not greet everyone.

Most synchronous <u>chat</u> software provides a list of who has entered the <u>chat</u>, so do not greet each new person with a "hello" when they arrive.

❏ Do not respond to each comment or question.

Respond only to those that address you specifically or to which your response will make a valuable contribution to the discussion.

❏ Keep the conversation focused on the topic.

Only post comments or questions that add value to the discussion.

❏ Note the time to develop social relationships.

Online relationships can be developed more effectively in small group <u>chats</u>, instant messages, or <u>email</u>, rather than during class time when many students are in the <u>chat</u> area together.

❏ Address your comments or suggestions.

Identify the individual you would like to respond to or ask a question of when you post to the <u>chat</u>. For example, "Dr. Robinson, in our readings I was somewhat confused by the terms 'cranial' and 'caudal'. Could you explain the difference?" or "Jane, how is your progress coming on the introduction section of our group project?"

❑ Take notes.

Especially if you will not have access to the <u>chat</u> transcripts, you should take notes on what is being discussed in the <u>chat</u>, either on paper or in a <u>word processing</u> document.

❑ Keep postings concise.

To the extent possible, keep your questions or comments short and to the point. If your question or comment is likely to take up more lines of text than are visible in the <u>chat</u> interface then divide the question into two parts.

❑ Participate.

Improve your comprehension by being an active participant in the discussions. Attempt to find the right balance of joining the conversation without dominating the conversation.

❑ Cut-and-paste.

Typically you will want to <u>cut-and-paste</u> links to other <u>Websites</u> (i.e., <u>URLs</u>) into your postings instead of typing them in; this will reduce the number of inverted letters or missing periods in links.

❑ Raise your hand with a blank message.

To gain the attention of the instructor or other host for a <u>chat</u>, simply post a blank message to the <u>chat</u> discussion. This is the equivalent of raising your hand when your <u>chat</u> software doesn't have other features for gaining the instructor's attention.

❑ Use <u>emoticons</u> and acronyms to express your feelings.

You should use the familiar <u>emoticons</u> and acronyms provided in chapter 6, on pages 124–125, to add non-verbal communication elements to your <u>emails</u>.

❑ Do not post "I am back".

If you lose connection or leave the discussion during the <u>chat</u>, do not inform everyone when you have returned. If you are absent for a long period of time due to technical problems write your instructor an <u>email</u> explaining the issues involved. This is one of the times when getting a transcript of the <u>chat</u> session would be useful to determine what information you may have missed.

❑ Do not multi-task.

For your college courses do not attempt to have more than one <u>chat</u> session going on at a time. Your comprehension of the discussion topics will be greatly decreased if your attention is divided among two conversations.

❏ Keep private conversations private.

If you want to ask a private question or make a comment to an individual student or the instructor, most <u>chat</u> software applications will permit you to "whisper" to other individual members in the <u>chat</u>. You may, however, want to try this function with a "whisper" that is not offensive to anyone in the <u>chat</u> just in case something goes wrong and everyone in the <u>chat</u> ends up viewing your private comments.

❏ Spelling and grammar are important.

Though people are typically more flexible on spelling and grammar during real-time <u>chat</u>s, it is still important to use correct spelling and grammar to the extent possible without slowing down the discussion. As a result you should be careful when typing and may want to use a <u>word processing</u> program to draft your postings before copy-and-pasting them into the <u>chat</u>.

Hot

❏ Leave misspelled words.

If you do misspell a word when posting to a <u>chat</u>, do not post another message correcting the misspelling (unless the misspelled word would significantly change the meaning of the message).

❏ Avoid sarcasm, idioms, slang, jargon, etc.

Do not use cultural or regional communication techniques that can easily result in miscommunication.

Hot

❏ Resist over-analysis.

Try not to read too much into statements made by others students or to take comments too personally. Miscommunications are common in <u>chat</u>s since many of the typical non-verbal communication tools (such as eye contact or body gestures) are not available.

❏ Patience is a virtue.

Be patient and ask questions when you are confused or believe that there may be a miscommunication.

❏ Cite and reference.

Provide accurate citation and reference information for any sources of information that you may use in your discussion, including <u>Webpage</u> <u>URL</u>s.

Hot

❏ Stay until the end.

Normally you will not want to leave the <u>chat</u> until the instructor has posted a message letting everyone know that the course-related <u>chat</u> has ended.

❏ Do not post "good-byes."

It is not necessary for you to announce when you are leaving the <u>chat</u> session. Your classmates and instructor will see your name leave the list of participants when you exit the <u>chat</u> area.

After the <u>chat</u>

❏ Review.

Go through the transcripts from the <u>chat</u> (or your notes) to determine if you should follow-up the discussion with <u>email</u> messages to your professor or fellow students.

❏ Summarize.

Sum up what you learned during the <u>chat</u> and/or what tasks you must complete next. Include this summary in your notes from the <u>chat</u> or along with your copy of the <u>chat</u> transcripts.

❏ Follow-up.

Immediately after completing the <u>chat</u>, <u>email</u> follow-up questions and comments, as well as your summary of what was discussed. Do this while the conversation is fresh in your mind.

Hot

❏ Improve your performance.

Identify strategies that would improve your comprehension and participation the next time you are going to participate in a synchronous discussion. Write these down in a document that can be saved to your course file <u>folder</u> in your computer.

❏ Keep a record.

Keep all files related to each <u>chat</u> session in a computer file <u>folder</u> where you can access them when preparing for future assignments, activities, or exams.

> **STUDENT-TO-STUDENT TIP**
>
> Read the discussion questions ahead of time and spend some quality time thinking about the answers to them.

Online <u>Discussion Boards</u>

<u>Asynchronous</u> discussions (normally in online bulletin or <u>discussion boards</u>) offer you the opportunity to carry on a conversation with your fellow students or professor at times convenient to you. Since each participant in the discussion can choose when to reply to the latest addition to the conversation, the flexibility in pace and length of the conversation can vary greatly. You can, however, use this additional time for responding to

HOW TO TUTORIAL
#22

HOW TO TUTORIAL
#29

messages to clarify your comments or questions to ensure that there are not miscommunications.

Before your participation in a discussion board

☐ Review earlier postings.

Prepare for the discussion by reviewing previous postings to the <u>discussion board</u> related to the conversation topic(s) on which you are going to focus.

☐ Review any rules or etiquette guide.

Often instructors will provide guidelines for participation in <u>discussion board</u> conversations in the syllabus. By following the rules and etiquette guidelines you can often avoid miscommunications.

☐ Clarify expectations.

Determine what the instructor expects of your postings, whether formal or informal, emphasizing quality or quantity, and so forth. Informal postings (like those that you would write to a friend) are common, but most often the clarity and precision of formal communications will be desired for online coursework.

☐ Examine a model posting.

Identify any model postings that an instructor may have provided to illustrate the desired level and types of participation.

☐ Verify continuing access.

Find out from the professor if you will continue to have access to previous discussions throughout the semester (or if older discussions will be removed or no longer be visible to students).

☐ Create a schedule.

Schedule times throughout each week of the semester when you will participate in the <u>discussion boards</u>. Include in this plan how much time you will spend responding to postings with your comments or questions. In order to fully participate in the discussions, in most courses you will want to schedule time at least every other day.

☐ Create a good study environment.

For example, turn off the television, ask your roommates not to interrupt you, turn off instant messenger programs, etc. (See chapter 4.)

During your participation in a <u>discussion board</u>

❑ Take your time.

Editing and reviewing your additions to the <u>discussion board</u> can help avoid miscommunications. Having time to revise and improve your comments or questions is an advantage of <u>asynchronous</u> discussions that you can benefit from.

❑ Do not respond to each comment or question.

Respond only to those that address you specifically or to which your response will make a valuable contribution to the discussion. Find a balance of quality and quantity with your additions to the discussion.

❑ Keep the conversation focused on the topic.

Only post comments or questions that add value to the discussion. Often you will want to <u>cut-and-paste</u> into your message the specific comment or question to which your response is referring.

❑ Keep to the topic of the <u>thread</u>.

Most <u>discussion boards</u> will <u>thread</u> the discussion (i.e., illustrate the order of the conversation) so you can see which postings are replies to which other postings. To the extent possible try to keep your comments or questions in the correct "<u>thread</u>" to provide consistency to the conversation.

❑ Use the subject line.

If your <u>discussion board</u> does not <u>thread</u> the discussion it is especially important to include in your posting specific information in the subject line regarding the posting to which you are replying. Including a copy of the original posting at the bottom of your posting is often useful in clarifying your response and reducing the chances for miscommunication.

❑ Write postings in a clear and expressive manner.

Most often you will want to write one or two well structured and thought-out paragraphs in a single posting to an online <u>discussion board</u>. Despite the fact that these paragraphs should have an introduction, supporting facts, and conclusion as in any well structured writing that you would submit for a grade in a college course, online discussion postings are typically short; most often you will want to limit the paragraphs in your postings to three to five sentences.

❑ Address your comments or questions.

Identify at the beginning of a posting if you would like a specific individual to respond. For example, "Dr. Robinson, in our readings I was somewhat confused by the terms 'cranial' and 'caudal.' Could you explain the difference?" or "Jane, how is your progress coming on the introduction section of our group project?"

❑ Provide a signature.

Although most <u>discussion board</u>s will include your name with the posting, it is always a good idea to include your name at the end of your messages.

❑ Participate.

Improve your comprehension by being an active participant in the discussions. Attempt to find the right balance of joining the conversation without dominating the conversation.

❑ Be discrete and polite.

Do not include anything in your <u>discussion board</u> postings that you would not typically write on a postcard; inevitably these discussions are rarely private.

❑ Cut-and-paste.

Typically you will want to <u>cut-and-paste</u> links to other <u>Websites</u> (i.e., <u>URL</u>s) into your postings instead of typing them in; this will reduce the number of inverted letters or missing periods in links.

❑ Spelling and grammar are important.

As a result you should be careful and may want to use a <u>word processing</u> program to draft your postings before copy-and-pasting them into the <u>chat</u>.

❑ Resist over-analysis.

Try not to read too much into statements made by others students or to take comments too personally. Miscommunications are common in <u>discussion board</u> conversations since many of the typical non-verbal communication tools (such as eye contact, body gestures) are not available.

❑ Avoid sarcasm, idioms, slang, jargon, etc.

Do not use cultural or regional communication techniques that can easily result in miscommunication.

❑ Cite and reference.

Provide accurate citation and reference information for any sources of information that you may use in your discussion, including <u>Webpage</u> <u>URL</u>s.

❏ Only post messages that add to the discussion.

Hot

Avoid short and pointless postings (such as, "I agree." or "I really like this.") that do not add substantial value to the discussion. Your postings to the discussion board should include examples and descriptive information about your comments or questions. No one wants to take the time to download multiple postings that merely say "Nice work."

After your participation in a **discussion board**

❏ Review.

Go through the many postings included in the discussion to determine if you may have missed any essential comments and/or if any follow-up communications with fellow students or the instructor is necessary.

❏ Summarize.

Hot

Sum up the major topics discussed in the online conversation and what you have learned from the discussion. Write this summary down and keep it for your records.

❏ Follow-up.

After an online discussion has ended, email follow-up questions and comments as well as your summary of what was discussed.

❏ Improve your performance.

Hot

Identify strategies that would improve your comprehension and participation the next time you are going to participate in an asynchronous discussion. Write these strategies down in a document that can be saved to your course file folder in your computer.

❏ Keep a record.

If discussion board postings will not remain available throughout the semester and you would like to keep information contained in one or more the postings, be sure to copy the posting(s) to a word processing document that you can save to your personal computer.

Email

Email is almost certainly the most common online communications tool used in college courses. Despite the fact that you are likely to have a great deal of experience in communicating with friends and family using email, the use of email in completing coursework should not be overlooked in

HOW TO TUTORIAL

#19

#26

preparing to be successful in college. Avoiding miscommunications and developing positive online relationships through <u>email</u> commonly requires that students pay additional attention before hitting the "send" button.

Before sending an <u>email</u>

❑ Review any rules or etiquette guide.

Examine any rules or guidelines required by the instructor for <u>emails</u> related to the course (such as, subject line requirements, naming attached files, etc.).

Hot

❑ Verify <u>email</u> addresses.

Confirm that you have correct <u>email</u> addresses for all those who are to be recipients of the <u>email</u>.

❑ Identify and organize any files.

Files that you may want to reference in an <u>email</u> should be easily accessible so you can find them. Have access to copies of previous <u>emails</u>, course syllabi, and other files related to the course so you can quote these resources as necessary in your <u>emails</u>.

❑ Relax.

If you are upset or angry, avoid writing any <u>emails</u> to your fellow students or the instructor for several hours.

❑ Create a schedule.

Each day you should schedule a time specifically for reading and replying to <u>emails</u>.

During an <u>email</u> conversation

❑ Use the subject line.

Include an accurate description of the <u>email</u> contents in the subject line.

❑ Include the previous message in a reply.

Often you will want to quote the original message in your reply to avoid possible miscommunications. This can also provide a record of the discussion for your later review. When including an original message in the reply, however, do not alter the original message in any way; typically you will not want to include more than the last message (i.e., do not include the previous five messages in your reply).

❏ Only forward course relevant emails.

Avoid forwarding email messages that do not directly relate to the course materials. Forwarding jokes and other miscellaneous emails should be saved for personal emails only.

❏ Review all messages carefully.

Prior to sending email messages, carefully review the message looking for misspelled words and grammar errors.

❏ Ask a friend to review important emails.

For important emails ask a roommate, fellow student, or friend to review the message. Clear and simple messages communicate most effectively.

❏ Don't store all of your messages in your email inbox.

Your email inbox will quickly become full of old messages and you will have a difficult time accessing important information if you do not develop a folder structure for storing email messages. When a message comes into your inbox, reply to it and save it in an appropriate folder that same day.

❏ Confirm software compatibility for attachments.

In order for the recipient to open a file that you have attached they must have the software application affiliated with the file (for example, the recipient must have Microsoft Word or a compatible application in order to view an attachment with the file extension .doc). You should verify that the recipient has the necessary software before sending a file.

HOW TO TUTORIAL
#19

HOW TO TUTORIAL
#26

❏ Describe attachments.

In your email message include a description of any attached files (including the name of the file and the software application used to create the file).

❏ Browse before you attach.

Many Web portals and email software applications require that you first identify the file you want to include as an attachment, this is often done by clicking on a "browse" button, and then attaching the file in a second step by clicking on the "attach" button.

❏ Ask before sending big files.

It is also good etiquette to ask before sending emails with large file attachments since the receiver may have to request additional server space to make room for the email(s). If you have numerous large attachments, include those within separate emails.

❑ Be cautious when receiving <u>attachments</u>.

Files that are attached to <u>email</u>s that you receive can contain files with computer viruses. If you do not know the sender of the <u>email</u> or if you are not expecting an attached file from an instructor or classmate, do not immediately open it. Take the time to <u>email</u> the sender in order to verify that they did intend for you to receive the file and that the file does not contain a computer virus. It is worth the extra time to be cautious since a computer virus can wipe away months of your work in just a few minutes.

`Hot` `Hot`

❑ Resist over-analysis.

Try not to read too much into statements made by other students or to take comments too personally. Miscommunications are common in <u>email</u> since many of the typical non-verbal communication tools (such as eye contact, body gestures) are not available.

❑ Be discrete and polite.

Do not include anything in your <u>email</u>s that you would not typically write on a postcard; inevitably these discussions are rarely private.

❑ Double-check recipients.

Always review the To:, Cc:, and Bcc: <u>field</u>s prior to sending any <u>email</u>. Often, in a hurry to complete our work, we will mistakenly add (or omit) an intended recipient to an <u>email</u> message. This can be both embarrassing (such as when an <u>email</u> to another project team member goes to the instructor) and sometimes destructive to the online relationships you have built.

❑ Include a signature.

At the end of every <u>email</u> message you should include a signature (i.e., name, <u>email</u> address, etc.).

❑ Keep the conversation focused on the topic.

Only post comments or questions that add value to the <u>email</u> conversation.

`Hot`

❑ Avoid sarcasm, idioms, slang, jargon, etc.

Do not use cultural or regional communication techniques that can easily result in miscommunication.

❑ Only send <u>email</u>s that add to the discussion.

Avoid writing short <u>email</u> messages that do not contain substantial information for the recipient. Rarely will a short <u>email</u>, like "I agree.,"

"Thank you.," or "Me too!" be useful to fellow students or your instructor. Take the time to compose messages with appropriate sentence and paragraph structures.

☐ Cut-and-paste.

Typically you will want to <u>cut-and-paste</u> links to other <u>Websites</u> (i.e., <u>URL</u>s) into your postings instead of typing them in; this will reduce the number of inverted letters or missing periods in links.

☐ Review the history.

When joining in an <u>email</u> conversation that has already been started by others, read the history of original <u>emails</u> that are most often included at the bottom of the <u>email</u> in reverse chronological order. This will provide you with the context of the more recent <u>email</u> messages.

☐ Remove <u>email</u> addresses from forwarded messages.

If you are forwarding an <u>email</u> message that contains the names and <u>email</u> addresses of multiple recipients who also received the original <u>email</u>, take a few minutes to remove those before forwarding the message.

☐ Cite and reference.

Provide accurate citation and reference information for any sources of information that you may use in your discussion, including <u>Webpage</u> <u>URL</u>s.

☐ Have multiple <u>email</u> accounts.

It is common for instructors to request that you use your college's <u>email</u> system (i.e., johndoe@mycollege.edu) since the college is responsible for maintaining access. Use this account for all of your course related <u>emails</u> and establish an alternate account for personal <u>emails</u>. You can often receive free <u>email</u> accounts for your personal communications (for example, at <http://www.hotmail.com>, <http://www.mail.com>, <http://mail.yahoo.com>, etc.).

☐ Use formatting to emphasize your ideas.

Hot

Use the bold, underline, and italics features of your <u>email</u> software applications to communicate more effectively.

☐ Use <u>emoticons</u> and acronyms to express your feelings.

You should use the familiar <u>emoticons</u> and acronyms provided in chapter 6, on pages 124–125, to add non-verbal communication elements to your <u>emails</u>.

☐ <u>Email</u> yourself.

Send <u>emails</u> to yourself as reminders of daily tasks to be completed.

❏ Number tasks or lists.

If you include a number of tasks or request for information in a single email, number them or use the bulleted list function of the email application.

❏ Review one last time.

Always review an email message one last time before sending it. Check spelling, grammar, punctuation, the recipient list, as well as the over-all impression of the email message.

After sending an email

❏ Keep a record.

File copies of all emails related to each college course you take in folders outside of your email inbox. You can delete these at the end of the semester after grades have been received, but until then you may want to refer to the email messages in preparing for exams or reviewing a conversation for clarity.

❏ Patience is a virtue.

Be patient while waiting for a reply. Instructors and classmates are not necessarily responding to their email messages at the same times you are checking your email.

❏ Courteous follow-up.

If you have not had a response to an email in more than 48 hours you can write a polite message to the recipient to see if the email was received.

Listservs

College instructors typically use listservs when they want to communicate the same message to all students in a course, or when they want to facilitate discussions that can include multiple students. You can use the listserv as an effective tool for communicating with multiple classmates.

Before participating in a listserv

❏ Sign up for a class listserv.

Listservs make it easy to email everyone in your college courses by simply addressing the email to the listserv address. In order to become a member of most listservs you will have to subscribe or register, though instructors do sometimes create a listserv for all students in the class so that you do not have to subscribe individually.

❏ **Save subscription information.**

`Hot`

When you have subscribed (or been registered by your instructor) for a listserv you should receive an email outlining how to send messages to the listserv, rules and etiquette guidelines, as well as information for how you can unsubscribe to the listserv. This is useful information that you should save.

❏ **Review any rules or etiquette guide.**

`Hot`

Often instructors will provide guidelines for participation in listserv discussions in the syllabus. By following the rules and etiquette guidelines you can often avoid miscommunications.

❏ **Hang out before participating.**

It is usually useful to review several messages posted by group member before sending your own message to the listserv. This will give you the opportunity to identify group norms and informal rules of etiquette.

During your participation in a listserv

❏ **Review the tips for sending emails. (See this chapter.)**

`Hot` `Hot`

Listserv messages are principally email messages that are sent to a large list of recipients, as a result the same suggestions and tips for sending email messages apply when sending messages to a listserv.

❏ **Check listserv replies.**

When replying to a message that you received from another member of a listserv you will want to examine the recipient field to make sure that you are replying to the individual and not to all members of the listserv.

❏ **Don't use listserv for private conversation.**

If you would like to respond to an individual regarding their posting to a listserv make sure that you address the reply message to the individual and not the listserv.

❏ **Always include your email address in the message.**

Often listservs will not indicate your email address in the "From:" field. In order for recipients to respond to you individually you should always include your email address in the text of the message.

❏ **Only send emails that add to the discussion.**

Avoid sending emails to the listserv that do not add new and valuable information to the discussion.

Hot

❏ Don't use vacation notices.

If you are going to be out of town or away from your <u>email</u> for an extended period of time do not establish a vacation message (i.e., a messaging response automatically sent to everyone who sends you an <u>email</u> letting them know that you are on vacation) without also informing the <u>listserv</u> manager that your subscription should be temporarily suspended.

After participating in a <u>listserv</u>

❏ Save and Review.

Go through the <u>listserv</u> messages to determine if you may have missed any essential comments and/or if any follow-up communications with fellow students or the instructor is necessary.

❏ Summarize.

Sum up the major topics discussed in the <u>listserv</u> conversation and what you have learned from the discussion. Write this summary down and keep it for your records.

❏ Improve your performance.

Identify strategies that would improve your comprehension and participation the next time you are going to participate in an <u>asynchronous</u> discussion. Write these down in a document that can be saved to your course file <u>folder</u> in your computer.

Online Group Projects

While group projects are commonly used in both high school and college courses, the utilization of online technologies to facilitate the group member roles and responsibilities is likely to be less familiar to most students. With more working adult students, as well as distance education students, in today's classrooms, the traditional strategies for successful group projects are changing, requiring the application of online technologies that provide greater flexibility for individual group members.

Before your participation in a group project

❏ Review.

Look at all of the information, rules, guidelines, and grading policies regarding the group project prior to beginning any work. These guidelines should also provide information on how groups will be assigned or formed during the course.

❏ Introduce yourself.

Take the opportunity to introduce yourself to the other group members. Include in your introduction some information about your schedule for the semester, your goals for the course, what roles you would like to have in developing a successful team, as well as your contact information.

❏ Verify contact information.

Hot

Make sure that you have accurate and up-to-date contact information for all group members. You should keep a *hard* copy of this information on paper in case you have technology problems later in the semester.

❏ Devise a communications strategy.

You will want a plan for the project that includes a schedule of meetings (i.e., both when and for how long), an explanation of the online communication tool(s) that will be utilized, as well as a decision on which group member will lead discussions. For example, a plan may state that your group will use instant messaging software for weekly meetings and email for other communications.

❏ Identify group roles.

Hot Hot

Prepare a plan for the group project that includes the roles of each member in completing the work (such as leaders, communicators, task managers, etc.) as well as the tasks that must be completed. The importance of group roles in the success of each team member is magnified when a project group moves to an online environment. In many cases it is best to have one group member that is responsible for communicating with the instructor with regards to the group project. This will reduce the number of opportunities for miscommunication.

❏ Assign tasks.

Each task should have an individual or team that is ultimately responsible for the successful completion of the task.

❏ Commit.

All group members should commit to being prepared for each meeting, allotting sufficient time for the group project, communicating with other group members openly, and being consistent in the quality and predictability of their interactions.[1]

> **STUDENT-TO-STUDENT TIP**
>
> Be assertive and "kindly critical." Learn to suggest alternatives and compromises when you disagree with a group member. Instead of blatantly saying "You're wrong," give the other person several suggestions to choose from regarding an alternative plan of action.

❏ Select a software standard.

To ensure that everyone in the group has access to all of the important files that will be created throughout the semester you will want to select a software standard. For instance, even if only one member has an older version of Microsoft Word, then other group members should <u>back save</u> their files to a version that ensures that all group members can access the files.

During your participation in a group project

❏ Follow-up on tasks.

Throughout the group project all team members must be responsible for successfully completing the required tasks they have been assigned.

❏ Maintaining your role.

Throughout the semester it is essential that all group members continue their functions within the group (such as, organizing meetings, taking notes, communicating with the instructor, keeping copies of all group files, etc.).

❏ Encourage good working relationships.

Do what you can to foster good group dynamics and relationships throughout the project. The importance of group relationships is elevated when group projects are relying on online technologies to facilitate the project.

❏ Share calendars online.

Use the shared calendars and <u>groupware</u> (see chapter 5) to facilitate scheduling meetings, sharing draft documents, and meeting deadlines.

❏ Patience is a virtue, but keep on top of group members.

Be patient with your classmates, but do not miss deadlines you have agreed upon as a group.

❏ Keep a record.

All files related to the group project (including <u>emails</u>, transcripts of synchronous <u>chats</u>, etc.) should be kept in a single location in your computer.

❏ Back-up.

Make weekly back-up copies of all files related to your group project.

☐ **Review and edit each other's work.**

Review and revise papers, <u>emails</u>, and other communications with group members to ensure clarity and reduce the odds of miscommunications.

☐ **Resist over-analysis.**

Try not to read too much into statements made by others students or to take comments too personally. Miscommunications are common since many of the typical non-verbal communication tools (such as eye contact, body gestures) are not available.

☐ **Cite and reference.**

Provide accurate citation and reference information for any sources of information that you may use in your discussion, including <u>Webpage</u> <u>URL</u>s.

☐ **Follow the group's communication strategy.**

Maintain the use of the agreed upon structure for online communications. For example, if the role of one group member is to lead online synchronous discussions then do not attempt to take over that responsibility during a <u>chat</u> session.

☐ **Track your progress.**

Use technology to share files, provide feedback to group members, track changes made in a Microsoft Word Document, indicate progress being made on the project, communicate with the instructor, and so forth.

HOW TO TUTORIAL

#5

After your participation in a group project

☐ **Follow-up.**

After completing an online group project send an <u>email</u> to each member of the project group thanking them for the contributions they made to the project. You do not know when you may be required to work with these individuals again.

☐ **Keep a record.**

Save copies of all final documents that the group submitted to the professor.

☐ **Improve your performance.**

Identify strategies that would improve your performance the next time you are going to participate in a group project. Write these down in a document that can be saved to your course file <u>folder</u> in your computer.

Online Exams

Taking an exam is commonly a stressful experience for students, and when the test is to be completed online the anxiety can be magnified for students who are not prepared. In preparing for an online exam you should prepare for the actual test items like you would for other similar exams, but in addition you will want to identify strategies that can effectively reduce any additional stress of having the test online.

Before an online exam

Hot ❑ **Review guidelines.**

Prior to completing an online test or exam review the guidelines for taking the exam provided by the instructor. Open book exams that are time limited are likely to be the most common given the limitations of current technologies, though proctored online exams (i.e., in a designated computer lab with a supervising staff member) are also used at many colleges and universities.

❑ **Verify format.**

Review any information provided by the instructor regarding the format of questions (such as short answer, multiple choice, essay, etc.).

❑ **Take practice exams.**

Find out from the instructor if there are online practice exams available for you to take prior to the graded exam.

❑ **Confirm that you have adequate software.**

Especially if you are going to complete an online exam on a computer other than your personal computer, prior to taking the exam determine if the required software is available on the machine you will be using. Additional software (such as a calculator and word processing application) may also be useful if permitted by the professor.

❑ **Study.**

Prepare for the test questions like you would for a classroom exam.

❑ **Apply time-appropriate constraints.**

In preparing for the exam, complete sample test questions within time constraints that match those possibly required for the online exam. For example, if you are going to be required to complete a 30-question exam in one hour, then prepare for the exam with no more than 2 minutes to answer each sample question.

☐ Create a good test-taking environment.

For example, turn off the television, ask your roommates not to interrupt you, turn off instant messenger programs, etc. (See chapter 4.)

☐ Identify the ideal time.

Often you will be able to complete an online exam at a time that is convenient to you (for example, any time on one of three consecutive days). Identify a time when you will have no interruptions or distractions.

☐ Prepare your resources.

Make sure that you have any permitted resources (such as books, notes, pen, paper, etc.) with you when you complete the exam.

☐ Relax.

Take a minute to close your eyes and calm down before entering the Webpage that contains the exam.

During an online exam

☐ Watch the time.

If the exam is timed, set a stopwatch or have a clock in view so you can keep track of how much time you have left to complete the questions. It is often useful to have an alarm or other signal to let you know when there is only 10 minutes left before the exam must be completed.

☐ Print a copy.

By printing out the exam you can give yourself several options. You can complete the exam on the paper copy and then transfer the answers over to the online version for submitting to the instructor, or you can keep a copy of each online answer you have selected just in case you lose your connection to the Internet or electrical power.

☐ Cut-and-paste.

In completing essay questions do not type your answer directly into the exam Webpage. First complete your answer in a word processing program to take advantage of spelling and grammar check features (as well as the thesaurus). When you have answered the question you can then cut-and-paste your response into the exam Webpage.

☐ Stay on the exam Webpage.

Do not attempt to go to another Website within the same browser window while you are completing the exam. Avoid hitting "forward" or "backward" to access information since you will commonly risk losing the answers you have already entered for the exam. Instead, open a second copy of your <u>Internet</u> browser, when allowed, to search for online information that may be useful in completing the exam (typically done by entering "<u>CTRL</u>" and "n" at the same time).

❏ Stay calm even if the technology doesn't work.

If a problem does occur with your technology, do not panic. Take careful notes of what has occurred and immediately <u>email</u> your instructor letting them know the specifics of the situation. Be sure to identify any error messages or other information that may have been provided.

❏ Review the exam before submitting.

Go through the online exam to guarantee that all of your intended responses are entered before hitting the submit button.

❏ Only submit once.

Typically you will only want to hit the submit button once. If an error does occur when submitting the exam, make another attempt and also <u>email</u> your professor about the situation. If possible include in that <u>email</u> a copy of the answers that you intended to submit from the printed copy of the test you have kept.

After an online exam

❏ Take notes.

Make note of the questions that you were unsure of your answer or that you could not answer. Immediately following the exam, review your textbook and notes to determine the correct answer.

❏ Check your grade.

Most online exams will provide you with an immediate score for multiple choice and short answer questions. If there was an essay component to the test you will likely have to wait a few days for those scores to be added to your grade.

❏ Improve your performance.

Identify strategies that would improve your performance the next time you are required to complete an online exam. Write these down in a document that can be saved to your course file <u>folder</u> in your computer.

Online Presentations

Of the course activities described in this chapter, online presentations are likely the adaptation most different from the traditional classroom activity. As a result, the use of online presentation is routinely limited and infrequent, often because the instructor is unfamiliar with strategies for making online presentations a successful teaching tool. When required, online presentations however are rarely done in a synchronous format unless being done with video or audio conferencing equipment. More commonly online presentations will require the sharing of Microsoft PowerPoint slide presentations that contain limited amounts of audio information.

Before the online presentation

❑ Review the guidelines.

Make note of software requirements, submission instructions, as well as requirements for presentation content.

❑ Plan your success.

Establish a plan for completing the online presentation. Managing your time is essential since the development of a successful online presentation often requires more time and effort than your typical classroom presentation.

❑ Confirm that you have adequate software.

Verify that you have the appropriate software for completing the presentation.

❑ Select a screen resolution of 800x600.

In order for the most number of fellow students to be able to properly view your presentation, you may want to set you your screen resolution to 800x600 prior to developing your presentation materials (especially Microsoft PowerPoint files that will be saved in the HTML format). This will be the most compatible screen resolution setting for most presentation software applications and computers.

❑ Send files 24 hours in advance.

`Hot`

At least 24 hours prior to your presentation you should provide any materials that you want other students or the professor to review or use during the presentation.

During the online presentation

❑ Confirm that everyone has a copy of your presentation.

Especially if you are going to be conducting a video or audio conference to accompany the slide presentation, make sure that everyone can view the slides before starting.

❏ Use the technology.

While presentation slides for the traditional classroom presentation should typically be limited to 5 words per line and 5 lines per page (providing minimal information that is significantly expanded upon by the presenter), online presentation commonly requires additional information in the presentation slides. Depending on the amount (i.e., length) of audio that will be incorporated with the online presentation slides (commonly limited to 10-15 seconds per slide with no more than 60-90 seconds for the entire presentation), the amount of information contained on the slides should vary.

`Hot`

❏ Avoid animated slide transitions.

Microsoft PowerPoint animations and slide transitions are generally lost when the presentation is saved to an HTML file format (and often when opened on a computer using a previous version of the software). As a result, do not spend a great amount of time working with these features.

❏ Use some personalized audio.

You can attach audio to accompany your online presentation slides. Audio dialogue to accompany the presentation slides can be inserted into a Microsoft PowerPoint presentation (this function is found in the "insert" pull-down menu of PowerPoint). Since audio files are large they should be used sparingly to provide information that requires additional explanation beyond the content of the presentation slides.

❏ Save as a PowerPoint Show (.pps).

You can save Microsoft PowerPoint presentations as a PowerPoint Show (or .pps) file that will automatically start for viewers in the full-screen presentation format.

❏ Save as a Hypertext Markup Language (.html or .htm).

You can save Microsoft PowerPoint presentations as a PowerPoint HTML (.html or .htm) file that can be used as a Website containing the presentation slides.

`Hot`

❏ Offer guidelines for asking questions.

If you are participating in a live audio or video conference to supplement the presentation slides then you provide participants with guidelines for asking questions.

After the Online Presentation

❏ Review.

Consider the feedback provided by the instructor.

❏ Follow-up.

After completing the online presentation, <u>email</u> follow-up questions and comments to your professor and/or classmates as appropriate.

❏ Improve your performance.

Identify strategies that would improve your performance the next time you are required to give an online presentation. Write these down in a document that can be saved to your course file <u>folder</u> in your computer.

Online Readings

While the typical college experience will introduce you to a variety of technologies (e.g., synchronous <u>chat</u>, <u>asynchronous</u> <u>discussion board</u>s, etc.), to be successful in most courses you will still want to be a proficient and effective reader. Increasing your comprehension when reading online materials is crucial to your success in any online learning experience.

Before you read

❏ Review.

Prepare for completing online readings by reviewing the required and recommended reading lists provided by the instructor.

❏ Determine the context.

Examine the required list of online readings (as well as other readings) within the context of the semester. This can provide you with a context for how readings relate to previous and future topics to be covered in the course.

❏ Select a preferred monitor resolution.

Experiment with varying monitor resolution settings (such as, 640x480, 800x600, or 1024x768 pixels) to determine which is best suited for your reading preferences.

❏ Create a good study environment.

For example, turn off the television, ask your roommates not to interrupt you, turn off instant messenger programs, etc. (See chapter 4.)

❏ Create a good reading environment.

For example, select a comfortable and supportive chair, as well as a computer set at the correct height. (See chapter 4.)

❏ **Confirm that you have adequate software.**

Verify that you have the necessary software for viewing online readings in the multiple formats that may be required (for example, Microsoft Word and Internet Explorer, Adobe Acrobat PDF, Netscape Navigator, etc.).

While you are reading

❏ **Define your goals.**

Based on the context of the reading within the course you should determine goals for reading the materials, making special note of specific information that you have learned by the time you complete the reading(s).

Hot

❏ **Identify the purpose.**

There are typically four potential purposes for reading: (1) understanding and comprehension, (2) evaluating critically, (3) practical application, and/or (4) pleasure.[2]

❏ **Preview.**

Examine the entire reading before starting a detailed read.

❏ **Select an appropriate pace.**

Determine an appropriate pace for your reading. For example, when reading detailed technical information, in order to better understand and comprehend the material, it may take more time than reading similar material for practical application.

Hot **Hot**

❏ **Become an active reader.**

Ask questions of yourself and take notes as you read through the materials.

❏ **Make a list of questions.**

Identify a list of questions that you should be able to answer when you have completed the reading.

❏ **Look for a pattern.**

When reading materials it is often useful to look for patterns in the text (such as, chronological, place, cause-effect, comparison-contrast, etc.).

☐ Take notes on the computer.

Depending on the permissions authorized by the creator of an <u>Adobe Acrobat PDF</u> document you may be able to take notes directly on the document. These notes will appear as sticky notes on the document and will not alter the original information. When using Microsoft Word you can add comments, which will appear to the right or along the bottom of the document (this function is found in the "insert" pull-down <u>menu</u> of Word). You can also take notes in a separate <u>word processing</u> file.

#6

#9

☐ Track changes.

When using Microsoft Word you can keep track of modifications made to the document by you and other viewers. The insertions or deletions of others will be illustrated in multiple colors depending on the viewer. This function, called "track changes" is found in the "tools" pull-down <u>menu</u> of Word.

STUDENT-TO-STUDENT TIP

To understand the concept of a Adobe Acrobat PDF file I like to think of it as a photograph of a document. You can not edit the file but you may attach comments to the text. The comments appear as sticky notes on the file.

☐ Review section titles and headings.

Use of the section titles and headings to provide clues as to the major concepts or ideas will allow you to focus on the broad content rather than specific words of each sentence.

#5

☐ Read the introductions and summaries.

Hot

Utilize the introductory and concluding paragraphs as guides for your reading.

☐ Keep a dictionary nearby.

Don't let a limited vocabulary reduce your understanding of the materials. You can also keep a <u>word processing</u> program (such as Microsoft Word) running on your computer in order to utilize its thesaurus (shift + F7) for words that may be less familiar.

☐ SQ3R.

Use the SQ3R process for increasing reading proficiency: Survey, Question, Read, Recite, Review. (See Pauk, 2000; Ellis, 2003.)

☐ Take reading breaks.

When reading from a computer monitor, take reading breaks at least every 30 minutes to rest your eyes.

After you read

`Hot`

❏ Review your questions.

Evaluate your notes on the reading to determine if you are able to answer the questions that you intended to answer by completing the reading.

❏ Review your notes.

Look over your notes for completeness, accuracy, and usefulness before closing the reading materials. Analyze the outline structure underlying your notes in comparison to the reading materials that you have just completed.

❏ Keep a record.

When permitted, save copies of online reading, along with your notes, for later review.

`Hot`

❏ Improve your performance.

Identify strategies that would improve your performance the next time you are required to complete online readings. Write these down in a document that can be saved to your course file <u>folder</u> in your computer.

Online (or Electronic) Portfolios

Online (or electronic) portfolios are increasingly becoming the means of demonstrating your skills, experiences, and accomplishments in college courses. These collections of assignments and activities, saved in their electronic format either as files on a disk or links on a personal portfolio <u>Webpage</u>, provide the professor with multiple measures of what you have learned and what skills you have gained in the course.

Before you create a portfolio

❏ Review the guidelines.

Instructors will commonly provide you with specific guidelines for online (or electronic) portfolios, including descriptions of each element that must be included as well as grading criteria.

❏ Examine sample portfolios.

Find out if sample portfolios from previous semesters are available to illustrate the instructor's expectations.

`Hot`

❏ Create a look-n-feel.

Establish a look-n-feel for your portfolio at the beginning of the semester (including color schemes, margins, fonts, and so forth). Use this for all word processing documents, Webpages, and other files that you create for the course.

☐ Confirm that you have access to adequate software.

Determine which software applications will be required for creating the elements of the online portfolio (such as, Microsoft Word, Adobe Acrobat PDF, etc.).

☐ Identify any additional hardware requirements.

Determine if additional computer devices will be required for creating the elements of the online portfolio (such as, a scanner, a digital camera, etc.). Often you will be able to check these out from a campus computer lab for use in class projects.

☐ Confirm adequate storage space on the college's server.

For an online portfolio, verify that you have adequate space on your college's or university's server for storing the many elements of the portfolio.

☐ Ask for help in creating Webpages.

`Hot`

If you are unsure of your skills for creating the necessary Webpages for an online portfolio, contact your college's or university's technical support services to identify any training that may be available to students.

While you are preparing a portfolio

☐ Back-up files.

When creating the elements of your online (or electronic) portfolio be sure to keep back-up copies of all files.

☐Follow through with your look-n-feel.

Throughout the semester design all of your assignments and activities to adhere with the look-n-feel that you have selected for your portfolio (including color schemes, margins, fonts, and so forth). Though you may not use every assignment or activity for your portfolio, this will save you time.

☐ Develop a structure for linking Webpages.

`Hot`

For an online portfolio, develop an initial Webpage that will link the viewer to the various elements of your portfolio. Produce this Webpage early in the semester and include the other elements of your online portfolio throughout the semester. Do not leave the creation of the online portfolio until the end of the semester.

❏ **Review grading criteria.**

Throughout the semester you will want to make sure that you are on target for success by reviewing the grading criteria since online (electronic) portfolios often have multiple elements.

After you have created a portfolio

❏ **Keep a record.**

Create a back-up copy that includes all the elements of your online (or electronic) portfolio.

❏ **Review the submission requirements.**

Before submitting the online (electronic) portfolio, examine the submissions requirements to make sure that you are making the project available to the instructor in the <u>file format</u> they require.

❏ **Improve your performance.**

Review the portfolios of other student to identify strategies that would improve your performance the next time you are required to develop an online (or electronic) portfolio. Write these down in a document that can be saved to your course file <u>folder</u> in your computer.

#20

#27

Turning in Assignments Online

Using online tools for submitting assignments and activities is quite common at most colleges and universities. Online submissions of coursework typically requires that you turn in the necessary file(s) by attaching them to an <u>email</u> message or by "uploading" them to an <u>educational portal</u> (such as WebCT or BlackBoard). From saving printing costs to flexibility in where you are when you submit the coursework, turning in files online has many advantages for you as a student.

Before turning in assignments online

❏ **Review the assignment requirements.**

Especially take note of the required file format, file-naming guidelines, and submission process desired by the professor.

❏ **Don't submit anything that hasn't been reviewed.**

Ask a friend, roommate, or classmate to review the final draft of any assignment or activity before submitting it to your instructor for grading. This will help you avoid a variety of errors that may cost you points.

While turning in assignments online

❏ Describe <u>attachments</u>.

When attaching an assignment or activity to an <u>email</u>, include a description of the assignment or activity being submitted, the name of the file being submitted, as well as the software application used to create the file (such as Microsoft Word or <u>Adobe Acrobat PDF</u>).

❏ Submit only once.

When "uploading" an assignment or activity to an <u>Internet</u> portal, click on the "submit" button only one time.

❏ Stay calm even if the technology doesn't work.

If a problem does occur with your technology, do not panic. Take careful notes of what has occurred and immediately <u>email</u> your instructor letting them know the specifics of the situation. Be sure to identify any error messages or other information that may have been provided.

❏ Check dates on files.

Double check that the file(s) you are submitting are the most recent and the ones that you intended to submit.

❏ Name the file with useful information.

Following any file-naming protocols provided by the instructor. For example, in the <u>file name</u> of each file you submit for grading, you may be required to include your name, the assignment number, your course section number, and/or the date. (See chapter 2.)

❏ <u>Back save</u> when necessary.

Often professors will require that you <u>back save</u> your files to a previous version of the application (for example, saving a Word XP file as a Word 2000 file instead). If this is required be sure that you do this before submitting the file for grading.

After turning in assignments online

❏ Follow-up.

For the first assignment or activity of the semester you may want to <u>email</u> your instructor letting them know that you have submitted the file (include the time and <u>file name</u> with the <u>email</u>). Once you have successfully submitted a file this verification is no longer necessary.

❏ Keep a record.

Save a back-up copy of all files that you submit for grading.

❏ **Patience is a virtue.**

If you do not receive immediate feedback regarding the assignment or activity, do not panic. Depending on the size of a class and the length of the assignments, grading can commonly take upwards of a week for many professors.

Hot

❏ **Keep track of your grades throughout the semester.**

Plan two or three times during the semester to review the online grade book for each of your courses. If grades are missing for assignments or activities that you have submitted weeks previously you should contact your instructor. You do not want to wait until the last week of classes to verify your grades.

Online Whiteboards

Success in most college courses requires that you effectively communicate with your classmates and professor. Often visual images can be used to avoid miscommunications, convey mathematical formulas, illustrate a relationship, and/or improve comprehension. The online whiteboard is the Internet's adaptation of the traditional classroom chalkboard.

Before using an online whiteboard

❏ **Determine your goals.**

Before selecting an online whiteboard as a tool for communicating with your classmates or instructor, determine which messages (or what information) is best expressed through illustrations on the online whiteboard.

Hot

❏ **Practice.**

Rehearse using the online whiteboard before selecting it as a tool. Using a computer's mouse to draw can be tricky, to say the least.

❏ **Consider a drawing tablet.**

If you are going to use the online whiteboard extensively in communicating with others, consider purchasing a drawing tablet. Shaped like a pencil and piece of paper, drawing tablets perform the functions of a computer's mouse while providing for accurate and detailed representations.

While using an online whiteboard

Hot

❏ **Use to add to discussions.**

Online whiteboards should be used when you consider it to be the most effective and efficient way to communicate a message. It is often best used as a supplement to other synchronous or asynchronous discussions.

❏ Make use of set shapes.

The set shapes (for example, circles, stars, squares, etc.) can be useful in drawing many illustrations and easier than drawing those shapes by free-hand with a mouse or drawing tablet.

❏ Vary your colors.

Use the multiple colors available in most online whiteboards to im-prove the effectiveness of your communications.

❏ Add text.

Commonly you want to add text to your online whiteboard illustra-tions, do this using the computer keyboard rather than drawing letters by freehand.

❏ Cut-and-paste.

Hot

Most online whiteboards allow you to cut-and-paste (or upload) images (such as pictures, PowerPoint slides, and others) to the whiteboard. You can then add to those images using the whiteboards tools.

❏ Save before starting a new illustration.

Save all illustrations before beginning subsequent drawings.

After using an online whiteboard

❏ Keep a record.

Save copies of the images you have created in the whiteboard. Often you will want to email copies of these images as attachments to others that participated in the online conversation.

❏ Improve your performance.

Identify strategies that would improve your performance the next time you use an online whiteboard. Write these down in a document that can be saved to your course file folder in your computer.

E-research

In the past most college students would spend hours in the library each week searching for resources for their coursework. For you, however, online technologies can be effectively used to provide flexibility in where you con-duct your research as well as reduce the amount of time necessary for find-ing the resources you require.

Before doing online research

`Hot` `Hot` ❏ **Identify objectives.**

Prior to conducting research online you should establish a list of objectives for the research. What information do you want to have when you have completed your research? What questions do you want to have answered when you have completed your research?

`Hot` ❏ **Determine what will be of value.**

Decide what types of information are going to be of the most value to you (such as empirical research, eye-witness accounts, statistics, narratives, rationale arguments, and so forth).

❏ **Select resources of value.**

Establish what types of resources are going to be of the most value to you based on the information you want to find (such as academic research journals, trade publications, books, magazines, statistical databases, and so forth).

`Hot` ❏ **Contact the library.**

Get in touch with your college or university library to determine which services and resources they have available online. Typically some services and resources will be available online (such as searching databases for journal articles and books), while others will only be offered on campus (such as access to recent journals or copies of most books).

❏ **Get training.**

Many college and university libraries provide training for students on using the many resources they have available, both online and on campus. Take advantage of these opportunities early in the semester. Often, online tutorials will also be available to students to supplement training provided by the library.

❏ **Review guidelines.**

Look over the specifications of the assignment or activity related to the research to determine requirements and expectations (for example, are you expected to reference at least five journal articles?).

`Hot` `Hot` ❏ **Don't plan to use online resources exclusively.**

Although you will want to use the online resources to supplement and reduce the research you will still have to do at a library, you should not expect to conduct all of your research online for a course assignment or activity.

While doing online research

❑ Evaluate all resources.

Information obtained from online resources, like online databases and Webpages, is often reliable but should also be evaluated with the same criteria as for print sources (see chapter 2).

❑ Expand your search.

Use search tools (such as, "and", "or", "not", "-", "+", etc.) to expand your search capabilities. (See chapter 2.)

❑ Use general searches along with database searches.

Search the World Wide Web for articles as well. Often journal articles that are not available in full text through online databases available through the library can be found online on journal Websites as samples or on the author's personal Webpage.

❑ Open links in new browser windows.

Save your starting point when exploring new links in new browser windows (right-click on the link and then select "open in new window").

#14

❑ Print sparingly.

Print only those pages that will be most useful to you. You can select individual pages to print by first previewing them in the print command of your Internet browser.

❑ Verify that you have accurate reference information.

Make sure that you have all of the necessary and correct information for resources you intend to cite in your coursework (such as the author, publication date, page numbers, accurate title, URL, date you accessed the Webpage, etc.).

❑ Don't forget outside resources.

Special libraries, government agencies, and advocacy groups make excellent starting points for topical research.

❑ Contact the author if all else fails.

If you cannot locate a journal article then you may want to search for the author's email address and inquire with them about receiving a copy of the article. Often they will be more than happy to provide you with a copy of their work in order to assist in your education.

❏ Don't be afraid to ask for help.

After significant attempts if you are still having problems finding useful information, contact your college or university library to seek the assistance of a librarian (or information specialist).

`Hot`

❏ Take careful notes.

Take notes about what you have learned from different online resources; often you will want to go back to information that you reviewed earlier.

After doing online research

❏ Review the resources.

Examine the resources you have obtained to ensure that they provide you with the necessary information for completing the assignment or activity.

`Hot`

❏ Double-check reference information.

Before leaving a <u>Website</u> or library verify that you have accurate citation information for all resources you plan to reference in the assignment or activity.

❏ Improve your performance.

Review your search strategies and identify ways to improve your online research techniques the next time you are required to conduct research for a course.

CHAPTER SUMMARY

Whether we realize it or not, each of us has a set of learning skills and study habits we use to succeed in the conventional classroom. Many of these skills and habits will, however, have to be transformed in order for you to have the same levels of success in an online course. In this case many of the skills you used in preparing for the classroom presentation will continue to be useful, although you will want to transform those skills for success in the new delivery system. The study tips offered in this chapter will help you adjust your learning skills, as well as develop new study habits, for being successful in online coursework.

As a review, for each of the following identify: (a) three things that you **will do** in the future, and (b) three things that you **won't do** in the future.

Real-time chat

Will do	Won't do
1.	1.
2.	2.
3.	3.

Discussion board

Will do	Won't do
1.	1.
2.	2.
3.	3.

Email message

Will do	Won't do
1.	1.
2.	2.
3.	3.

Email attachment

Will do	Won't do
1.	1.
2.	2.
3.	3.

Online exam

Will do	Won't do
1.	1.
2.	2.
3.	3.

Online reading

Will do	Won't do
1.	1.
2.	2.
3.	3.

Online research

Will do	Won't do
1.	1.
2.	2.
3.	3.

CHAPTER SEVEN   SKILLS CHECKLIST

After completing this chapter you should be able to do the following. If there are skills below that you may not be able to do, take a few minutes to review the chapter, focusing on those areas that you may have missed the first time through.

❏ I can effectively participate in online real-time chats.

❏ I am prepared to participate successfully in online discussion boards.

❏ I can organize and manage online group projects.

❏ I have the skills to successfully take online exams.

❏ I can make effective online presentations.

❏ I can use email to communicate with classmates and instructors.

❏ I know how to use a listserv to communicate in my courses.

❏ I am prepared to be an active reader.

❏ I can create an effective online (electronic) portfolio.

❏ I can turn in assignments online.

❏ I know how to use an online whiteboard.

❏ I can conduct online research for course assignment and activities.

❏ I know how to evaluate online resources for reliability, quality, and usefulness.

ADDITIONAL RESOURCES

Additional resources on topics covered in this chapter are available on the Website: **<http://collegesurvival.college.hmco.com/students>.**

NOTES

1. Based on Winograd and Moore, 2003.
2. Carter, C., J. Bishop, and S. Kravits. *Keys to Effective Learning.* 3rd ed. Upper Saddle River, New Jersey: Pearson Prentice Hall, 2002.

8

Getting Motivated, Staying Motivated

As we have discussed previously, the social network of an online student is one that must be developed intentionally through involvement with other students and the instructor. This social network, in most cases, also will serve as a foundation for the necessary motivation required to succeed in college. As distracting events occur you will want to have a motivational support system on which you can rely. From fellow students who provide encouragement when your grades aren't as high as you had hoped, to friends that won't push you to join the softball team when your studies must take priority, getting motivating and staying motivated requires the assistance of others.

In the end, however, your success in any college course is primarily your responsibility. Of course there will be some instances when an inexperienced online instructor may not provide sufficient support for your success, but in the majority of cases students that fail to succeed in college courses are not successful due to their own actions. In some cases they are not prepared for the demanding study schedule of online course assignments and activities, while in other cases they do not spend the time during the first weeks of the course to establish adequate study habits for preparing for online exams. Likely the most common reason for lack of success in a college course is, nevertheless, a decrease in the student's motivation as the course continues through the semester.

For many of us, the opening excitement of initially learning more about a topic can generate some unrealistic expectations. We can often over estimate the time we have available and even convince ourselves that we will be interested in all of the tedious facts that will be covered. Yet, when the reality of daily course requirements sets in (such as <u>discussion board</u> postings and online readings that take place during our favorite television shows), is when our motivation is most challenged.

> **STUDENT-TO-STUDENT TIP**
>
> Begin the semester with enthusiasm. Line up the sites you want visit, the books and articles you want to read, and the people you want to contact before you begin. Then, jump into the course.

Adding to the threats to your motivation will be some of the unique characteristics of online coursework. Many of the conveniences offered through online coursework may also present many motivational challenges. Ask any of your friends or colleagues who have tried working exclusively out of their home office about the challenges of staying motivated when your office (or classroom) is only steps from your bed or television. Likewise, while taking and completing online assignments and activities there will be many tempting distractions that aren't there while you are sitting in the classroom. Few conventional classrooms offer cable television, <u>instant messaging</u>, <u>email</u>, phone calls, and other distractions like those you will have while completing your assignments online.

Strategies for getting motivated and staying motivated will require your attention throughout any college course, especially in courses that use online technologies. In this chapter we will discuss strategies for finding and keeping your motivation throughout the entire course. After all, motivation that only lasts through the first few weeks is never enough to ensure that you are successful.

Selecting Courses

As a student it is most difficult to sustain your motivation throughout a semester when you enter a course with little or no motivation to be successful. It is possible that you will not be highly motivated for all of your courses in college. If you select courses in which your odds of success are low (see chapter 3), then finding and maintaining your enthusiasm throughout the course will however require additional attention and resources. Typically, your likelihood of success in a course is closely related to your motivation. Consequently, whenever possible you should select courses where your motivation is greatest.

For example, if your academic interests tend to provide you with more motivation in the applied sciences, then taking a theoretical physics course as an elective is likely to be more of a challenge to your motivation that semester than taking a course in applied physics. While you may not always be able to dictate what courses you take, if you have been successful in taking courses that utilize online technologies and you are given the option to take one of multiple course sections that is taught online, then you should consider your motivation in the course when making your decision.

Finding an Application

By enrolling in a course you are hopefully motivated to be successful; however, that may be defined within the context of your experience. Initial motivation to enroll in a course is unfortunately not enough to keep you motivated throughout the course and ensure your success. Finding the motivation to maintain your learning skills and study habits will often require different strategies throughout a course. Grades may motivate you at times, but at other points (often in the same course) career or personal ambitions may be the better motivator.

Hot

Throughout any college course you should try to link the topics you are studying to their application outside of the course context. Focusing on how the knowledge and skills you learn from your biology class will be useful to you as an environmental engineer after college can encourage you to maintain your concentration when studying for an exam. Likewise, linking any course topic to other personal interests can be useful to maintain motivation. For example, though you may not be interested in a career in journalism, learning to communicate effectively through writing will likely be a useful skill even if you intend to practice sports psychology after you have graduated. Focusing on the impact that the course may have on your long-term goals may also help provide you with the enthusiasm necessary to be successful in English 101. And while the links may not always be as strong as the examples we have provided, trying to find a link can help sustain your motivation.

Keeping Your Goals in Mind

A mix of long- and short-term goals can provide a foundation for your motivation in college. Both your long- and short-term ambitions can be used throughout any college course to sustain your motivation since there will be times when graduating with honors doesn't have the same motivational impact as getting a better grade than your study partner.

✔ Link your long- and short-term goals to help ensure that using either as a source of motivation will keep you on the right path.

✔ Setting your goals in measurable terms will help you better assess where you are, where you want to be, and how to know it when you have arrived.

✔ Since most of us quickly forget the details of our goals (for example, do you recall the New Year's resolution that you set last year), putting your long- and short-term goals down in writing is an essential step in using them as a motivational strategy. When you write goals down, you are also more likely to stick with them until they are achieved.

✔ Keep a copy of the file with your goals on your computer's <u>desktop</u>, or print out a copy that can be posted on the bulletin board next to your desk. No matter where you keep the goals you should review them every few weeks to ensure that they remain fresh in your memory.

Developing Your Motivational Support System

You will want to develop a learning support system to lend a hand when finding the motivation to keep up with the course requirements becomes too much. Your support system may be made up of fellow students, co-workers, roommates, family, or just about anyone else who is willing to help you get and stay motivated in order to achieve success.

✔ At the beginning of each semester identify at least two individuals that you can rely on when your motivation slips. These should be responsible classmates, family, or friends that will encourage you to maintain successful study habits. Be sure to let them know that you may come to them during the semester for motivational support, this will help ensure that they can provide you with useful assistance when (and if) the time comes.

✔ Peer feedback is a crucial element to motivation. In developing your motivational support you should contact other students in your courses to exchange draft assignments and activities for review. By providing each other with supportive feedback, not only are you more likely to remain motivated but often you will also have greater academic achievement.

✔ Find a mentor that can help prepare and guide you throughout your college experience. Your mentor should not be your peer, rather he or she should be an experienced student who has a record of being successful in college courses and who is willing to commit time to helping you be successful. Most often you will want to select a mentor who has been successful in your major or a similar major since they will have experiences in the courses that you are taking.

✔ Motivation is a two-way street and you can't expect others to always provide the encouragement. You will also be called upon throughout your college experience to help others make difficult decisions and maintain their motivation. Be encouraging and help them to accomplish their goals as well.

| Hot |

ACTIVITY 8-1   Have you missed something?

As a review, read the following statements then circle *True* or *False* for each one.

1. **True–False**   By finding an application of course topics to your work or professional goals you can improve your motivation.

2. **True–False**   A mentor should be a peer with about the same amount of experience in college courses as you have.

3. **True–False**   You are more likely to achieve goals that you have written down.

4. **True–False**   Your friends and family should know about the study habits you plan to use to be successful in your college courses.

5. **True–False**   If you are motivated at the beginning of the semester you will stay motivated until the end the semester.

Visualizing Your Success

Visualizing your success doesn't necessarily mean that you should close your eyes and picture yourself walking across the stage at graduation dressed in the valedictorian's gown. Though many students use literal visualization as an effective motivational strategy, you can simply focus your thoughts on many of the benefits of your pending success and still find the necessary inspiration to succeed. This type of visualization is more analogous to what most of us do when purchasing a lottery ticket for a multi-million dollar prize. We daydream about the luxurious life we will live after we have won that week's lottery drawing. In the same manner we can daydream (i.e., visualize) about our success in college.

Communicating with Your Instructor

Your instructor will typically be an excellent source of motivation. They will not only know you personally through the course, but they will also know your past performance, upcoming course requirements, and have a general understanding of why the topics covered in the course should be of interest. All of which can be useful in improving your motivation throughout the semester.

Hot

✔ When you are struggling to sustain your motivation <u>email</u> your professor and ask a few questions that may be helpful in revitalizing your motivation. For example, in a college algebra course you could ask the instructor to suggest any books that would provide you with exercises and examples of college algebra within the context of your major, business management.

#24

✔ Request feedback from the instructor on your performance in the course at any point in the semester. Do not wait until the final week of classes to determine what grade you will have to get on the final exam in order to be successful. By maintaining a running approximation of your grade throughout the semester you can hopefully avoid a "helpless" situation where your likelihood of success is minimal.

#31

✔ If family or other personal illnesses result in reduced motivation during the semester you should contact your instructor immediately. Often instructors are willing to make individual arrangements that may reduce your stress levels and improve your motivation. In addition, most colleges and universities offer a variety of support services (from counseling to tuition refunds) on which your instructor should have information.

Being an Active Participant

Hot Hot

Likely the most useful strategy for sustaining enthusiasm throughout the semester is to remain an active participant in the course. When you have fallen behind or lost touch with other students in the course it is often difficult to revive the motivation you had at the beginning of the course. Throughout the semester remain involved in course discussions, group projects, and other activities since these will each help you sustain your motivation. Asking questions, providing valuable comments, and organizing study groups are all techniques for maintaining your connection to the course.

Rewarding Yourself Throughout the Semester

Nothing is as rewarding or fun as celebrating our successes. So why wait for the end of the course to celebrate? Set intermediate goals throughout the course that will provide you with milestones. Milestones that when accomplished successfully are worth celebrating. If you receive an "A" on the midterm, enjoy an evening at the movie you have been waiting to see (with a big bag of popcorn, of course). Master the skills necessary for uploading new <u>Website</u> graphics; treat yourself to your favorite ice cream.

E-learning Experiences

Throughout elementary school I participated on a variety of little league baseball teams, none of which ever managed to win more than a game or two per season. Since my teams were always so bad, my parents could not wait to celebrate until my team won a game (at the time my favorite way to celebrate my successes was a trip to Dairy Queen for ice cream). If they had, I would still be waiting for my ice cream. Therefore they found the little things to reward; I didn't strike out after the first three pitches or I stopped the ball from going behind me in the outfield. Now for those on the winning teams, these wouldn't have seemed like events worth celebrating, but to me they would be the highlights of my baseball career. And though I didn't go on to participate in high school or college sports, one of the lessons I learned from those early experiences was to reward yourself whenever you can.

The same is true in college; you should celebrate even the smallest victories. Whether it is going out with friends after you finish the research for your term paper, or having pizza when you get a B on your Physics lab report, treating yourself to something special (i.e., ice cream, a movie, a night out with friends) will you keep on top of your tasks and avoid procrastination.

Developing Healthy Habits

The health of your body is very influential in your motivation to be successful in college. Maintaining healthy habits like a balanced diet, consistent exercise, and adequate rest, are all essential ingredients to sustained motivation and a successful college experience. Consider for a moment how difficult it is to concentrate on your studies or keep a positive attitude about your courses when you have a cold or the flu.

✔ Review your eating habits every few weeks to determine if you are getting an adequate balance of nutritional foods. Stay away from eating too many fatty, sugary, or salty foods, and don't go on drastic diets that may not provide you with adequate nutrition.

✔ Exercise on a regular basis, and especially around times when you are studying long hours (such as, during end-of-the-semester exams).

 ✔ Manage your time to ensure that you are able to get sufficient amounts of sleep each night. At a minimum you should get at least 6 hours of sleep each night, and it is often best to sleep for regular periods each night (for example, always going to sleep between 10:00 and 11:00 P.M. and waking between 7:30 and 8:30 A.M.).

✔ Schedule routine visits to your doctor and dentist. Preventative medicine can keep you on track to success; after all the last distraction you want from studying for your mid-term exam is a toothache or other medical emergency.

Activity 8-2   Have you missed something?

As a review, complete the following statements by marking the correct phrase.

1. When you are having a hard time staying motivated in a college course, you should not...
   a. contact your instructor to get feedback and suggestions on your performance.
   b. put off doing any assignments or activities for the next week.
   c. talk to classmates about study strategies they are using to be successful.

2. In order to visualize your success in college courses you should...
   a. close your eyes tightly and meditate on quiz questions.
   b. play soft music in the background as you study.
   c. relax and think about accomplishing your goals.

3. To stay healthy and perform your best on your course assignments and activities, you should...
   a. adopt a diet with no fat or sugar.
   b. exercise regularly.
   c. try to stay up all night studying once a week.

CHAPTER SUMMARY

Finding and maintaining your motivation throughout the semester is essential for your success in college. By using the goals you have set for yourself as a guide and adopting several strategies suggested in this chapter, you can improve your motivation as well as create a support system of friends and family that offer encouragement when you struggle to stay motivated. No matter how excited you are about your college courses, at some point during your college experience academic or other events are likely to test your motivation for success. By planning appropriately and developing useful motivational habits with your study skills, you can overcome these obstacles to success and achieve your goals.

CHAPTER EIGHT   EXERCISE

To begin the exercise you will want to have access to the World Wide Web using a Web browser (such as, Netscape Navigator or Microsoft Internet Explorer, etc.). In addition, you will want to open a new document in a word processing program (for example, Microsoft Word).

STEP ONE: Using the Web browser access your course Website (or educational portal) using the login and password provided to you by the instructor or institution. When you have entered the course Website or portal you will want to enter the area that includes the course syllabus. Within the course syllabus identify the assignments and activities that will be used to grade your performance in the course.

STEP TWO: Copy-and-paste the course assignments and activities from the syllabus into a new word processing document. After each course assignment insert into the word processing document your goal for the assignment or activity (such as the grade you want to receive on the assignment or activity).

STEP THREE: For each assignment and activity identify a potential reward to give yourself when you successfully accomplish your goal. The rewards don't have to be big, but they should be something that you would consider to be a treat for being successful.

STEP FOUR: For each assignment or activity, identify at least one positive use for the knowledge or skills you are demonstrating. This can be a constructive use in another college course you are taking (or planning to take) or a valuable skill that you can (or will) apply in your profession.

STEP FIVE: Identify for the course at least two people (such as classmates, friends, family, etc.) that can help encourage you throughout the semester for the selected course.

STEP SIX: Review the above list whenever you struggle to stay motivated in the selected course.

CHAPTER EIGHT SKILLS CHECKLIST

After completing this chapter you should be able to do the following. If there are skills below that you may not be able to do, take a few minutes to review the chapter, focusing on those areas that you may have missed the first time through.

❏ I can find outside applications for the topics covered in my college courses.

❏ I am able to keep both my long-term and short-term goals in mind throughout the semester.

❏ I have a motivational support system that can encourage me.

❏ I have informed the members of my motivational support system of my goals and desired study strategies.

❏ I can visualize my success.

❏ I have the contact information for my instructor so I can contact them if I require feedback, questions answered, or encouragement.

❏ I am an active participant in my courses.

❏ I have adopted healthy eating, sleeping, and exercise habits.

❏ I have identified rewards that I can give myself throughout the semester when I am successful.

❏ I have completed the chapter 8 activities.

ADDITIONAL RESOURCES

Additional resources on topics covered in this chapter are available on the Website: **<http://collegesurvival.college.hmco.com/students>.**

References and Recommended Readings

Anderson, T. and H. Kanuka. *E-research: Methods, Strategies, and Issues.* New York: Allyn and Bacon, 2003.

Blanchard, K. *The One Minute Manager Meets the Monkey.* New York: Quill, 1989.

Ellis, D. *Becoming a Master Student.* 10th ed., New York: Houghton Mifflin, 2003.

Harnack, A. and E. Kleppinger. *Online: A reference guide to using Internet sources.* Boston: Bedford St. Martins, 2001.

McVay, M. *How to Be a Successful Distance Learning Student: Learning on the Internet.* Boston: Pearson Custom Publishing, 2000.

Pauk, W. *How to Study in College* . 7th ed. New York: Houghton Mifflin, 2001.

Wahlstrom, C., B. Williams, and P. Shea. *The Successful Distance Learning Student.* Belmont, CA: Wadsworth, 2003.

Watkins, R. "Are You Prepared to be a Successful Online Learner: An E-learner Self-Assessment." In Biech, E., ed. *The 2003 Pfeiffer Annual: Training.* San Francisco: Jossey-Bass-Pfeiffer, 2003.

Winograd, K. and G. Moore, *You Can Learn Online.* Boston: McGraw Hill, 2003.

Glossary[1]

Adobe Acrobat PDF: A suite of programs developed by Adobe Systems that allows you to place documents formatted by most any word processing (e.g. Microsoft Word), presentation (e.g. Microsoft Powerpoint), or desktop publishing (e.g. PageMaker) program to be read by users of different platforms (i.e., Macintosh or Microsoft Windows) and allows you to view a document exactly as the person wrote it. (Also see Tutorial 7 on page T16.)

Antivirus program: A utility that checks emails, memory, and disks for computer viruses and removes those that it finds. Since new viruses corrupt, you should periodically update the antivirus program's virus definitions on your computer; though some programs will now do this automatically over the Internet.

Asterisk: A character when used in a search of computer memory (such as when searching for a specific file on a CD-ROM) or the World Wide Web that acts as a wild card that can stand for any unspecified file name or search term.

Asynchronous: Communications that do not necessarily take place at the same time (such as, email, discussion boards, etc.).

Attachment: A file that is attached to an email or other Internet communication. The contents of an attachment usually do not appear within the body of the email message.

Back up: To copy files from one storage area (e.g., hard drive, floppy disk, CD-ROM) to another to prevent their loss in case of disk failure.

Back save: To save a file in a format that can be read by previous versions of the software application. For example, to save a document in Microsoft Word XP as a file that is compatible with Microsoft Word 1997.

Bookmark: A marker used in a program such as a Web browser or a help utility that allows you to go directly to a specific Webpage.

Discussion board (Bulletin Board System or BBS): An electronic communication system that allows users to leave messages, review messages, and upload and download software.

Chat (real-time chat, Internet relay chat, or IRC): To communicate in real-time (i.e., synchronous) on a computer network using typed messages. A person chatting with another person or group of people on the network (for example, the World Wide Web) types a message and waits for the other party to type in a response.

---

1. Definitions based on: Kleinedler, S. Ed. *Dictionary of Computer and Internet Words: An a to z guide to hardware, software, and cyberspace.* New York: Houghton Mifflin, 2001.

Ctrl (control key): A key on IBM PC and compatible keyboards that is pressed in combination with another key(s) to produce an alternative function (for example, "ctrl" + "c" will copy highlighted text).

Cookie: An item, such as a file, that is used to relate one computer transaction with a later one. For example, certain Webpages download small cookie files that hold information that can be retrieved by other Webpages on the site (such as, name, address, recent purchases, credit card numbers, etc.).

Coursework: The assignments, activities, research, exams, or other tasks that are required of students in successfully demonstrating their mastery of course topic.

Central Processing Unit (CPU): The part of a computer that interprets and executes instructions.

Cut-and-paste: To cut part of a document or a graphic file and then insert or paste it into another place in the document or into another document or file.

Desktop: In a graphical user interface, an onscreen metaphor of your work, just as if you were looking at a real desktop cluttered with folders full of work to do. The desktop consists of icons that show files, folders, and various documents.

Domain Name System (DNS): A database system that translates textual network domain names into numeric Internet addresses.

Download: To transfer a copy of a file from a central source to a peripheral device (such as, CD-ROM, DVD, etc.) or a computer. You can download a file from a network file server to another computer on the network (for example, from the World Wide Web) or from a discussion board.

Educational portal: An educational Website considered as an entry point to other Websites that commonly include online tools like grade books, real-time chat, discussion boards, online whiteboards, and other course resources.

Email: A feature that lets a computer user send a message to someone at another computer using the Internet. Email, or electronic mail, can duplicate most of the features of paper mail, such as storing messages in "in boxes" and "out boxes," message forwarding, providing delivery receipts, and sending multiple copies.

Emoticons: A combination of characters used in email messages, chats, or discussion boards to represent a human emotion or attitude (such as, happiness, laughter, sadness, etc.).

Field: In a database or on a Webpage, a space where a single item of information can be entered into a record. For example, name, address, telephone numbers, and other information.

File directory: A way to organize files into a hierarchical structure. The top directory is often called a root directory that is labeled with a letter (such as, "C:\" for a computer's hard drive, or "E:\" for a computer CD-ROM drive; though these can be set by the user to be alternative letters). All directories below the root directory are considered subdirectories and represent the file folders and files contained in the storage device represented by the root directory (for example, "C:\myfiles\assignment1.doc" would represent the file "assignment1.doc" in the "myfiles" folder on a computer's hard drive that is labeled with a "C:\" root directory).

File format: The format that a program uses to encode data on a disk. Some formats are proprietary, and a file so encoded can only be read by the program that has created the file. Today companies often share formats so that users can save files in one program in the format of another company's program (for example, in Microsoft Word you can save the file in the Corel WordPerfect file format).

File name: The name given to a file so that it can be distinguished from other files. In most operating systems you cannot include the following characters in a file name: " ' | \ / [ ] , ? * < >

Folder: In a graphical user interface, an organizing structure that contains multiple files and is analogous to a directory.

Footer: In word processing, printed information (especially title, page number, or date) placed in the bottom margin of a page and repeated on every page or every other page of the document (also see, header).

Groupware: Software that helps organize the activities of users in a group that uses a network (such as the World Wide Web). Examples of groupware include software that allows users to share calendars, plan meetings, distribute electronic newsletters, etc.

Header: In word processing, printed information (especially title, page number, or date) placed in the top margin of a page and repeated on every page or every other page of the document (also see, footer).

Homepage: The first screen containing information that you see when you arrive at a Website.

Host: A computer containing data or programs that another computer can access over a network (such as the World Wide Web).

HTML (hypertext markup language): A coding system used on the World Wide Web to format text and set up links between documents.

HTTP (hypertext transfer protocol): A protocol used by the World Wide Web to govern the transfer of data.

Icon: In a graphical user interface, a picture on the screen that represents a specific file, directory, window, or program.

Internet: A matrix of networks that interconnects millions of supercomputers, mainframes, workstations, personal computers, laptops, and hand-held devices. The networks that make up the Internet all use a standard set of communications protocols, thus allowing computers with distinctive software and hardware to communicate.

Listserv: A mailing list manager used for the distribution of email among the list's members.

Menu: An onscreen list of available options or commands. The options are usually highlighted by a bar that you can move from one item to another.

Menu bar: A horizontal bar that runs across the top of the screen or the window and holds the names of available menu options.

Modem: A device that converts data from digital signals to analog signals and vice versa, so that computers can communicate over telephone lines, which transmit analog waves.

Operating system: Software designed to control the hardware of a specific computer system in order to allow users and application programs to employ it easily. The operating system mediates between hardware and software applications.

Personal Digital Assistant (PDA): A lightweight, handheld computer, often featuring software applications that provide calendars, calculators, address books, and other useful resources. New models commonly have an internal modem and cellular phone to be used as a link to a larger computer or the World Wide Web.

Pop-up menu: A menu that appears on the screen in response to a user action (such as a right-click on the mouse) and is separate from the primary application menus.

Pull-down menu: A pop-up menu that appears directly beneath the item selected on a menu bar.

Real-time chat (Internet relay chat or IRC): A network of Internet servers through which individual users can hold real-time online conversations. Instant messaging is a type of real-time chat.

Search engine: A program that allows you to perform searches for data on the World Wide Web.

Server: In a network, a computer that stores files and provides them to other computers.

Shortcut: In Microsoft Windows, a file that points to another file (such as a software application, word processing document, or Webpage).

Signature: A short text message that can be automatically included at the end of each email and that contains contact information (such as name, address, phone number, email address, etc.).

Software: The programs, programming languages, and data that control the functioning of the hardware and direct its operations.

Surf: To browse through information presented on the Internet by casually following links you might think lead to something of interest.

Synchronous: Communications that take place at the same time (such as, real-time chats or instant messaging).

Thread: A series of messages on a certain topic that have been posted on a discussion board, typically using visual indicators to illustrate which messages are replies to which other messages.

URL (uniform resource locator): The specific name or identifier of a file on the World Wide Web.

Web Browser: A program, such as Microsoft Internet Explorer or Netscape Navigator, that allows you to find and access documents from anywhere on the World Wide Web.

Webpage: A file on the World Wide Web that is accessible using a Web browser.

Web portal: A Website considered an entry point to other Websites.

Web server: A computer on which server software has been installed and that is connected to the Internet, allowing the computer to accept requests for information using the HTTP protocol.

Website: A set of interconnected Webpages, usually including a homepage, generally located on the same server, and prepared and maintained as a collection of information by a person, group, or organization.

Window: A rectangular portion of a display screen set aside for a specific purpose.

Wizards: An automated instructional guide that is a feature of some Microsoft and other software applications. Wizards can provide application shortcuts for accomplishing specific tasks.

Word processing: The act or practice of using a computer to create, edit, and print out documents such as letters, papers, and manuscripts.

About the Authors

Ryan Watkins, Ph.D.

Ryan Watkins, Ph.D. is an Assistant Professor of the Educational Technology Leadership program at the George Washington University in Washington, DC. His doctoral degree in Instructional Systems Design is from Florida State University, and he has additional formal training in both change management and program evaluation. Ryan has designed and taught courses, both online and in the classroom, in areas of instructional design, needs assessment, research methods, as well as technology management. Previously, he worked as an assistant professor of instructional technology and distance education at Nova Southeastern University, and as a member of the research faculty in the Office for Needs Assessment and Planning at Florida State University. He is an active member of the International Society for Performance Improvement (ISPI) and has served as vice president representing the United States in the Inter-American Distance Education Consortium. (CREAD).

Ryan is a co-author of *Strategic Planning for Success: Accomplishing high impact results* (2003; Jossey-Bass), and *Useful Educational Results: Defining, prioritizing, and achieving* (2001; Proactive Publishing). He has published more than 35 articles on the topics of distance education, needs assessment, strategic planning, return-on-investment analysis, and evaluation. He also provides workshops and related consulting services on distance education, needs assessment, and strategic decision making. For more information please visit <http://www.ryanwatkins.com>.

Michael Corry, Ph.D.

Dr. Michael Corry is an Assistant Professor and Director of the Educational Technology Leadership program at the George Washington University. Dr. Corry is intimately involved with course design, delivery, and management of this pioneering program delivered via distance education. Dr. Corry's research interests include distance learning theory, distance learning policy, faculty development, asynchronous learning, the integration of technology into K-12 and higher education settings, instructional design, and human-computer interaction. He has numerous publications and presentations related to his research interests. He has also designed and delivered faculty development workshops involving technology. Dr. Corry holds a Ph.D. from Indiana University in Instructional Systems Technology. Before coming to the George Washington University he taught at Indiana University as well as at the high school level in Utah.

Acknowledgements

We would like to express our appreciation and gratitude for the encouragement we have received from our friends and family throughout the writing of this book. We would especially like to thank the following people for their support: Doug and Judi Watkins; Christina Gee; Monte and Julie Watkins; Deborah, Brandon, Rachel, Ryan, Murray and Donna Corry.

We are also grateful for the many colleagues and students that have participated in the development of the many strategies and tips that are found in this book, including the online students of the Educational Technology Leadership program at the George Washington University; Bill Booz, Diane Atkinson, Amy Lynch, Chih Tu, Bill Robie, Ralph Mueller, Mary Futrell, Stephen Joel Trachtenberg (all of the George Washington University); Doug Leigh (Pepperdine University); Roger Kaufman, Leon Sims, Dale Lick (Florida State University); Mike Simonson, Charlie Schlosser, Mary Ellen Maher, Sue Fassanella, Marsha Burmeister (Nova Southeastern University); Lya Visser, Jan Visser (Learning Development, Inc.); Atsusi Hirumi (University of Central Florida).

In addition we would like to acknowledge the colleagues that provided reviews of the draft manuscripts in preparation for the book. These include the following:

Marla Barbee, *South Plains College,* TX
Cecelia R. Brewer, *University of Missouri—Kansas City*
Elaine Gray, *Rollins College,* FL
Amy Hawkins, *Columbia College,* IL
Gary L. Heller, *University of Phoenix—Idaho Campus*
Dana Kuehn, *Florida Community College at Jacksonville*
Jennifer Lindquist, *Thomas University,* GA
Mary McKenna, *Kaplan College,* IA
Jennie Scott, *Pima Community College,* AZ
Robert A. Stuessy, *Midlands Technical College,* SC
Kimberly J. Verdone, *University of Pittsburgh,* PA
Kate E. Wrigley, *University of Connecticut—Storrs*

Lastly, we would like to express our gratitude for the support and guidance provided by the staff of Houghton Mifflin Corporation. Especially the following individuals who made significant contributions to this book, Mary Finch, Shani Fisher, Andrew Sylvester, and Tamela Ambush.

Contents

Tutorials

Overview of Tutorials

The purpose of this portion of this book is to provide you with tutorials for some of the most common tasks used in online learning. It provides guidelines on how to work both with Windows and Macintosh computers, Microsoft Word, Adobe Acrobat PDF, Microsoft Internet Explorer, Netscape, Blackboard and WebCT. It also provides a tutorial on how to troubleshoot problems that might occur.

The tutorials do not cover every aspect of each of these areas, but they address the most commonly used functions in online learning. Our hope is that you will use these tutorials as you are working on your computer and have them by your side.

The tutorials have been designed using step-by-step instructions along with pictures similar to what you will see on your computer. The tutorials were also designed using the most common versions of software. However, software versions change frequently. Therefore, your version of the software may be different than the one's pictured in the tutorials. If this is the case, don't fret, in most cases the tutorials will still provide you with the necessary guidance to help you out.

Check out the book's Website for updated and additional tutorials. The Website address is **<http://collegesurvival.college.hmco.com/ students>.**

HOW TO TUTORIAL

Checking your Computer's Hardware Profile in Microsoft Windows

Before starting a course with online course materials you should verify the hardware profile for your computer. This is important to know when installing software, trouble shooting technical problems, and verifying that you have the minimum configurations to participate in the online portion of your course. This tutorial is designed for Microsoft Windows 98 users, but may be applicable to other Microsoft Windows users as well.

1. To begin, in Microsoft Windows 98, double click on the "My Computer" icon on the screen or select it from the "Start" menu. A window should pop up that looks similar to the one below.

2. Double click on the "Control Panel" icon and a window should pop up that looks similar to the one below.

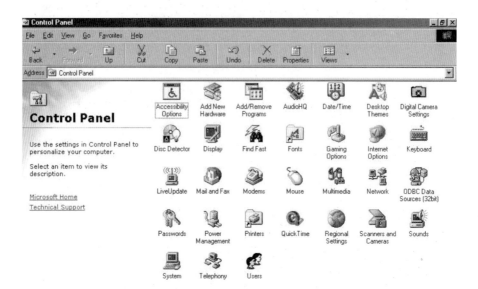

3. Scroll down (if necessary) and double click on the "System" icon and a window should pop up similar to the one below.

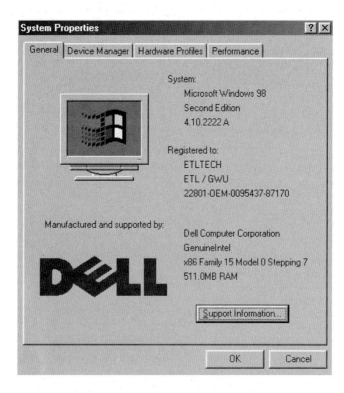

4. Note the four tabs across the top of this new window (General, Device Manager, Hardware Profiles, and Performance). Click on the "General" tab and you will find information about your operating system, system processor (chip), and RAM.

5. If you click on the "Device Manager" tab you should get a window that looks similar to the one below.

6. In the Device Manager you can find out a lot about the hardware in your computer. You can double click on any of the items on the list and you will find out more details about that device. For example, if you want to find out about your monitor, double click on the word "Monitors" in the list and you will get more information. You can do this with any of the devices on the list.

HOW TO TUTORIAL

Creating Folders and Staying Organized in Microsoft Windows

One of the nicest features of Microsoft Windows is the ability to create folders to organize and save your work. If you do not organize your files in some way, as you add more and more files to your computer it will be harder and harder to find what you are looking for.

1. To create folders and organize files begin by clicking on the "Start" button at the bottom left-side of the screen. Then select "Programs" from the list. Then select "Windows Explorer" from that list. A window should pop up that looks similar to the one below.

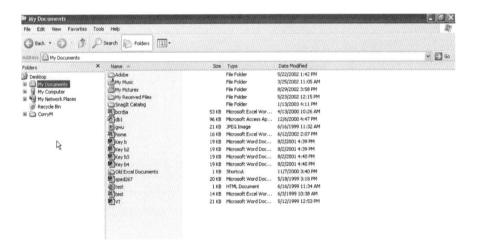

2. The window you are now seeing is divided up into two areas. The area on the left lists the drives and folders in your computer. The area on the right will be used to see the details of what is in each of your folders.

3. Since most of you will have a hard drive in your computer labeled the "C" drive, we will use that letter in our examples. If you know that your hard drive is a letter other than "C," then substitute that letter for the letter "C" in our examples.

4. In the left-hand side of the screen, try double clicking on the letter "C." It should expand and contract the list of current folders in your hard drive.

5. Now let's add a new folder that you will use to save files for a fictional course you are taking called "HMCO 101."

6. To create this folder click on the letter "C" in the left-hand side of the screen. Then single click on the "File" pull-down menu at the top left-hand side of the screen. Then single click on "New" from the list. Then single click on "Folder" from the list. It should look similar to the picture below.

7. Once you do this, on the right-hand side of the screen a new folder should be created titled "New Folder" and the cursor should be positioned on the title. At this point, you can simply type in the name you want for the new folder and hit the "Enter" key. For our example, why don't you type "HMCO 101" for the title and then hit the "Enter" key. You should then have a new folder on the right-hand side of the screen titled "HMCO 101" and your screen should look similar to the one on the following page.

8. Now that you have this new folder, you can save any files that you want into it. You can also move existing files into it by dragging and dropping them into your new folder.

HOW TO TUTORIAL

Checking Your Computer's Hardware Profile on a Macintosh Computer

Before starting a course with online course materials you should verify the hardware profile for your computer. This is important to know when installing software, trouble shooting technical problems and verifying that you have the minimum configurations to participate in the online portion of your course. This tutorial is designed for Macintosh users.

1. To begin, on your Macintosh computer, click on the "Apple" icon on the top left-hand corner of the screen. Then, click on the "Apple System Profiler" option.

2. Once you have clicked on the "Apple System Profiler" option, you should get a new window that has six tabs across the top (System Profile, Devices and Volumes, Control Panels, Extensions, Applications and System Folders).

3. Note the six tabs across the top of this new window. Click on the "System Profile" tab at you will find information about your operating system, RAM and system processor (chip), network configuration (if any), printer (if any) and ROM.

Tutorials

Creating Folders and Staying Organized on a Macintosh Computer

One of the most powerful options in a Macintosh computer is the ability to create folders to organize and save your work. If you do not organize your files in some way, as you add more and more files to your computer it will be harder and harder to find what you are looking for.

1. To create folders and organize files begin by double clicking on the "Hard Drive" icon on your screen. A new window should open up that lists the various folders on your Hard Drive.

2. Any folders that already exist in your hard drive are displayed in this window. Now you will be able to create new folders that you will use to save files for different purposes—for example, to organize files for a course that you are taking.

3. To create this folder, click on "File" pull-down menu located at the top left-hand side of the screen. Then click on "New Folder" option from the list. Once you do this, in the bottom of the window a new folder should be created titled "Untitled Folder" and the cursor should be positioned on the title.

4. At this point, you can simply type in the name you want for the new folder and hit the "Enter" key. Note that once you type in the new folder name and hit enter that the folder may then be moved into alphabetical order within the list of folders. Now that you have this new folder, you can save any files that you want into it. You can also move existing files into it by dragging and dropping them into your new folder.

Tracking Changes in a Microsoft Word Document

Microsoft Word contains a powerful feature that allows you to track changes made to a document. This feature, like adding notes, is mostly used when more than one person is reading and editing a document. In general, here's how it works. First, one person may write a paper. Then, a second person may review it and make some changes. If the second person uses "track changes," then all the changes they make to the paper will be marked in such a way that they are easy to identify. Then, when the first person gets the paper back, they can easily see what changes the second person has made to the paper. The first person then has the opportunity to either accept or reject those changes. As you can imagine this is very important when doing a group paper.

1. If you want to track the changes made by someone else in a Microsoft Word document, begin by opening the document. Once you have the document opened, click on the "Tools" pull-down menu from the top of the screen. Then click on the "Track Changes" option. Then select "Highlight Changes." Your selections should look similar to the screen below.

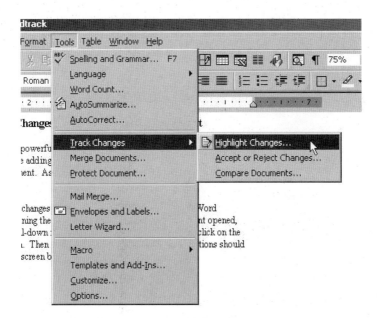

ee a window that looks something like the one below. At this
o the left of "Track Changes While Editing." Also, make sure

Tutorials

2. Now, you should see a window that looks something like the one below. In this window check the box to the left of "Track changes while editing." This turns on the track changes option. Also, make sure "Highlight changes on screen" is checked. This will enable you to easily see the tracked changes on the screen. The "Highlight changes in printed document" box is optional. This option allows you to see the tracked changes when you print the document. Click "OK" to turn on "track changes."

3. Now, try making some edits to your document. You will see two things happening. The first thing you will see is that all changes are underlined. The second thing you will see is that a horizontal line appears on the left-hand side of the page where the changes occur. This same thing will occur when someone else makes edits or changes to the document.

4. You can accept or reject changes to your document by clicking on the "Tools" pull-down menu from the top of the screen. Then click on the "Track Changes" option. Then select "Accept or Reject Changes." Your selections should look similar to the screen below.

5. Now, you should see a window that looks something like the one below. At this window you can move from "tracked change" to "tracked change" in your document and individually elect to accept or reject each change. You can also accept all the changes or reject all the changes at once. Click on the "Close" button when you are done.

Accept or Reject Changes		? ✕
Changes No changes selected. Use Find buttons or select a change.	**View** ⦿ Changes with highlighting ○ Changes without highlighting ○ Original	⬅ Find ➡ Find
Accept	Reject	Accept All	Reject All	Undo	Close

6. To turn off track changes in your document, click on the "Tools" pull-down menu from the top of the screen. Then click on the "Track Changes" option. Then select "Highlight Changes." A new window should pop up. At this window un-check the box to the left of "Track changes while editing" and click "OK." This will turn off track changes.

7. Please note that in order to have track changes on for the next person who reads the document, you should turn it on before you save your document, and then save your document.

HOW TO TUTORIAL 6

Adding Notes or Comments to a Microsoft Word Document

Microsoft Word has a powerful feature that allows you to add notes to the document. This feature, like track changes, is mostly used when more than one person is reading and editing a document. This is very useful when doing a group paper.

1. The Adding Notes or Comments feature of Microsoft Word gives you the ability to add comments to a document without actually changing the text. To do this start by clicking on the "View" pull-down menu at the top of the screen. Then click on the "Toolbars" option. Then click on the "Reviewing" option. Your selections should look similar to the screen below.

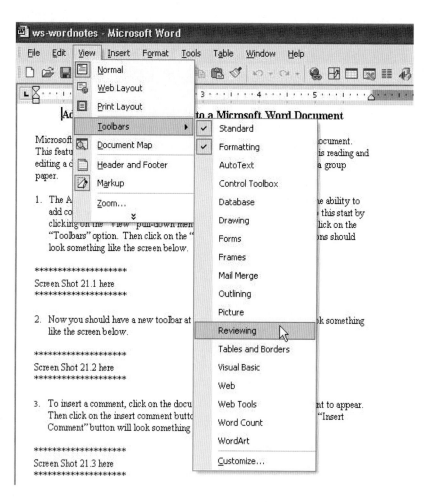

2. Now you should have a new toolbar at the top of your screen. It will look similar to the screen below.

Final Showing Markup   ▾ Show ▾ ⤵ ⤴ ↯ ▾ ⤬ ▾ 🗔 ▾ 📄 📥 ▾

3. To insert a comment, click on the document where you want the comment to appear. Then click on the "Insert Comment" button on the reviewing toolbar. The "Insert Comment" button will look similar to the one below.

4. Put your cursor in the document where you want the comment or note to appear, and then click on the "Insert Comment" button.

5. Type in your comment in the area provided and then click on the "Close" button. Your comment is now available for others to read.

6. To delete a comment, simply click on the comment and then click on the "Delete Comment" button on the reviewing toolbar. The "Delete Comment" button looks similar to the one below.

⤬ ▾

If you receive a Microsoft Word document that contains comments, you can identify them because their location will be highlighted. You can read the comment by placing your cursor over the highlighted area and leaving it there for a few seconds. The comment will then be displayed.

Understanding Adobe Acrobat PDF Software

Adobe makes a very useful piece of software called Acrobat that is used in many courses that have online components. The Adobe Acrobat software is used to create PDF files. Therefore, sometimes people call the software Adobe PDF or simply PDF software.

The Acrobat Software comes in two versions—the full version and the reader only version. The reader only version is free and can be downloaded from the Adobe Website <http://www.adobe.com>.

Many of you may already have downloaded this "reader-only" version of the software at some point because many documents on the Web can only be accessed if you have this reader. The "reader-only" version does exactly what you would think, it allows you to read Adobe Acrobat PDF files. But that is all it will allow you to do. It will not allow you to create your own PDF documents or to add personal notes to existing PDF documents.

The full version of the Adobe Acrobat PDF software does allow you to do many more things than just read PDF files. Two of the most important things it allows you to do are to create your own PDF documents and to add personal notes to existing PDF documents. Because the full version contains these important features, your course instructor may require that you have it to participate in the online portions of your course. If you need to purchase the full version of the software, please note that many times students will get a significant discount on the retail price of the software. Therefore, consult with your school's bookstore or computer store about getting the discounted price. Also, before you buy the full version of the software, you should consult with your school to find out if they already have it installed on certain computers on campus.

HOW TO TUTORIAL 8

Creating an Adobe Acrobat PDF Document

Many courses that are completely or partially online will require you to submit documents in Adobe PDF format. This format is used because it is a common interface that maintains the settings and formatting of your original document. Creating an Adobe PDF document is just like making a photocopy of a piece of paper. The only difference is that with PDF documents you make the copy completely digitally using your computer. Once you create an Adobe Acrobat PDF copy of your original document, then you can easily attach the Adobe Acrobat PDF file to an email and send it to another student or your instructor(s). You can also put your Adobe Acrobat PDF file into a Digital Drop Box in either Blackboard or WebCT. Note: This tutorial assumes that you have already properly installed the full version of Adobe Acrobat PDF Software to your computer.

1. To create an Adobe PDF document, start by opening the document you want to copy or convert into the PDF document. For example, if you have a paper that you wrote using Microsoft Word, you would open the file for the paper in Microsoft Word.

2. Once you have opened your Microsoft Word file, click on the "File" pull-down menu at the top left-hand side of the screen. Then click on the word "Print" in the list. You should get a screen that looks similar to the one below.

Print   ? X

Printer

Name:	HP LaserJet 1100 (MS) ▼ Properties
Status:	Idle Find Printer...
Type:	HP LaserJet 1100 (MS)
Where:	LPT1: ☐ Print to file
Comment:	☐ Manual duplex

Page range

- ⦿ All
- ○ Current page   ○ Selection
- ○ Pages: [   ]

Enter page numbers and/or page ranges separated by commas. For example, 1,3,5–12

Copies

Number of copies: [1]

☑ Collate

Print what:	Document ▼
Print:	All pages in range ▼

Zoom

Pages per sheet:	1 page ▼
Scale to paper size:	No Scaling ▼

Options...   OK   Cancel

3. In the window that appears, locate the white box to the right of the word "Name." The white box should have a down arrow in the right side of the box. Click on the down arrow and you should get a drop-down list similar to the one below.

4. Now, single click on the "Adobe PDFWriter" option on the drop-down list. That option should then appear in the white box. You have now told your computer that you want to print or create an Adobe PDF document of your file. To actually create the Adobe PDF file, click on the "OK" button.

5. After you click on the "OK" button, you should get a screen similar to the one below.

6. Since you are creating a file and not actually printing the document, your computer needs to know what you want to name the Adobe Acrobat file and where to save it. Therefore, on this screen, type in the name for your Adobe Acrobat PDF file and select the folder where you want it saved. Then click on the "OK" button.

7. After you click the "OK" button, Adobe Acrobat will automatically open your newly created PDF file so that you can see what it looks like.

HOW TO TUTORIAL  9

Adding Individual Notes to an Adobe Acrobat PDF Document

Adding individual or personal notes to Adobe Acrobat PDF documents can be a great way to share ideas or get feedback or grades on work you have done. Because of this reason, this is one of the most common uses of Adobe PDF file in online course work. *Note:* this tutorial assumes that you have already properly installed the full version of Adobe Acrobat PDF Software to your computer.

1. To add notes to an Adobe PDF document, start by clicking on the "Start" button at the bottom left-hand corner of the screen in Windows. Then click on "Programs." Then click on "Adobe Acrobat." Then click on "Acrobat Exchange." You should get a screen that looks similar to the one below.

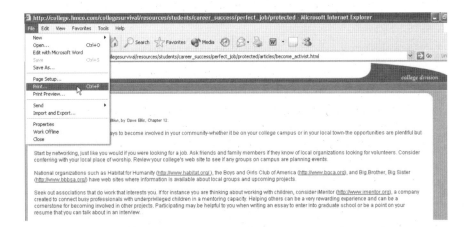

2. Once you have this screen, you need to open the file where you want to add a personal note. You can do this by clicking on the "File" pull-down menu at the top left-hand corner of the screen. Then select the "Open" option and then select the file you want to open and click on the "Open" button. This should open up the PDF document you wanted. For this example, we have opened up a document that looks similar to the one below.

3. Now let's add a personal note to this Adobe PDF document by find-ing the spot on the document where we want the note to appear. The personal note will act just like a "Post It" note. You will paste it on the document, but you will not actually change what is in the document. To add a note, start by clicking on the "Notes" button lo-cated on the taskbar near the top of the screen. The "Notes" button should look similar to the screen below.

4. At this point, your cursor should change shape and look like a crosshair. Once your cursor looks like a crosshair, position it where you want the note to appear and click and drag your cursor making a box about the right size for your note. You should get a window that looks similar to the one below.

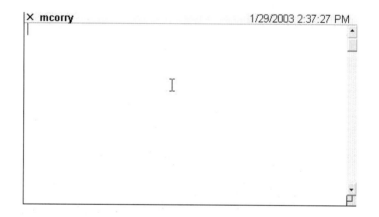

5. In this box, type your personal note. Once you are done typing your note, single click on the top left-hand corner of your note area and it will close up and look like a "Post It" note stuck to the document.

Creating an Adobe Acrobat PDF Document

Many courses that are completely or partially online will require students to submit documents in Adobe PDF format. This format is used because it is a common interface that maintains the settings, etc. of your original document. Creating an Adobe PDF document is just like making a Xerox copy of a piece of paper. The only difference is that with PDF documents you make the copy completely digitally using your computer. Note, this tutorial assumes that you have already properly installed the full version of Adobe Acrobat PDF Software to your computer.

1. To create an Adobe PDF document, start by opening the document you want to copy or convert into the PDF document. For example, if there was a paper you wrote using Microsoft Word, you would open the file for the paper in Microsoft Word.

6. You, or the person reviewing the document, can double click on the note to open it. You can also add additional comments by double clicking on it and typing. You can add as many individual notes throughout a document as you like.

7. Once you have added all the notes you like, make sure you save the document and notes by clicking on the "File" pull-down menu and selecting either "Save" if you want to keep the same name or "Save As" if you want to change the name of the file.

Saving Favorites in Microsoft Internet Explorer

In Microsoft Internet Explorer you can make a list of your favorite Web-pages so that you can easily find them again.

1. Go to the web page you would like to add to your "favorites" list.

2. Once you have the Website on your screen, click on the "Favorites" pull-down menu. It should look similar to the screen below.

3. Then click on the "Add to Favorites" option. This will add the Website to your list of favorite web pages. To go back and see if it was added, click on the "Favorites" pull-down menu and it should appear at the bottom of the list. If at any time in the future you want to visit the Website, simply click on the Website name in your "Favorites" pull-down menu and it will automatically take you there.

HOW TO TUTORIAL   **11**

Organizing Favorites in Microsoft Internet Explorer

Once you have started to create a list of your favorite Webpages in Microsoft Internet Explorer, you can do several things to help you keep the list organized.

1. Click on the "Favorites" pull-down menu.

2. Then click on the "Organize Favorites" option. You will get a window that looks similar to this:

3. All of your favorites and any folders containing favorites will be shown on the right hand side of this window. From this window you can create a new folder and give it a name. You can then put your links to your favorite web pages into that folder. For example, if you wanted to create a new folder you would begin by clicking on "Create Folder." Then a new folder will appear in the window. Then you would give the new folder a name. In this example, we have named this folder "Publishers". Now you have a new folder and can add some of your favorites to that folder. It should look similar to the screen on the following page.

Organize Favorites

To create a new folder, click on the Create Folder button. To rename or delete an item, select the item and click Rename or Delete.

[Create Folder]   [Rename]

[Move to Folder...]   [Delete]

New Folder
Favorites Folder

Modified:
2/26/2003 3:18 PM

- Channels
- Imported bookmarks
- Links
- Media
- Software Updates
- Graphics
- My Documents
- Temp
- Houghton Mifflin Company
- Publishers

[Close]

4. To add favorites to a folder, begin by clicking on the favorite and then clicking on "Move to Folder." A new window will appear which will look similar to this:

Browse for Folder

Click the folder that you want to move the selected files to.

- ⭐ Favorites
  - Channels
  - Imported bookmarks
  - Links
  - Media
  - Publishers
  - Software Updates
  - Temp

[OK]   [Cancel]

5. To move the favorite to the new folder, simply click on the name of the folder where you want to keep the favorite and click OK. The favorite will automatically be moved to the new folder. The only thing left is to click the "Close" button.

6. In the future, if you want to find your favorite web page, simply click on the "Favorites" pull-down menu and then click on either the favorite or the folder where the favorite is saved.

HOW TO TUTORIAL  12

Printing Lectures in Microsoft Internet Explorer

While working on the online portion of your course, you may find it helpful to print your lecture or course materials. This is important if you like to read at places other than your computer. Steps 1 and 2 will discuss how to print an entire Webpage. Steps 3 and 4 will discuss how to print a portion of the page.

1. To print lectures or course materials in Internet Explorer, start by going to the Website that has the materials and then clicking on the "File" pull-down menu at the top of the screen. Then select the "Print" option. Your selections should look similar to the picture below.

2. You will now have a window that looks similar to the one below. Click the "OK" button. This should print the Webpages you have open.

3. If you want to only print a portion of the Webpage, begin by clicking on the "File" pull-down menu at the top of the screen. Then select the "Print Preview" option. You should get a window that looks similar to the one below.

4. You can scroll through the printable pages using the right and left arrow keys. Once you have determined the page(s) you want to print, click on the "Print" button at the top left-hand corner of the window. You should get a window that looks like the "Print" window above. Instead of clicking on the "OK" button at this point, click on the blank circle to the left of the word "Page." Type in which pages you want to print and then click on the "OK" button.

HOW TO TUTORIAL

Caching Materials for Viewing Offline with Microsoft Internet Explorer

Microsoft Internet Explorer allows you to cache (or save) Web materials to view at a later time when you are not connected to the Internet. This is important if you want to cache online course materials and then read them at a different time.

1. To cache or save a Website to view offline at a later time, start by going to the Website you want to cache. Then click on the "Favorites" pull-down menu at the top of the screen and select the "Add to Favorites" option. You will get a screen that looks similar to the one below.

Add Favorite

Internet Explorer will add this page to your Favorites list.   OK

☐ Make available offline   Customize...   Cancel

Name: Houghton Mifflin Company   Create in >>

2. Click on the box to the left of the phrase "Make available offline" and then click on the "OK" button.

3. Before you log off of the computer click on the "Tools" pull-down menu at the top of the screen and then select the "Synchronize" option. You should get a window that looks similar to the one on the following page.

Tutorials

Items to Synchronize

To ensure that you have the most current data when working offline, you can have Windows synchronize the data on your computer and the data on the network so that both are up to date.

Select the check box for any items you want to synchronize.

Name	Last Updated
🔄 Offline Web Pages	
☑ 🌐 Houghton Mifflin Company	
☑ 🏠 My Current Home Page	

Properties

Synchronize   Setup...   Close

4. Make sure any of the Webpages you want to read offline have a check mark next to them, and then click on the "Synchronize" button. Internet Explorer will then take a couple of minutes to synchronize all the Websites you have selected.

5. Now, go to the "File" pull-down menu at the top of the screen and select the "Work Offline" option.

6. You can now log off of the Internet. At a future time, you can simply open Internet Explorer and select the Website you want to view from the Favorites list. Do this by clicking on the "Favorites" pull-down menu and selecting the Website you want to view. It will open up just as if you were connected to the Internet.

7. One note of caution—the next time you log onto Internet Explorer, make sure the first thing you do is to go to the "File" pull-down menu at the top of the screen and select the "Work Offline" option. This will switch you back to working online. If you don't do this, you will remain in offline mode.

Please note that the ability to cache materials to view offline is not available in Netscape.

HOW TO TUTORIAL   14

Opening New Windows in Microsoft Internet Explorer and Netscape Communicator

In Microsoft Internet Explorer and Netscape Communicator many times you will want to have more than one window open at the same time so that you can view more than one Website at the same time. This is possible by opening new windows.

1. To open a new window while in Internet Explorer or Netscape, start by clicking on the "File" pull-down menu at the top of the screen. Then select the "New" option and then the "Window" option in Internet Explorer or the "Navigator Window" option in Netscape. Your selections in Internet Explorer should look similar to the picture below. Your selections in Netscape (not pictured) are very similar.

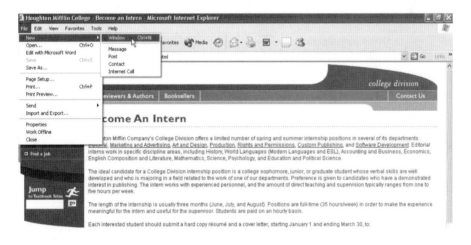

2. Now you should have a new window. The new window will initially look just like the one you left. However, you can type in a different web address and go to the new Website.

3. You can switch back and forth between Websites by clicking on the toolbar icons at the bottom of the page. The toolbar in Internet Explorer should look similar to the picture below. The toolbar in Netscape (not pictured) is very similar. The different Websites' icons have the Internet Explorer or Netscape symbol in front of them. Please note that you can have many Websites open at once.

HOW TO TUTORIAL

Saving Bookmarks in Netscape Communicator

In Netscape Communicator you can bookmark your favorite Webpages so that you can easily find them again. Bookmarking is a great tool because it saves you a lot of time by not having to search for Websites again and again. It also saves you time because you don't have to type in Website addresses. Here's how to bookmark a Website in Netscape:

1. Go to the Webpage you would like to add to your favorites list.

2. Once you have the Website on your screen, click on the "Communicator" pull-down menu. Then click on "Bookmarks." Your options should look something like the screen below.

3. Then click on the "Add Bookmark" option. This will bookmark the Website. To go back and see if it was bookmarked correctly, click on the "Communicator" pull-down menu and then "Bookmarks". The name of the Website you bookmarked should appear at the bottom of the list. If at any time in the future you want to visit the Website, simply click on the "Communicator" pull-down menu, select "Bookmarks," then click on the Website you want to visit and it will automatically take you there.

HOW TO TUTORIAL 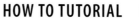 16

Organizing Bookmarks in Netscape Communicator

Once you have started to bookmark your favorite Webpages in Netscape Communicator, you can do several things to help keep the list organized.

1. Click on the "Communicator" pull-down menu and click on "Bookmarks."

2. Then click on the "Edit Bookmarks" option. You will get a window that looks similar to this:

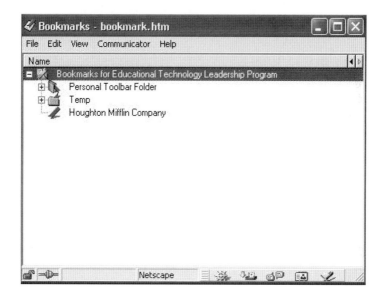

3. All of your bookmarked Websites and any folders containing bookmarks will be shown in this window. From this window you can create a new folder and give it a name. You can then put your bookmarks into that folder. For example, if you wanted to create a new folder you would begin by clicking on the "File" pull-down menu. Then you would click on the "New Folder" option. Then a new folder will appear in the window. Then you would want to give the new folder a name. In this example, we have named this folder "Publishers". Click OK and you now have a new folder and can add some of your bookmarks to that folder. It should look similar to the screen on the following page.

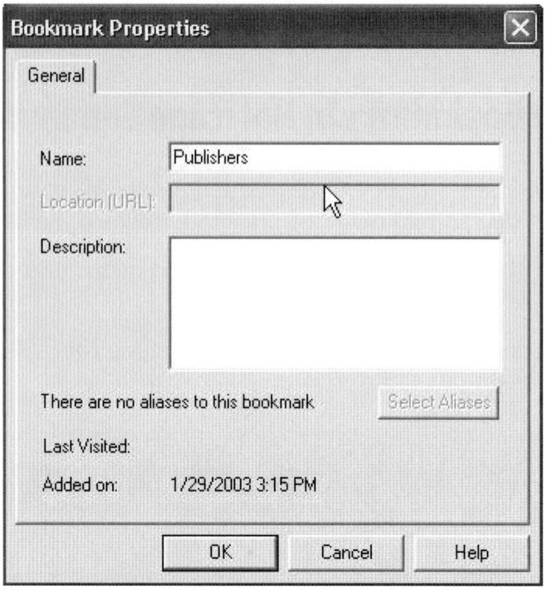

Bookmark Properties ☒

General

Name: Publishers

Location (URL):

Description:

There are no aliases to this bookmark   Select Aliases

Last Visited:

Added on: 1/29/2003 3:15 PM

OK   Cancel   Help

4.   To add bookmarks to a folder, begin by putting your cursor over the bookmark. Then click and drag the bookmark onto the folder where you want it to be saved. If we were to move a bookmark into the Publishers folder, the end result would look something like the window below. The only thing left is to do is click on the "File" pull-down menu and then click on the "Close" option and your bookmark will be saved in the new folder. It should look similar to the screen below.

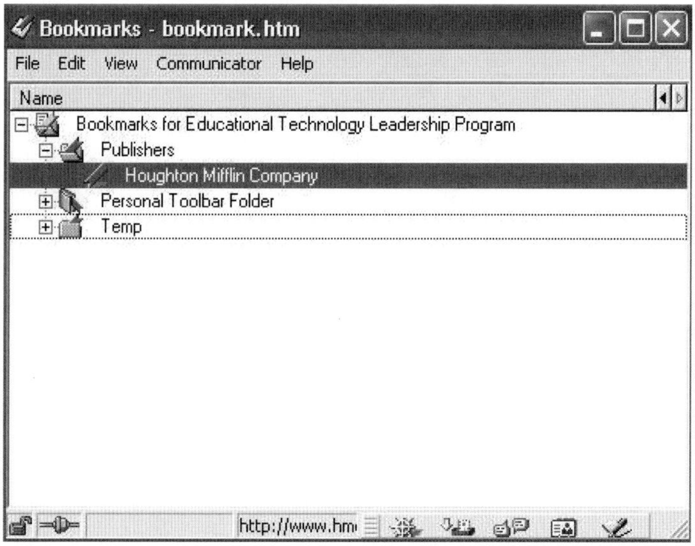

Bookmarks - bookmark.htm

File   Edit   View   Communicator   Help

Name

Bookmarks for Educational Technology Leadership Program
   Publishers
      Houghton Mifflin Company
   Personal Toolbar Folder
   Temp

http://www.hm

5. In the future, if you want to find your bookmarked web page, simply click on the "Communicator" pull-down menu and then click on "Bookmarks." Then click on either the bookmark or the folder where the bookmark is saved.

HOW TO TUTORIAL

Printing Lectures in Netscape Communicator

While working on the online portion of your course, you may find it helpful to print your lecture or course materials. This is important if you like to read at places other than your computer. Steps 1 and 2 will discuss how to print an entire web page. Steps 3 and 4 will discuss how to print a portion of the page.

1. To print lectures or course materials in Netscape, start by going to the Website that has the materials and then clicking on the "File" pull-down menu at the top of the screen. Then select the "Print" option. Your selections should look similar to the picture below.

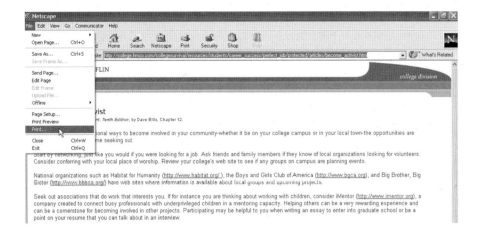

2. You will now have a window that looks something like the one on the following page. Click the "OK" button. This should print the web pages you have open.

Print

Printer

Name: HP LaserJet 1100 (MS)   Properties...

Status: Ready
Type: HP LaserJet 1100 (MS)
Where: LPT1:
Comment: ☐ Print to file

Print range   Copies

⦿ All   Number of copies: 1

○ Pages from: 1   to:

○ Selection   ☑ Collate

                    OK   Cancel

3. If you want to only print a portion of the web page, begin by clicking on the "File" pull-down menu at the top of the screen. Then select the "Print Preview" option. You should get a window that looks similar to the one below.

4. You can scroll through the printable pages using the "Next Page" and "Previous Page" keys. Once you have determined the page(s) you want to print, click on the "Print" button at the top left-hand corner of the window. You should get a window that looks like the "Print" window above. Instead of clicking on the "OK" button at this point, click on the blank circle to the left of the word "Pages." Type in which pages you want to print and then click on the "OK" button.

HOW TO TUTORIAL 18

Finding Your Course Materials in Blackboard

Once you have logged into your course in Blackboard, it is important to understand where you will find your course materials (announcements, calendars, lectures, etc.). The location of these items may vary from course to course, but there are some general guidelines you can follow.

1. To begin, start by exploring the buttons found on the left-hand side of the screen.

2. Below is a general idea of what you might find when exploring each of these areas.
   - Announcements—This link will include announcements from your course instructor and those people who maintain the Blackboard system for your school. These announcements can be very important, so check them regularly.
   - Course Information—This link is where you might find general course information like the name of the course, how many credits it is worth and when it meets.
   - Staff Information—This link will include information about your course instructor and teaching assistants. Check here for information about office hours.
   - Course Documents—This link is where you will find a lot of the materials relating to the course. These items are similar to course lectures such as papers you should read and lecture notes from your instructor.
   - Assignments—As indicated in the title, this link is where your assignments will be located. Obviously this is a very important part of the course site.
   - Communication—This link is where you will find things like how to send an email to your classmates or instructor, the virtual discussion board, the virtual classroom or chat, the class roster, and group pages.
   - Discussion Board—This link is a short cut to the same discussion board that you might find under the Communication button. The Discussion Board is very important because this is where you can share thoughts and ideas with everyone in the course by posting messages and replying to other's messages.
   - Groups—If you are assigned to a group, this link is where your group will access important information.
   - External Links—This link is where you will find external links to other Websites that are important to your course.

- <u>Tools</u>—This link allows you to do many things such as putting assignments into the digital drop box, editing your home page and personal information, maintaining your personal and course calendar, checking your grades, and keeping an address book.
- <u>Resources</u>—This link is a button that might link you to other general resources that may or may not be specifically course related. For example, some instructors might put recommended readings here.
- <u>Course Map</u>—This link will provide you with a map of what is in your course. Some people like to use this to navigate quickly through the material you are expected to cover in the course.

Tutorials

Sending an Email and Adding an Attachment in Blackboard

One of the most important items when working online is the ability to communicate with classmates and your instructor. A great way to do so is by using the email function in Blackboard.

1. To send an email using Blackboard begin by clicking on the "Communication" button located on the left-hand side of the screen.

2. Then in the middle of the screen, click on the option that says "Send E-mail." See the example below:

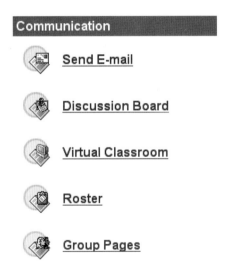

3. Once you have clicked on "Send E-mail," in the middle of the screen you will have several options about who to send your email to. For example, you might have the option of sending it to everyone in the class, or just a certain student or group, or to your course instructor.

4. If you want to send an email to your course instructor(s), begin by clicking on the "All Instructors" link. You should get a screen that looks like the following (but with your email address in the "From:" line and your instructor's name in the "To:" line).

5. At this point, you should fill in the "Subject" line of the email and the "Message" area. Now, before you send your email, there are other options also available to you including adding a file attachment to the email. If you wish to add an attachment to your email, click on the "Add" button under the "Add Attachments" section. If

All Instructors

❶ Enter Message Details

To: Corry, Mike; Designer, Blackboard; Vendor 2, HMCo;
From: mcorry@gwu.edu
Subject:
Message:

❷ Set Message Options

☐ Send Copy of Message to self

❸ Add Attachments

(Add)

❹ Submit

Click **"Submit"** to finish. Click **"Cancel"** to abort this process.

(Cancel)   (Submit)

you do not wish to add an attachment to the email, simply click on the "Submit" button and your email will be sent.

6. If you wish to add an attachment to the email message and you have clicked on the "Add" button under the "Add Attachments" section then you should have a screen that looks similar to this:

All Instructors

❶ Select File

Click "Browse" to select your file and then click "OK" to add the file to your message

[Browse...]

❷ Submit

Click **"Submit"** to finish. Click **"Cancel"** to abort this process.

(Cancel)   (Submit)

7. At this point, click on the "Browse" button and find the file you wish to attach. Once you have located and chosen the file to attach, the name of the file should show up in the box to the left of the "Browse" button.

8. Then, simply click on the "Submit" button and your email and attachment will be sent.

HOW TO TUTORIAL  **20**

Turning in Assignments in Blackboard

As you work your way through college you will probably be required to turn in assignments online from time to time. Many courses will have you do this using the Digital Drop Box in Blackboard. The Digital Drop Box is like a mailbox slot where you drop off items for your instructor.

1. To submit an assignment using the Digital Drop Box, begin by clicking on the "Tools" button on the left-hand side of the screen.

2. Then click on the option that says "Digital Drop Box."

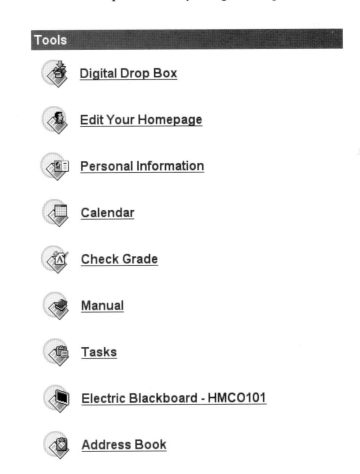

3. Once you have clicked on "Digital Drop Box," you should then submit your assignment to your instructor by clicking on the "Send File" button.

4. At this point, you should fill in the "Title" box and the "Comments" area with information about your assignment. At this point, click on the "Browse" button and find the assignment file you wish to send to your instructor. Once you have located and chosen the file to send, the name of the file should show up in the box to the left of the "Browse" button.

Digital Drop Box

❶ File Information

Select file: [- ▼]

OR upload new file:

Title: | Second Assignment |

File: | figure 2.3 | (Browse...)

Comments: | Here is my second assignment. |

❷ Submit

Click **"Submit"** to finish. Click **"Cancel"** to abort this process.

(Cancel)   (Submit)

---

5. Then, simply click on the "Submit" button and your assignment will be sent to your instructor and a message will be sent to your email account confirming that your assignment was sent successfully.

Tutorials

Participating in the Virtual Classroom or Chat in Blackboard

One of the most exciting things about Blackboard is the ability to have synchronous conversations with other classmates or your instructor using the Virtual Classroom or Chat function. Synchronous means that the conversations are occurring in "real" time with all participants in the chat room at the same time.

1. To participate in a Chat session, begin by clicking on the "Communication" button on the left-hand side of the screen.

2. Then click on the option that says "Virtual Classroom."

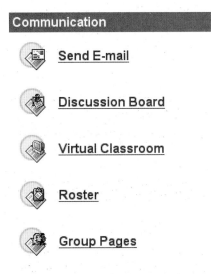

3. Once you have clicked on "Virtual Classroom" in the middle of the screen you will have two options—to enter the virtual classroom or to browse archives. To participate in a live chat session, click on the "Enter Virtual Classroom" link. You may get a message at this point indicating that it is loading the Chat software. This may take a couple of minutes. Once the Chat software loads, it should look similar to the screen on the following page.

4. At the top of the screen you can see the word "Location" and a blank box to the right of that word. You can go to a Website by typing in the Website address in that blank box. The Website will appear in the large white area below the word "Location."

5. At the left-hand side of the screen you have tools that you can use to draw pictures or make notations that everyone in the chat room can see. You can also draw or make notations on a Website. Take a minute to try out some of those tools by clicking on them and then drawing on the right-hand side of the screen.

6. To have a synchronous conversation with others who are in the chat room, simply type in your question or comment in the blank box at the very bottom of the screen and hit enter. Your message will then appear in the box just above where you originally typed it. The message will then be seen by everyone in the chat room.

7. To see everyone who is in the chat room click on the "user info" tab. On the left-hand side of the screen you will see a list of everyone who is in the chat room. You can click on their name to find out more about them. Before you start playing in the chat room and sending messages, it might be a good idea to find out who is there.

8. You can also send a private message directly to your course instructor from the chat room by clicking on the "questions" tab. Then you can type your question in the box on the right-hand side of the screen and click the "Send" button to send it to your instructor.

9. To leave the chat room, click on the "X" at the top right-hand corner of the screen.

HOW TO TUTORIAL

Posting to a Discussion Board in Blackboard

One of the most common tools used in online learning is the discussion board. Discussion boards allow students and instructors to carry on conversations over a period of time.

1. To post to the discussion board in Blackboard, begin by clicking on the "Communication" button on the left-hand side of the screen.

2. Then in the middle of the screen, click on the option that says "Discussion Board."

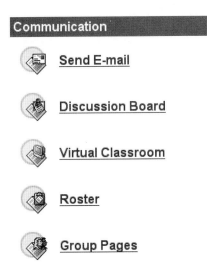

3. Once you have clicked on "Discussion Board," you will see all the discussion topics or forums that have been created. To post a message to a particular discussion forum, click on the name of the discussion you want to post to. This will take you to a screen that will look similar to the one below.

Discussion Board

Add New Thread

VIEW UNREAD MESSAGES ▼

EXPAND ALL ⊞ COLLAPSE ALL ⊟
SEARCH ?

SHOW OPTIONS

⊟ My thoughts	Corry, Mike	Fri Jan 24 2003 4:10 pm
Re: My thoughts	Corry, Mike	Fri Jan 24 2003 4:27 pm
Its Important to be Well-Rounded	Corry, Mike	Fri Jan 24 2003 4:22 pm

Sort By: [Default ♦]

(OK)

4. In discussion boards, messages are usually organized by "threads." Threads are simply a common topic that more than one person wants to comment on. That keeps everyone interested in a certain topic by posting messages at the same place to the same thread. If you want to add your own comments or start a thread, click on the "Add New Thread" button at the top of the screen. You will get a screen that looks similar to the one below.

Discussion Board

Create New Message

Current Forum: Week 1 Discussion - Becoming a Master Student
Date: Wed Jan 29 2003 12:59 pm
Author: Corry, Mike

Subject: [   ]
Message: [   ]

Options: ● Smart Text ○ Plain Text ○ HTML
☐ Post message as *Anonymous*
Attachment: [   ] (Browse...)

(Preview) (Cancel) (Submit)

5. In this screen, fill in the "Subject" box with the subject of the thread and fill in the "Message" box with your first message in the thread. Then click on the "Submit" button and your thread will be created and your message added.

6. Now, in the middle of the screen you can see any threads and messages that have already been posted to this discussion forum. You can read those messages by simply clicking on the title of the message. They will look similar to the screen below.

Discussion Board

◄◄ Previous Message   Next Message ►►

Current Forum: Week 1 Discussion - Becoming a Master Student
Date: Fri Jan 24 2003 4:22 pm
Author: Corry, Mike < mcorry@gwu.edu >
Subject: Its Important to be Well-Rounded

I think it is important to be well-rounded. How can I do this and also become a master student?

(Reply)

◄◄ Previous Message   Next Message ►►

Current Thread Detail:
Its Important to be Well-Rounded   Corry, Mike   Fri Jan 24 2003 4:22 pm

(OK)

7. You can respond or reply to anyone else's message after reading it by clicking on the "Reply" button. After you click on the "Reply" button, type your message in the message box and click on the "Submit" button. Your reply to someone else's message will now be posted.

Finding Your Course Documents and Assignments in Blackboard

It is very important for you to be able to find your course materials or documents in any online course.

1. To find your course materials in Blackboard, begin by clicking on the "Course Documents" button on the left-hand side of the screen.

2. Then in the middle of the screen, you will see the course materials that have been prepared by your instructor.

Course Documents

Current Location: Top

📁 **Start Here**

📁 **External Links**

📁 **First Step**

📁 **Time**

📁 **Memory**

📁 **Reading**

📁 **Notes**

📁 **Tests**

📁 **Thinking**

📁 **Communication**

📁 **Diversity**

📁 **Resources**

📁 **Health**

3. Your course materials may be listed as a series of links to documents. If this is the case, simply click on the title of the document to access it.

4. Another important location in Blackboard that may contain course materials is in the Assignments area. To access the Assignments area, begin by clicking on the "Assignments" button on the left-hand side of the screen.

5. Then in the middle of the screen, you will see the assignments that have been prepared by your instructor.

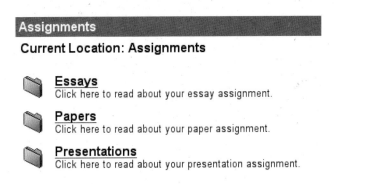

Assignments

Current Location: Assignments

Essays
Click here to read about your essay assignment.

Papers
Click here to read about your paper assignment.

Presentations
Click here to read about your presentation assignment.

6. Again, your course assignments may be listed as a series of links to documents. If this is the case, simply click on the title of the document to access it.

HOW TO TUTORIAL 24

Finding Your Assignment Grades and Feedback in Blackboard

Almost all students want to know about their grades. Blackboard provides a simple way of checking your grades.

1. To find your grades in Blackboard, begin by clicking on the "Tools" button on the left-hand side of the screen.

2. Then in the middle of the screen, click on the option that says "Check Grade."

Check Grade

User Information

Average Points/Assessment:	N/A
Assessment Average:	0%
Total Points:	0

Scores

Date Added	Item Sort items by: Item Order Date Added Name Type	Score	Points Possible	Weight	Class Avg.
Jan 24, 2003	Ch01 Practice Quiz (Quiz)	-	10	%	N/A

✔ Completed
🔒 In Progress
- No Information
! Needs Grading
? Grading Error

(OK)

---

3. Once you have clicked on "Check Grade," in the middle of the screen, you will see all the information about your grade in the course. This includes both summary information as well as detailed information.

4. Some instructors may also provide feedback on assignments that you submitted using the Digital Drop Box. If this is the case, you can access that feedback by clicking on the "Tools" button on the left-hand side of the screen.

5. Then in the middle of the screen, click on the option that says "Digital Drop Box." Any feedback sent back to you from your instructor would be listed in this area. You can access the file by clicking on the name of the file.

HOW TO TUTORIAL

Finding Your Course Materials in WebCT

Once you have logged into your course in WebCT, it is important to understand where you will find your course materials (announcements, calendars, lectures, etc.). The location of these items may vary from course to course, but there are some general guidelines you can follow.

1. To begin, start by exploring the buttons found on the left-hand side of the screen.

> Course Menu
> Homepage
> **e-Learning Hub**
> Calendar
> Student Homepages
> Discussions
> Mail
> Chat
> Course Content
> Assignments

2. Below is a general idea of what you might find when exploring each of these areas:

   • Homepage—This link provides a general overview for the course and the information will vary depending on what your instructor decides to include. Some of the links you might find here include links to the start of the course, quizzes, course lectures (content) and external links. Note: Some of the links on the home page might be duplicated under other links on the left-hand side of the page (e.g., course lectures found in Course Content).

   • E-Learning Hub—This link is where you might find general information and resources about E-learning. This may include frequently asked questions and answers, articles about E-learning, and how to use WebCT.

   • Calendar—This link will include a calendar that you can use to organize your schedule and the schedule for the course. The calendar might include dates for assignments, readings, and quizzes.

   • Student Homepages—This link is where you will find an area where you can create and maintain your own home page. You can also view the home pages of other students in the class.

   • Discussions—The discussion board is very important because this link is where you can share thoughts and ideas with everyone in the course by posting messages and replying to other's messages.

Tutorials

- Mail—This link is where you will be able to send an email to your classmates or instructor. This is a very important area when communicating in the course.
- Chat—This link is where you can go to participate in a synchronous (real time) chat with other classmates and your instructor. Again, this can be a very important part of course communication.
- Course Content—This link is where you will find a large majority of the course materials (lectures, readings, etc.). You will probably spend a lot of time in this part of the course site.
- Assignments—This link is where you will find more information about your course assignments. This might include directions, due dates, how to submit and assignment, etc.

3. In addition to the links on the left-hand side of the page, many WebCT courses will provide a link at the top of the screen to the "Course Map." This will give you an overview of the entire course. You might find the course map useful when trying to navigate through the course.

HOW TO TUTORIAL   **26**

Sending an Email and Adding an Attachment in WebCT

One of the most important items when working online is the ability to communicate with classmates and your instructor. A great way to do so is by using the email function in WebCT.

1. To send an email using WebCT begin by clicking on the "Mail" button located on the left-hand side of the screen.

2. Then in the middle of the screen, click on the option that says "Compose Mail Message." It should look similar to the screen below.

Compose Mail Message

Send to	[ ] [Browse...]
Subject	[ ]
Message	[ ]

Height of edit area [12 ⬍] [Resize]   ○ Don't wrap text ● Wrap text

Equation [Create new equation ⬍] [Equation editor]

Attachments: [   ] [Browse...]   [Attach file]

There are no files attached.

[Send] [Preview] [Cancel]   [Save draft]

3. Once you have clicked on "Compose Mail Message," a new window will open and you will have several options about who to send your email to. For example, you might have the option of sending it to everyone in the class, to a certain student, to a specific group or to your course instructor(s).

4. If you want to send an email to your course instructor(s), begin by clicking on the browse button to the right of the "Send to" box. You should get a screen that looks something like the one on the following page. Click on the name of your instructor and then click on the "Done" button.

[Done] [Cancel]

Select one or more people to receive your
message:

amy dunaway
Test Student
Mike Corry Test Student
paul vansickle

5. At this point, you should fill in the "Subject" line of the email and the "Message" area. Now, before you send your email, there are also other options available to you including adding a file attachment to the email. If you do not wish to add an attachment to the email, simply click on the "Send" button and your email will be sent. If you wish to add an attachment to your email, click on the "Browse" button to the right of the "Attachments" box. If you wish to add an attachment to the email message and you have clicked on the "Browse" button to the right of the "Attachments" box then you should have a screen that looks similar to this:

Desktop ⊞			🖥 🗊 ⏰
Name			**Date Modified** ⬍
▽ desktop stuff			7/29/02
📄 figure 1.1			Today
📄 figure 2.1			Today
📄 figure 2.2			Today
📄 **figure 2.3**			Today
📄 figure 3.1			Today
📄 figure 3.2			Today

[Show Preview]

⑦   [Cancel] [Open]

6. At this point, find the file you wish to attach. Once you have located and chosen the file to attach, click on the "Open" button and the name of the file should show up in the box to the left of the "Browse" button.

7. Now, click on the "Attach File" button and the name of your attached file should be seen below the "Browse" button.

8. Then, simply click on the "Send" button and your email and attachment will be sent.

HOW TO TUTORIAL 27

Turning in Assignments in WebCT

As you work your way through your course you will probably need to turn in assignments. Many courses will have you do this using the Upload or Submit features in WebCT.

1. To submit an assignment in WebCT, begin by clicking on the "Assignments" button on the left-hand side of the screen.

2. Then in the middle of the screen, click on the name of the assignment you are submitting. You should then see a screen that looks similar to the one below (you may have to scroll down).

Online Becoming a Master Student, 2/e by Gray/Ellis: CORRY01
Home › **Assignments** › Second Assignment

Assignment: Second Assignment
Return to <u>Assignments</u>

Assignment Information

Maximum grade	100
Due date	March 29, 2003
Instructions	Submit Your Second Assignment Here
Assignment files	None
Submissions	You can only submit your assignment once. No re-submission is permitted.
Notification	The instructor will not be notified via email when you submit this assignment.

Submit Assignment

Status	Not Submitted
Student files	None
	To upload your completed assignment, click **Upload file**.

`[ Upload file ] [ Remove files ]`

Notification	If you want to be notified when your assignment has been successfully submitted, enter your email address.

`[                          ]`

After you have uploaded your completed assignment, you must click **Submit assignment**.

`[ Submit assignment ]`

3. At this point, you should click on the "Upload file" button. Then click on the "Browse" button to the right of the "Filename" box.

4. At this point, you should find the assignment file you wish to send to your instructor and click on the "Open" button. Once you have located and chosen the file to send, the name of the file should show up in the box to the left of the "Browse" button. Now click on the "Upload" button. You should get a screen that looks similar to the one on the following page.

Home ▸ **Assignments** ▸ Second Assignment

Assignment: Second Assignment
Return to Assignments

Assignment Information

Maximum grade	100
Due date	March 29, 2003
Instructions	Submit Your Second Assignment Here
Assignment files	None
Submissions	You can only submit your assignment once. No re-submission is permitted.
Notification	The instructor will not be notified via email when you submit this assignment.

Submit Assignment

Status   Not Submitted

Student files   To view a file, click its filename.

Files	Modification Date	Size
☐ figure 2.3	January 29, 2003 1:22pm	42.1 kB

To upload your completed assignment, click **Upload file**.

[**Upload file**] [**Remove files**]

Notification   If you want to be notified when your assignment has been successfully submitted, enter your email address.

[   ]

After you have uploaded your completed assignment, you must click **Submit assignment**.

[**Submit assignment**]

5. Then, simply check the box to the left of your file name and click on the "Submit assignment" button and your assignment will be sent to your instructor. If you want an email confirmation, fill in your email address in the appropriate box before submitting the assignment.

HOW TO TUTORIAL   **28**

Participating in Chat in WebCT

One of the most exciting things about WebCT is the ability to have synchronous conversations with other classmates or your instructor using the Chat function. Synchronous means that the conversations are occurring in "real" time with all participants in the chat room at the same time.

1. To participate in a chat session, begin by clicking on the "Chat" button on the left-hand side of the screen.

2. Then in the middle of the screen, you may have several chat rooms available for your use. They should look something like the screen below. Click on one of them. In this example, we are going to click on the link that says "Room 1."

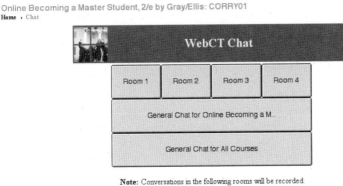

Online Becoming a Master Student, 2/e by Gray/Ellis: CORRY01
Home › Chat

Note: Conversations in the following rooms will be recorded:
Room 1, Room 2, Room 3, Room 4.

3. Once you have clicked on "Room 1" you will get a new window. It should look similar to the screen below.

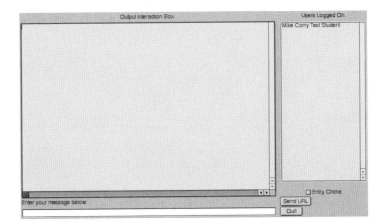

4. The box on the right-hand side of the screen lists the users currently in that chat room.

5. To have a synchronous conversation with others who are in the chat room, simply type in your question or comment in the blank box at the very bottom of the screen and hit enter. The question or comment will then appear above in the "Output Interaction Box" for everyone in the chat room to see and respond to.

6. At the bottom right-hand side of the screen you can see the "Send URL" button. You can go to a Website by clicking on that button and then typing in the Website address in that blank box that appears. The Website will be opened in a new window. Others in the chat room can also view the Website and you can comment on it.

7. To leave the chat room, click on the "Quit" button at the bottom right-hand corner of the screen.

HOW TO TUTORIAL 29

Posting to a Discussion Board in WebCT

One of the most common tools used in online learning is the discussion board. Discussion boards allow students and instructors to carry on conversations over a period of time.

1. To post to the discussion board in WebCT, begin by clicking on the "Discussions" button on the left-hand side of the screen. You should see a screen similar to the one below.

Online Becoming a Master Student, 2/e by Gray/Ellis: CORRY01
Home ▸ Discussions

Select a topic to see its messages

Compose Discussion Message   Search   Topic Settings

Topic	Unread	Total	Status
All	3	5	
Main	3	5	public, unlocked
Notes	0	0	public, unlocked

2. Then in the middle of the screen, click on the word "All" under "Topic." Your screen should look similar to the one below.

Online Becoming a Master Student, 2/e by Gray/Ellis: CORRY01
Home ▸ Discussions ▸ All

Discussion messages: All
Return to Discussions

Compose Discussion Message   Search   Mark All As Read   Update Listing
Select topic: All ⬍   Show all / Show unread   Threaded / Unthreaded
Select all Select none   Apply to selected message(s) below Compile ⬍ Go

Status	Subject	Topic	Author	Date
▼ 2/4	☐ 🔍 First Week's Discussion A...	Main		
✉	☐ First Week's Discussion A...	Main	Mike Corry Test Student	January 28, 2003 4:24pm
✉	☐ ↳ Re: First Week's Discussi...	Main	Mike Corry Test Student	January 28, 2003 4:27pm
✉	☐ ↳ Re: First Week's Discussi...	Main	Mike Corry Test Student	January 28, 2003 4:34pm
✉	☐ ↳ Re: First Week's Discussi...	Main	Mike Corry Test Student	January 28, 2003 4:47pm
▼ 1/1	☐ 🔍 Second Week's Postings	Main		
✉	☐ Second Week's Postings	Main	Mike Corry Test Student	January 28, 2003 4:37pm

3. You should now see all of the discussion topics or forums that have been created. If the arrow(s) on the left-hand side is/are not pointing downwards, then click on it and it will point down. This allows you to see all the postings in the discussion area. To post a message to a particular discussion forum, click on the name of the discussion you

want to post to. This will take you to a screen that will look similar to the one below.

Subject First Week's Discussion Area
Previous Thread Next Thread Close

Reply   Reply Privately   Quote   Download
Message no. 1
Posted by **Mike Corry Test Student** on Tuesday, January 28, 2003 4:24pm

In this area post messages about this week's course topic.

Previous Message Next Message

Previous Thread Next Thread Close

4. Now click on the "Reply" button and type in your message in the "Message" box. When you are satisfied with your entry, click the "Post" button. Your reply to the previous message will be posted and you will be taken back to the main discussion board screen.

5. In discussion boards, messages are usually organized by something called a "thread." Threads are simply a common topic on which more than one person wants to comment. This keeps everyone interested in a certain topic by posting messages at the same place to the same thread. If you want to add your own or start a new thread, click on the "Compose Discussion Message" button at the top of the main discussion board screen. You will get a screen that looks similar to the one below.

Compose Discussion Message
Topic   [Main ↕]
Subject [   ]
Message [   ]

Height of edit area [12 ↕] [Resize]   ○ Don't wrap text ● Wrap text
Equation [Create new equation ↕] [Equation editor]

Attachments: [   ] [Browse...] [Attach file]
There are no files attached.

[Post] [Preview] [Cancel]

6. In this screen, fill in the "Subject" box with the subject of the thread and fill in the "Message" box with first message in the thread. Then click on the "Post" button and your thread will be created and your message added.

7. Now, in the middle of the screen you can see any threads and messages that have already been posted to this discussion forum. You can read those messages by simply clicking on the title of the message.

HOW TO TUTORIAL  **30**

Finding Your Course Content in WebCT

It is very important for you to be able to find your course materials or documents in any online course. In WebCT, course materials or documents can be found fairly easily.

1. To find your course materials in WebCT, begin by clicking on the "Course Content" button on the left-hand side of the screen.

2. Then in the middle of the screen, you will see the course materials that have been prepared by your instructor.

3. Your course materials may be listed as a series of links to documents. If this is the case, simply click on the title of the document to access it.

4. Another important location in WebCT that may contain course materials is in the Assignments area. To access the Assignments area, begin by clicking on the "Assignments" button on the left-hand side of the screen.

5. Then in the middle of the screen, you will see the assignments that have been prepared by your instructor.

Online Becoming a Master Student, 2/e by Gray/Ellis: CORRY01
Home ▸ Course Content

ONLINE BECOMING A MASTER STUDENT

Table of Contents

Module Overview and Guide
▼ **First Step**

Module 1 Opener
Module 1 Topic Case Study

Module 1 Case Study Reflective Journal
Power Process Article: Ideas are Tools
Power Process Case Study: Ideas are Tools
Power Process Case Study: Ideas are Tools Reflective Journal
Module 1 Emotional Intelligence Scenario

▼ **Time**

Module 2 Opener
Module 2 Topic Case Study
Module 2 Case Study Reflective Journal
Power Process Article: Be Here Now
Power Process Case Study: Be Here Now
Power Process Case Study: Be Here Now Reflective Journal
Module 2 Emotional Intelligence Scenario

▼ **Memory**

Module 3 Opener
Module 3 Topic Case Study
Module 3 Case Study Reflective Journal
Power Process Article: Love Your Problems
Power Process Case Study: Love Your Problems
Power Process Case Study: Love Your Problems Reflective Journal
Module 3 Emotional Intelligence Scenario

▼ **Reading**

6. Again, your course assignments may be listed as a series of links to documents. If this is the case, simply click on the title of the document to access it.

HOW TO TUTORIAL 31

Finding Your Assignment Grades and Feedback in WebCT

Almost all students want to know about their grades. WebCT provides a simple way of checking your grades.

1. To find your grades in WebCT, begin by clicking on the "Assignments" button on the left-hand side of the screen.

2. Then in the middle of the screen, you will see all the assignments you have submitted. If they have been graded it will say "Graded" under the "Status" column and the grade will appear under the "Grade" column. It should be similar to the screen below.

Online Becoming a Master Student, 2/e by Gray/Ellis: CORRY01
Home ▸ Assignments

Assignments

Current date: January 29, 2003 1:29pm

Title	Availability	Grade	Status
First Assignment	From: Immediately Due: January 28, 2003 5:00pm	98 / 100	Graded
Second Assignment	From: Immediately Due: March 29, 2003 1:00pm	-- / 100	Not Submitted

3. To see more detailed feedback about the assignment, click on the graded link. There may be instructor comments included in this detailed feedback or you may want to open the graded file and look for comments there. To open the graded file click on the file name under the "Files" column in the "Graded Files" section of the screen.

HOW TO TUTORIAL   32

Troubleshooting Problems

Computers and technology have made it possible for us to do things easier than in the past. For example, we can now pay our bills, send mail to friends, and edit papers much faster and easier than only a few short years ago. However, nothing is perfect and computers are no exception. With that in mind, it is important to understand that at some point you will have problems with your computer hardware or software and you will need to fix those problems or get help to do so. The purpose of this tutorial is to give you some guidance on how to troubleshoot problems you might face.

1. When it comes to troubleshooting problems the first place to start is by using the "Help" function that is available on most software. The "Help" function usually contains detailed information to help you solve the most common problems associated with the software. It also can provide details about "how to" do certain tasks within the software. For example, you would use the "Help" function to figure out how to change the margins in a Microsoft Word document. The "Help" function is usually found as a pull-down menu on the top of your screen. It is usually the pull-down menu furthest to the right of all the pull-down menus. Once you click on it, it will look similar to the following:

2. Once you have clicked on the "Help" pull-down menu, the best place to start is usually the "Contents and Index" option. Click on that option. Each software's "Contents and Index" area might look a little different, but once you have selected this, then there should be a way to select the "Index" option. In Microsoft Word, it would look similar to the following:

```
┌─────────────────────────────────────────────────────────────────┐
│ Help Topics: Microsoft Word                              [?][X]  │
├─────────────────────────────────────────────────────────────────┤
│  ┌────────┬───────┬──────┐                                       │
│  │Contents│ Index │ Find │                                       │
│  └────────┴───────┴──────┘                                       │
│                                                                   │
│   1 Type the first few letters of the word you're looking for.   │
│   ┌─────────────────────────────────────────────────────────┐   │
│   │                                                         │   │
│   └─────────────────────────────────────────────────────────┘   │
│                                                                   │
│   2 Click the index entry you want, and then click Display.      │
│   ┌─────────────────────────────────────────────────────┬──┐   │
│   │ 3-D effects                                         │▲│   │
│   │ a pplications                                       │ │   │
│   │ abstracts                                           │ │   │
│   │ accessibility for people with disabilities          │ │   │
│   │ action items, exporting from PowerPoint to Word     │ │   │
│   │ ActiveX                                             │ │   │
│   │ add-in programs                                     │ │   │
│   │    loading                                          │ │   │
│   │    overview                                         │ │   │
│   │    troubleshooting                                  │ │   │
│   │    unloading                                        │ │   │
│   │ addition, = (Formula) field                         │ │   │
│   │ additional file converters                          │ │   │
│   │ addresses                                           │ │   │
│   │    delivery point                                   │ │   │
│   │    envelopes                                        │ │   │
│   │    inserting                                        │▼│   │
│   └─────────────────────────────────────────────────────┴──┘   │
│                                                                   │
│              ┌─────────┐  ┌───────┐  ┌────────┐                 │
│              │ Display │  │ Print.│  │ Cancel │                 │
│              └─────────┘  └───────┘  └────────┘                 │
└─────────────────────────────────────────────────────────────────┘
```

3. Once you are in the "Index" area, you can type in a word related to your problem in the blank box at the top. The software will find any related topics and display them in the window in the bottom. Then click on any one of those topics and click on the display button. The help topic details will then be displayed. If you don't find the information you need, simply go to the "Index" area and type in a different word.

4. If you are unable to find the solution to your problem using the software's "Help" function, then you should try to get help through your college desk. Most schools have their own computer help desk for students, faculty, and staff. If your problem involves a school computer, software, or Internet access, then you should contact them before contacting the software manufacturer. There is usually no cost to access school help desks, so you might want to contact them first. In addition, each software manufacturer maintains a help desk that you can reach either via the telephone or Internet. Accessing the help desk via the telephone usually involves a charge (except for the first few weeks you own the software). Accessing via the Internet is sometimes free, but you have to wait longer to get your answer. If you choose to use the telephone help desk option, the phone number will be in your software's printed documentation. If you can't find that documentation, try locating the number on the manufacturer's Website. That is also where you will find access to the Internet help desk. Note: The help desk is sometimes called technical support.

5. Before you contact any help desk you should have certain information available that you will need to provide to the help desk. Below is a list of the basic information you should have available and how to get it:

• <u>Version of the software</u>—Software comes in many different versions. To find out what version of a software package you own, open the software and click on the "Help" pull-down menu at the top of the screen. It should look similar to the first screen shot above. Click on the option that says "About" and then the name of the software. In the first screen shot above, it says "About Microsoft Word." Once you click on that option, a new window will open and tell you what version of the software you own.

• <u>Type of computer you own and the operating system</u>—The type of computer you own is going to be either a Windows computer or a Macintosh computer. You can find out how to determine your computer's operating system by referring to the tutorials "Checking Your Computer's Hardware Profile in Microsoft Windows" or "Checking Your Computer's Hardware Profile on a Macintosh Computer" in this book. An example of an operating system is Windows 98.

• <u>What the problem is and when it occurs</u>—When you contact the help desk, they are going to ask you to explain what the problem is and when it occurred. It is helpful if you write that information down before you contact the help desk so that you can clearly communicate it to them.

• <u>Error messages</u>—If the reason you are contacting the help desk is because you are getting an error message make sure you have written down exactly what the error message says and what you were doing when it appeared.

Tutorials

Index